CN00760413

INTO THE HEART OF TASMANIA

'*Into the Heart* is a powerful and gripping detective story about Tasmania's deep and recent past and why it matters today. It is a subtle exploration of Aboriginal history, a profound reflection on the place of Tasmania in world conversations about human evolution, and an intriguing journey in quest of understanding. Historian Rebe Taylor pursues an English collector on ship, foot and bicycle as he sets out to plumb the mystery of human origins; she eavesdrops on his conversations and sifts all the clues that he has left behind—in Britain and the antipodes, in the archive and the field, in language and places, and in words and stone. As we look over his shoulder, the people he is studying come surprisingly into focus. Perhaps only now can we understand the stories they are trying to tell.'

Tom Griffiths, Professor of History and Director, Centre for Environmental History, Australian National University

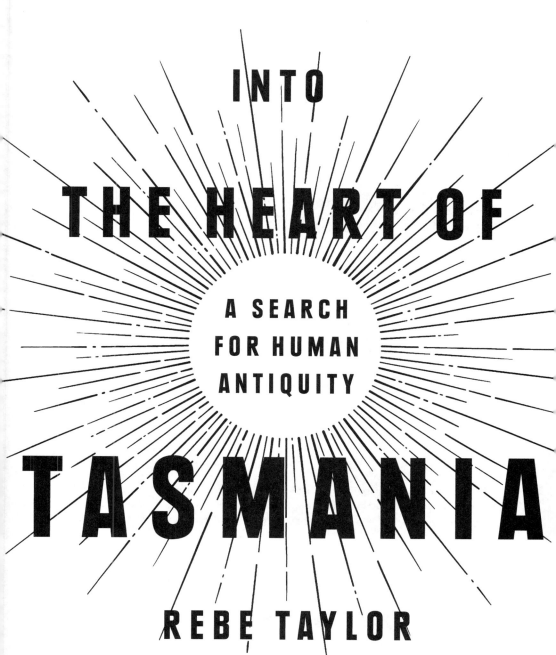

INTO
THE HEART OF

A SEARCH
FOR HUMAN
ANTIQUITY

TASMANIA

REBE TAYLOR

MELBOURNE UNIVERSITY PRESS
An imprint of Melbourne University Publishing Limited
Level 1, 715 Swanston Street, Carlton, Victoria 3053, Australia
mup-info@unimelb.edu.au
www.mup.com.au

First published 2017
Reprinted 2017
Text © Rebe Taylor, 2017
Design and typography © Melbourne University Publishing Limited, 2017

This book is copyright. Apart from any use permitted under the *Copyright Act 1968* and subsequent amendments, no part may be reproduced, stored in a retrieval system or transmitted by any means or process whatsoever without the prior written permission of the publishers.

Every attempt has been made to locate the copyright holders for material quoted in this book. Any person or organisation that may have been overlooked or misattributed may contact the publisher.

Note on front cover: The stone artefact is an illustration of an English 'eolith' (a supposed stone 'tool') from the 1913 journal paper announcing the discovery of 'Piltdown Man' in Sussex, one of 'the most infamous hoaxes in science'. The John Glover painting depicts Tasmanian Aborigines dancing with Hobart in the distance. Glover's depiction is probably 'ethnographically correct', but the only place where they could gather in such numbers in 1835 was on Flinders Island, where they had been forcibly removed by the colonial government. See Greg Lehman, 2016, p. 285.

Text design and typesetting by Cannon Typesetting
Cover design by Design by Committee
Printed in Australia by McPherson's Printing Group

National Library of Australia Cataloguing-in-Publication entry
    Taylor, Rebe, author.
    Into the heart of Tasmania: a search for human antiquity/Rebe Taylor.

9780522867961 (paperback)
9780522867978 (ebook)

Includes bibliographical references and index.

Aboriginal Tasmanians—History.
Aboriginal Tasmanians—Social life and customs.
Anthropology—Tasmania—History.
Archaeology—Tasmania—History.

Contents

To Peter, Hugo and Neve.

Author note

With the exception of names of ancestors, Aboriginal names and words in this book appear in lower case. This follows the style of palawa kani, the revived form of the original Tasmanian Aboriginal languages, a program led by the Tasmanian Aboriginal Centre. I respect that some writers prefer to place Tasmanian Aboriginal language names in italics, but for consistency I have used only roman text.

This book uses the terms 'Aboriginal' and 'Aborigines' rather than 'Indigenous'. This is the preference of the Tasmanian Aboriginal community. Other names for Aborigines also appear in the context of their times.

Into the Heart of Tasmania also includes scientific theories about, and descriptions of, Aboriginal culture and people that belong to other writers and other times. Some of these theories, like the older names for Aborigines, are not, by today's standards, appropriate. Even some relatively recent scientific ideas may appear culturally insensitive. In quoting these ideas and by repeating older names for Aborigines I do not mean any disrespect or to cause offence to the Tasmanian Aboriginal community.

I also wish to remind readers that while this book describes collecting thousands of stone tools, it is illegal to interfere with, or to remove any Aboriginal cultural artefacts from anywhere in Tasmania.

Prologue: The gift

kutalayna, Tasmania, 17 April 2011

The smoke curls around his grey beard, his ochred cheeks, through his curly hair, into his blue eyes. He welcomes it, fans it so it drifts over those gathered around the fire, listening in silence. And then he speaks, softly:

yah ta wah ti wah warrawah (greetings from the spirits).

mena lagata nala neminah tagarilia coyetea nena (I tell you our Earth Mother family loves you).

palingina mumirimina walantanalinany (welcome to mumirimina Country all round).

We are here today to heal this place, kutalayna, our community, and everyone in Brighton. We will leave kutalayna in a graceful way to show respect to our ancestors, and ourselves who have conducted our protest with strength and grace.

… I ask the spirits to heal kutalayna, heal the Tasmanian Aboriginal community and, all of the people of Brighton. Our struggle has been a long one to protect kutalayna, and our struggle continues.

The construction workers and the police are watching, waiting for the ceremony to end before they start work. Before they arrest him.

He is nearly finished. He takes a packet from his pocket, and opens it with care: ashes, gathered from the fire at the Aboriginal Tent Embassy at Old Parliament House, Canberra, which burns day and night. He spreads them over the crackling branches: 'This is a symbol of our sovereignty, and pride in our heritage.'

It is done. His son falls in by his side. The group circles around them, offering solace and protection. They begin to walk out. The police stand solid in thick leather jackets, black gloves and sky-blue hard hats. The protestors approach slowly. A thin young man dressed only in a white loincloth and his sister in a black singlet and an apron of furs are painted head to toe in ochre; a stark contrast to well-attired police.

They are not allowed to pass. A brave and professional young woman makes a plea for the use of police discretion; they will leave quietly. But the decision has already been made.

He knows this. The standoff is pointless. He asks his community members to stand aside, and to let him and his son pass through, and they are led away to the waiting paddy wagon.

In April 2009 the Tasmanian State Government had begun construction of the Brighton Bypass, a 9.5-kilometre road, costing $191 million, to divert traffic off the Midland Highway, away from the Hobart suburbs of Brighton and Pontville. The bypass would have to cross the Jordan River. The proposed site for a bridge was kutalayna, known to the Tasmanian Aboriginal community as a long-time seasonal meeting place of the mumirimina people. In September 2009 the protestors had prevented construction starting. Twenty were arrested. By February 2010 the government commissioned archaeologists to determine the age and significance of the site. The University of Melbourne determined an age for the sediments and artefacts at the bottom of the excavation of about 41,000 years. This is 'the oldest site in Tasmania, and among the oldest in Australia'. In fact the age of kutalayna is 'beyond the first southern expansion of *Homo sapiens* elsewhere in the world'.[1]

The Aboriginal community campaigned to reroute the bypass without success. By December 2010, they set up a protest camp to prevent construction. Some non-Aboriginal locals supported it, others slowed their cars down as they passed so they could lower their windows and spit at the protestors. The owners of the land adjoining the site would build a bonfire, crack open some beers and make a lot of noise.

Aaron Everett, an Aboriginal Heritage Officer, lived on the site for nearly a year. The sit-in cost him his job. He was arrested four times, and his father, Jim Everett, three times. By early 2011, both were under court orders not to enter the site. But in mid April 2011 Aaron phoned his dad, who was up on Flinders Island in the Bass Strait, and told him to fly back to Hobart and come to kutalayna. Tomorrow. They had one day to heal the site before the bulldozers came. Before it was too late.

When Jim walked back onto kutalayna, he did so with hurt and a sense of loss. But still he sought the healing for all, even those who did not ask for the gift, who perhaps did not deserve it. It was given quietly, in the knowledge that few would ever learn about it. It was given without the expectation of reciprocity.

I have known Jim for over fifteen years. He has inspired and assisted my writing, guided my understanding of history, and been a key part of my education. This book is written in the spirit of reciprocity for what he has given, and what other Tasmanian Aboriginal people have also given me, including Clinton Mundy, Patsy Cameron and Greg Lehman.

At first it seems an odd sort of a gift. It begins with the journey of an Englishman to Tasmania nearly a century ago to collect stone tools. To the living Aboriginal community the removal of artefacts is wrong—as Clinton Mundy reiterated to me, 'No stone tools should ever have been taken from anywhere in Tasmania, at any time in history.' Ernest Westlake took away over 13,000 artefacts, creating the largest single collection of Tasmanian stone implements ever formed, and as he did so he assumed that the Tasmanian Aborigines were the most primitive race on earth and that they were extinct.

Westlake shared the blindness of his generation, of his scientific discipline, and of his Empire. Yet, through his story, we are led to see what the collector could not perceive: an Aboriginal people with a complex culture and a deep past. We are led into the living, beating heart of Tasmania.

The decision

London, 1908

Ernest Westlake walked up the broad steps of the British Museum and, passing through that famous colonnade, stepped into a cramped and busy entrance hall. He did not follow the other visitors to see the Egyptian and Greek antiquities towering in the ground-floor galleries, but took the most direct route to where his interests lay. Up the Principal Staircase, lined with first-century Indian Buddhist carvings, he entered the Central Saloon. British Iron Age arrowheads, Bronze Age helmets and Neolithic stone axes regressed down to the prehistoric stone tools from British and French caves; made by the 'races of men of whom we have no history'.[1] The Early Stone Age was his particular enthusiasm, but knowing this room well he walked on, past the swords of the Anglo-Saxon Room and the tea sets in the Asiatic Saloon, until he reached the entrance to the Ethnographical Gallery.

Five open-ended galleries stretched before him, extending almost the length of the eastern wing of the Museum's upper floor. At once elongated and dense, the gallery reflected the spread of Empire. Glass cases reached up the walls and across the floors, each case packed with objects from the colonised world. Their origins were indicated in red on maps that hung from their doors; a guidebook sketched out their contents. On the right in the second and third rooms were artefacts

One of the ethnographical galleries, British Museum, Donald Macbeth, 1908
[© The Trustees of the British Museum]

from the 'brown races' of Micronesia and Polynesia: feather-work cloaks and helmets from Hawaii and jade paddle-shaped battleaxes from New Zealand. On the left, the collections from the 'black races' of the Pacific, Melanesia and Australia: boomerangs and spear throwers described as the 'inventions among tribes who had no knowledge of the bow'.[2] Near these wooden implements hung the 'portrait of a Tasmanian belonging to a now extinct race'.[3] A black man looked out from under a helmet of thick and matted hair, dressed in skins and shell necklaces, and holding a spear.[4]

Then Westlake's attention was arrested. It was a display he had not seen before, at least not this large and varied: a hundred stones, packed together under the peaked glass roof of a floor cabinet, where he could gaze down upon them. Some were no bigger than his thumbnail, others almost as big as his fist. They varied in shape—round, spherical, square, squat, tall, peaked and pointed—and were an assortment of colours: pearly white, sandy brown and even hard black. They had been broken for reasons that made the cabinet seem absurd: to crack a bone, skin a wallaby, prise open an oyster. The map on the cabinet indicated the island of Tasmania, southeast of mainland Australia. A few pasted labels offered the opaque names of towns and beaches: 'Port Sorell', 'Ironhouse', 'Westwood'.[5]

The pieces of stone made a sudden and inspiring impression upon him. They reminded him of stones he knew well, stones he had collected and held in his hands in a warm and quiet valley in the Auvergne region, central France. They shared the same rough, chipped angles and shapes, as if they had been made without plan or design. In France he had turned the stones over in his hands in wonder, unsure and excited, the sun on his back, the village church bell tolling in the distance: had he really found the tools of an unknown Stone Age race?

That question had driven him to keep exploring. Westlake dug down to a geological depth he estimated to be 100,000 years old. He unearthed a mass of tools. French customs stopped him on his way home, complaining he was taking too much of 'the soil of France'. He reduced the collection from 100,000 to 4000 artefacts. He was yet to present the evidence to the scientific community, but he could already hear the sceptics: the Auvergne stones were naturally broken rocks; it was beyond reason to claim artefacts of such antiquity and crudity could be man made.

The stones in front of him now would prove that it was possible. If the Tasmanians had made stone tools of such simplicity, why not also the early Europeans? Culture was evolutionary; even the most advanced civilisation had to begin somewhere. The Tasmanian Aborigines had evidently *not* progressed; they had evidently been one of the most primitive races to have lived in modern times. But that made their tools so useful. They could authenticate his French artefacts. While the two cultures were admittedly remote in space and time, and the comparison between them could never be exact, it would be sufficiently close to prove the human origin of the European flint and to show that the level of culture was essentially the same.[6]

Westlake knew instantly what he must do. It was a big decision. He was a widower and his children were still young. He was financially independent, but no longer prosperous. But at stake was determining the true depth of European human antiquity. He must then, at the earliest opportunity, travel to Tasmania and bring back his own collection of Aboriginal stone tools.

Pitt Rivers Museum Annexe, Oxford, January 2000

I am the only researcher in the small archives reading room. Its upstairs window reveals none of Oxford's romantic parapets or domes, just a dull and wintry Banbury Road. The archivist says little except to complain about the cold and I am left largely alone in my task. I wonder where to begin. Which box, which folder? I know almost nothing of this archive, or of the man who created it. I decide upon his letters, for they begin at the start of Westlake's journey to Tasmania, and are written to those he loved: 'My dear Children', he unfailingly addressed them. Aubrey, fifteen, and Margaret, twelve, were living

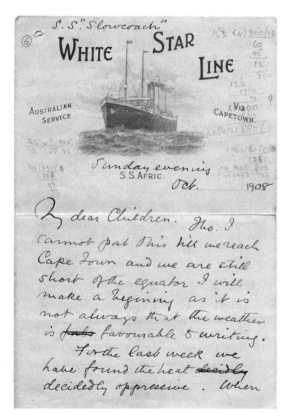

Letter from Ernest Westlake to Margaret and Aubrey Westlake, begun 24 September 1908 [© Pitt Rivers Museum, University of Oxford Pitt Rivers Museum Manuscript Collections, Westlake Papers, Box 2, Folder 1a, folio 6 recto]

variously at school or with their uncle and his family. For nineteen months Westlake wrote to them at least once a week: eighty-five letters in all as he travelled from the docks at Liverpool, to Melbourne, across Tasmania and back to London. In the absence of a diary, they record Westlake's journey and research.

Westlake travelled to some of the remotest parts of Tasmania during the age of steam. It took seven hours to travel from Hobart to Launceston by train. Many places could be reached only by boat. Westlake had a tent and rode a bicycle, which was sometimes loaded with several kilograms of stones. He walked when the terrain was too rough, or when his bicycle broke down. He slept on sand hills, under bushes, in sheds and abandoned houses. There were many months when Westlake was in Hobart, reading in the archives, or in Launceston, photographing stone tools. Then his letters took a reflective turn, and I learned about his political ideas, religious beliefs, even his dreams.

After several weeks of reading and transcribing in the cold reading room, I felt I knew this odd, clever and tenacious 50-something-year-old man. Then I turned to his field books. Six of them, each small enough to fit into a pocket, their pages often dense and not always easy to read, as if the notes were written on a knee or a makeshift table. The first one, however, was rather dull, neat and sparse: a collection of lists, names and notes, mostly without context. But the second began suddenly in the middle of an intense and personal recollection recorded by Westlake in November 1908: Truganini, the 'Last' of the Tasmanian Aborigines, was remembered as laughing and crying and scared of dying. Other memories, just as striking, followed: stories passed down from the 'Black War' of 1826–34 filled with blood and shootings, more recent memories of the Aborigines incarcerated on Flinders Island in the Bass Strait, and at the old convict station at Oyster Cove, south of Hobart. The notebooks reveal a community coming to terms with a difficult past at the beginning of a new century in a recently Federated nation. They are filled with repentant shame, are also littered with attempts to apportion blame, but foremost they emphasise that the history of settlement has ended. Westlake was reminded over and over again by the settler descendants he spoke to that the Aborigines had all gone; they were 'extinct'.

But then I encounter the voices of living Aboriginal people, first on the islands of the Bass Strait—the children and grandchildren of the Aboriginal women and their Straitsmen husbands who pioneered the settlements from the early nineteenth century—and then at Nicholls Rivulet, south of Hobart—the children of Fanny Smith (née Cochrane), who had passed away in 1905. The little notebooks were filled with Aboriginal knowledge: word lists and phrases, plant foods, hunting methods, medicines, and spiritual practices and beliefs.

Westlake called the Islanders and the Smith family 'half-castes'. He thought that the language and cultural information they gave him was useful, and was more than he had expected to find, but he called it 'second hand'. He assumed it did not belong to the people who spoke of it, but to their parents or grandparents; those whom Westlake called the 'Blacks', and whose culture he presumed was extinct and gone.[7] But how was it gone when he was writing it down? Why was this knowledge passed on if not so it would be kept and continued?

Westlake's imperception was typical, but his tenacity was unique. His determination to uncover every possible source of information about Tasmanian Aborigines led him to find what other researchers before him had missed. No one previously had made the effort to visit the Smith family. Few thought it was worth going to see the Islanders. Those who did had been met with a silence that they assumed was ignorance, but was in fact born from mistrust, and an agreement not to share their cultural knowledge with outsiders. But Westlake was not shunned by the Islanders or by the Smith family. His archive is the richest collection of Tasmanian Aboriginal culture formed in the twentieth century, and offers a way to see and understand how that culture was retained and practised. But has its value been recognised?

An archive dismissed

In 1991, NJB Plomley, a historian and honorary research associate at the Queen Victoria Museum and Art Gallery in Launceston, published Westlake's interview notes in the field books as *The Westlake Papers*. He edited Westlake's notes substantially, cutting and moving text, but without indicating how, which makes his edition an unreliable source for researchers.[8] Plomley also dismissed the value of Westlake's interviews with Aboriginal people. He derogatively called them 'half-castes' and 'mixed-bloods'. He thought the interviews with Fanny Smith's children confirmed only that their mother had known 'nothing of the Aboriginal way of life, and clearly had no wish to learn anything'. The interviews with the Bass Strait Islanders demonstrated to him that they had learned 'nothing of the way of life of their Aboriginal forbears'. But for 'few words' the Aboriginal language had 'clearly been lost, as well as almost everything else, quite early'.[9]

Plomley's reading of Westlake's papers was coloured by recent politics. From the 1970s the Tasmanian Aboriginal community began to publicly and stridently fight for rights to land and education, for the return of their ancestors' bodies from museums, and for recognition that they were not extinct. Plomley was a conservative scholar who had spent his career researching their history. He did not believe they had the right to call themselves 'Aboriginal'. He likened their ceremonial cremation of repatriated ancestral remains to the violence of the white settlers towards Aborigines on the early frontier.[10] The invective seems out of place in the introduction to Westlake's papers, but Plomley did not want to miss the opportunity to add his voice to a wider debate between Tasmanian Aboriginal people and the scholars who studied their cultural history.

Much of the hostility had begun with a controversy stirred by an Australian archaeologist. In 1965, Rhys Jones deduced that the first Tasmanian Aborigines had reached their island by foot, before the end of the last Ice Age, 10,000 to 12,000 years ago, when rising seas had created the Bass Strait. By 1977, Jones proposed that isolation had caused the Tasmanian Aboriginal culture to simplify.[11] Then, as the narrator of the popular 1978 film *The Last Tasmanian*, Jones drew a figurative parallel between simplification and extinction, asking even if Europeans had never discovered Tasmania, had the Aborigines nonetheless been 'doomed' by the devastating effects of isolation?[12] The idea caused a fracture between the Tasmanian Aboriginal community and the academy that lasted for decades.

Jones's controversial thesis had an important connection to Westlake's interviews. The notion of simplification hinged foremost on two supposed cultural losses: the ability to catch fish with scales and the art of making fire. But both Aboriginal and settler Tasmanians described knowledge of these skills repeatedly to Westlake, as Jones knew. He had been the first Australian scholar to study Westlake's collections in the Pitt Rivers Museum. He later wrote that Westlake helped lay 'the foundations for Tasmanian field archaeology'. It was perhaps the sheer size of the stone tools collection that prompted the compliment, for Jones dismissed Westlake's evolutionary theory and his archive. He did, however, first read Westlake's notebooks carefully. While Westlake never wrote down his questions, Jones had known that he had often asked, 'Did the Tasmanians know how to make fire …?'[13] Jones disregarded the answers because they dated over a century after first contact.

Jones was adhering to the parameters of his discipline. Historical sources had to be largely unaffected by the 'tide of history' for archaeologists to trust they could inform the deeper past. The requirement troubled Westlake, too. He was pleased and surprised by the wealth of information he was given in Tasmania, but he never saw it as a 'pure' or truly authentic record of Aboriginal culture. That, he assumed, had gone.

A new lifeworld

The threads of traditional continuity are present in Westlake's papers. Many of the descriptions of cultural practice, including fishing and fire making, are echoed in far earlier historical records. What was changed by 1908 was the context of those traditions. Tasmanian Aboriginal people had indeed adapted, often in order to survive and endure.

Despite these changes, generations of Tasmanian Aborigines did hand down important traditional knowledge that present-day descendants continue to remember. Tasmanian Elder Patsy Cameron in her 2011 book *Grease and Ochre*, describes that out of her ancestral history—the Aboriginal women and their white husbands who pioneered the Bass Strait Island settlements—there emerged a new generation and community defined not by loss, but by the 'transformative power' of their island environment and of the 'blending' of their cultures, economies and traditions. This fusion created what Cameron calls a 'new lifeworld'.[14]

Westlake's interviews offer insight into that 'lifeworld' and to the handed-down traditional knowledge, revealing the ways Tasmanian Aboriginal cultural practices in both the islands and the Nicholls Rivulet communities had been maintained. But this realisation has only been possible to explain with the guidance of Tasmanian Aboriginal people. They include, among others, those whose ancestors pioneered the Bass Strait Islands: Patsy Cameron, Jim Everett and Buck (Brendan) Brown, and the descendants of Fanny Smith: Cheryl Mundy and Clinton Mundy. Their guidance has been crucial, for it has meant perceiving that which Westlake failed to see.

Westlake saw neither the depth of Tasmanian Aboriginal antiquity nor the wealth of its continued existence because he was looking for something else: the artefacts and facts that would validate an imagined phase of European history. Westlake did not understand the true value of his collections. In noting the discord between his intention and his actual achievement something is learned.

Westlake's papers have taught me to ask myself: How do *I* see the past? How do I see Aboriginal peoples and cultures in the archive, or indeed, in the present? Am I looking in order to prove a point? To advance my discipline? To educate my fellow Australians? To even chastise them? None of these things are necessarily wrong, but it is important to consider how these goals might colour my vision. It is important to ask myself: Can I look into the past, or even at the present, can I cross cultures, and actually learn something new? Can I see what is before me? Can I actually see a new 'lifeworld'?

It has been a long journey just to get to the point of asking these questions. But then, a journey that follows Westlake is full of curious and circuitous turns.

Sandy Balls, New Forest, Hampshire, April 2000

The taxi driver thought it was hilarious. 'Sandy Balls?!' he exclaimed, 'Isn't that what you get when you go to the beach?' He found his own joke raucously funny. I found it added to my apprehension about what exactly I was doing going to an oddly named English caravan park, when I was meant to be researching Tasmanian Aboriginal history.

One of the first things I noticed when I arrived was a traditional 'gipsy' caravan parked near the entrance gate, complete with carvings, colourful paintwork and wooden front steps. Then I met Jean Westlake, the granddaughter of Ernest, whose house stood nearby. She explained to me that the caravan was bought by Westlake shortly before his marriage, with the dream that he and and his wife Lucy would travel, or even live in it. They never did, but Westlake always kept the caravan. He even lived in it during the final years of his life.

I spent several nights in Jean's house. It was surrounded by a large permacutlure garden, which provided most of our vegetarian meals. Once outside the garden gate, we were in the Sandy Balls holiday park. It was run by her brother on land originally bought by Ernest Westlake in 1919 to host the Order of Woodcraft Chivalry. Westlake established the movement with his son Aubrey in 1916, as a non-militarist alternative to the Scouts, open to boys, girls and adults. The Order sought post-war regeneration by offering an opportunity to return to nature, and to learn the skills of woodcraft and the code of chivalric conduct lost through urbanisation and industralisation.

Jean's historical tour began in the Sandy Balls Forest. I learned that its name was old and sensibly given; the land was a series of dunes created by an ancient river. Amid the dense fir trees Jean led me to a clearing, the 'Folkmoot Circle', where members of the Order, dressed in ceremonial robes and carrying heraldic banners, had gathered annually by a sacred fire. Jean loaned me a bike and we rode together past fields that had once grown the flax that Ernest Westlake's father Thomas had turned into sailcloths in his nearby mill. We reached the village of Fordingbridge, where Ernest Westlake had been born, and we visited his first home, bearing a plaque commemorating that the

'Father of the Order' had been born there in 1856—as Jean pointed out, it was in fact 1855.

Next door stood the hall that his father had built to host evangelical services for the villagers and his workers. We then visited the impressive family home Thomas Westlake built after he made his fortune, the one his son lost through mismanagement. Ernest Westlake was a scientist with little knowledge of money. Our tour ended at the modest wooden cottage at Godshill, Ernest Westlake's last home. Chris Charman, Westlake's grandson through his daughter Margaret, lived there. Chris described Ernest Westlake as a 'recluse' who had struggled with even a casual conversation. The idea seemed at odds with the 'Father of the Order' who dressed in ceremonial robes. But then, across the space of a day and the radius of a few miles, my key impression of Westlake was one of contrasts and eccentricities.

By early summer, shortly before I was due to return to Australia, I learned that the Oxford University Museum of Natural History had recently acquired Westlake's English stone tools and fossils collected from around the time he began his interest in geology in the 1870s to around 1900. When I requested to look through the related papers, I was surprised to be given only one box. The collection had been formerly held in the University of Southampton, where geologist Justin Delair had studied it at length. Delair's two subsequent papers referenced archival papers I could not find in the single box I had been given.[15] When I later met Delair, he assured me that there had to be more.

The day before I was due to fly out, I travelled with the Natural History Museum's geology curator to Newham village, near Oxford, where the deconsecrated church was being used as a museum store. On the church's upper floor we encountered Westlake's English geological collection: a series of wooden boxes that created a wall as high as my head and the length of the large room. Over several hours we removed boxes containing letters, notebooks and other papers. I spent the remainder of the day in front of a photocopier in the Natural History Museum. It was not until I was back home that I was able to read the papers properly. I saw they contained, among other subjects, Westlake's research notes into psychical phenomena, including dream premonitions and ghosts, as well as his plans to build a health sanatorium in outer London. I was reminded of what Justin Delair had warned me about Westlake: 'He's like a stone in a pond: the more you look, the more ripples you've got to chase'.[16]

Stories in Stone

I submitted my dissertation in 2005, but I felt my work on Westlake had only just begun.[17] My PhD had not been able to capture all the ripples of Westlake's life. Further, I knew from talking to Tasmanian Aboriginal people that it was important to their community to gain access to the unedited interviews. Plomley's edition had not only cut and moved text around, but Westlake's little sketches were missing, along with his marginalia and cross-references. Without his letters, Westlake seemed absent. Much is missing from Plomley's publication, such as twenty-one tourist guides used by Westlake for travel in Tasmania, twenty exercise books filled mostly with Westlake's notes from Tasmanian colonial records and newspapers, and 230 photographs of stone implements captured by Westlake in Launceston in 1909. Researchers with a range of interests might benefit from accessing his papers and I certainly thought no one else should have to try to piece together the various parts of Westlake's life and unpublished archives as I had done.

In 2008, archivist Gavan McCarthy and I spent a week in the Pitt Rivers Museum, in a beautiful, new on-site reading room. Using a digital camera and portable lights, we captured the entire Westlake papers relating to his Tasmanian archive. Two years later, when I was pregnant with my second child, archivist Mike Jones returned to Oxford and, using the same camera and lights, captured the entire Westlake papers in the Oxford University Museum of Natural History. In 2013, Jones, McCarthy and I finally published *Stories in Stone: An annotated history and guide to the collections and papers of Ernest Westlake (1855–1922)*, which includes more than 8000 images with added contextual historical information. *Stories in Stone* does not include

Westlake's papers relating to the Order of Woodcraft Chivalry, which are held in a separate archive and have been drawn upon to create a large two-volume history.[18] All the references to Westlake's papers in this book are discoverable in *Stories in Stone*. Of course, traffic may occur the other way: the archive might be the gateway into this book.

It is rare that a historian has their chief archive available online for readers. You can go and query my interpretation, or travel beyond my focus on his Tasmanian journey to carry out your own exploration of Westlake's life and work. Indeed, I hope you do. Just beware the many ripples in the pond.

The collector

Ernest Westlake had spent his life dedicated to stones. He grew up and lived in Victorian rural England, but he occupied a more ancient world. He walked on the Roman roads of Hampshire's New Forest, he found Palaeolithic stone artefacts in the newly cut railroad lines, and he saw fossils from ancient seas in the buttresses of his local church. The shape of a stone, the stratum in which it lay, revealed for Westlake millennia-long changes in a landscape and its place in the history of the world. Westlake was an amateur geologist, a gentleman scholar and a collector with a passion and enthusiasm beyond the ordinary.

Modern innovations granted Westlake's view into the ancient past. From the early nineteenth century, industrial mining and rail works brought to light buried oceans and landforms and extinct animals and plants, offering geologists the ability to map the depth of earth's history. From the realisation of deep geological time came a radical rethinking of human history.

The year Westlake turned four, 1859, Charles Darwin published *On the Origin of Species*, challenging Biblical creationism by linking humans to animals by the transmutation of species. In the same year, English geologists published reports that dated the earliest stone tools back to the last Ice Age (or Pleistocene), a time of woolly mammoths and glaciers.[1] These revelations came at a time of expanding Empire and encounters with other cultures. Anthropology and archaeology emerged as disciplines of discovery and comparison, mapping human culture in technological stages from the 'primitive' Stone Age to the 'advanced' Industrial Revolution era. These developments became collectively known as the 'Darwinian revolution'.[2] Westlake grew up in its wake. He understood human history to be determined, progressive and successful. This view inspired and directed his lifework.

At University College London in the early 1870s, the young evangelical Quaker was asked to distinguish his faith from the rational exploration of science, and to question Creationism in favour of evolutionism. Westlake retained his devotion to Christ, but he returned home to Hampshire determined upon a career that would advance the knowledge and depth of human and geological history within an evolutionary framework. His first project was a history of his own county, followed by a survey of the chalk fossils of Britain. Westlake took to fieldwork with enthusiasm. He loved the outdoors and being alone. He never joined the academy and published little. His first desire, and his principle occupation, was collecting.

By the turn of the twentieth century, Westlake had amassed around 10,000 British stone tools and fossils—the collection I saw stacked in boxes in the upper floor of Newnham Church. It was the first of three huge collections that he would form. From 1901, Westlake began to search for stone tools that he believed pre-dated the Pleistocene.

In 1865, Sir John Lubbock set out in his *Pre-Historic Times* four 'great epochs' of prehistoric man: the Old Stone Age (the Palaeolithic) the New Stone Age (or Neolithic—distinguished by polished tools), the Bronze Age, and the Iron Age. It was not long after these definitions were established that some scientists found evidence for what they argued was human activity pre-dating the Palaeolithic epoch. Their evidence was the stone artefacts they called 'eoliths'—*eo* meaning 'dawn' and *lithic*, 'of stone'—but they were not universally accepted. While it was accepted that the Palaeolithic humans must have had ancestors, the question as to whether eoliths could be accepted as the evidence of their existence became one of the most heated and important debates for early archaeology. 'Eolithic' stone tools appeared much like rocks broken by natural causes, such as river water or shifting glaciers. The limits of the early archaeology made discerning the differences difficult. And the immense age of eoliths stretched the boundaries of reason.[3]

Westlake was convinced by his finds of Eolithic stone tools in Hampshire from 1901. His largest collection of eoliths, however, was formed in the Auvergne, discovered while on a cycling holiday in 1904. He spent several years excavating and transporting the collection, but he was yet to present his findings and try to convince the eolith sceptics, who by then far outweighed the supporters. It was this challenge that inspired Westlake's instantaneous decision in the British Museum, when he was convinced that a comparison between the French and Tasmanian artefacts would demonstrate beyond all reasonable doubt that his eoliths were genuine, and that European human antiquity would thus be demonstrated to date back at least 100,000 years.

'squeezing other races out of existence'

Westlake walked into the British Museum in 1908 a geologist. The project that the collections there inspired him to take on transformed him into an anthropologist. He took to the discipline with enthusiasm. He was accepted as a Fellow of the Royal Anthropological Institute of Great Britain in 1910, although he never regarded himself as a professional.[4]

When Westlake left England in 1908 he had no expert or extensive knowledge of the Tasmanian Aboriginal culture or history. The first 'fact' he would probably have known about Tasmanian Aborigines was what had made them famous among the British public: their supposed extinction. When he was fourteen years old, the death of the 'Last' Tasmanian Aboriginal man, William Lanne in Hobart, was reported widely in the British press. Lanne's death was newsworthy not only because it supposedly marked the certain end to an entire race as a result of British colonisation, but also because of the scandalous mistreatment of his remains. Hobart hospital surgeons dissected Lanne's body without authorisation and under the cover of night, and then sent his head, as arranged, to the Natural History Museum in London.[5]

Lanne's mutilation caused public outrage in Hobart and internationally. When James Bonwick's book *The Last of the Tasmanians* was published months later, there were staged public readings, extensive debates and discussions. The book outlined in detail the destruction of the Aborigines, and laid the blame squarely at the feet of the colonial government.

Westlake's generation grew up with the story of Tasmania as a lesson in the cost and nature of colonisation. It was a lesson that was intended to evoke melancholy and regret. Westlake's letters home from Tasmania echoed this sentiment, and his grandchildren remembered him speaking of such 'shame' years later.[6] Westlake's feelings were as much about the loss to science caused by extinction, but he also felt as a pacifist a genuine disquiet over the violence of the frontier. Westlake showed none of the triumph that British historian Tom Lawson observes was common among popular British responses to the supposed extinction. Even when regret was voiced, it was often 'tinged with pride' over the demonstrated 'might' of the Empire. Months after Lanne's mutilation, *The Times* predicted with vainglorious relish, 'English-speaking men are destined to cover the planet, squeezing other races out of existence ... until, the red Indian promises to disappear and the aboriginal Tasmanian has actually vanished.'[7]

Westlake did not share the 'colonial curiosity' of many British, who sought out public displays of Tasmanian Aboriginal bones in museums. Their human remains were plundered covertly from graves, exchanged in 'favours' and deals, and housed in private and public collections the world over, but the desire was as much for the sake of possession as rare curiosities, trophies of superiority, as for any scientific intention.[8] Westlake did, however, collect prints of the photographs taken of residents of the Oyster Cove Aboriginal Establishment while he was in Hobart, which are part of his archive. Circulated widely and repeatedly from the 1870s, these images became what Julie Gough reflects was the 'enduring face of Aboriginal Tasmania for more than a century'; the representatives of a dying race.[9]

Residents of the Oyster Cove Aboriginal Station, Bishop Francis Nixon, around 1858–60.
Back row (left to right): Drayduric (Sophia), Coonia (Patty), Drunameliyer (Caroline);
front row: Wapperty, Meethecaratheeanna (Emma), Mary Ann Arthur (seated on chair),
Calamarowenye (Tippo Saib), Plowneme (Flora), Truganini [National Library of Australia,
nla.obj-140385483]

As a student of geology, Westlake would have encountered some references to the culture status of Tasmanians, which probably informed
his immediate and certain appraisal of their stone tools in the British
Museum. John Lubbock's book was a foundation text for students
of archaeology and geology, and it defined the term Palaeolithic for
the first time. To illustrate the early Stone Age, Lubbock pointed to
the 'Van Diemaner' (Tasmanian Aboriginal) as a representative culture.[10] The idea may have been inspired by Edward Burnett Tylor,
who apparently had seen the only Tasmanian stone artefact available
in England a few years earlier, and concluded it to be at the same level
of culture as European artefacts dating back to the recently discovered
Pleistocene epoch. Tylor went on to transform nineteenth-century
anthropology into a science through the application of evolutionary theory. One of his first books, the 1865 *Researches into the Early
History of Mankind and the Development of Civilization*, was probably
another of Westlake's foundation texts, and it declared, 'the Natives of

Van Dieman's Land, whose dismal history is closing in total extinction, are among the lowest tribes known to Ethnology'.[11]

Tylor's conclusion anticipated a correlation between the ideas of extinction and 'low' cultural status that soon came to explain and justify the colonisation of Tasmania as a natural law of human progress. Charles Darwin's 1871 book, *The Descent of Man*, which Westlake would certainly have encountered, explained the effects of colonisation in Tasmania in this way: 'when civilised nations come into contact with barbarians the struggle is short,' and ends in their 'victory', for the cultivation of land is 'fatal ... to the savages, for they cannot, or will not, change their habits'.[12]

Westlake did not translate Darwin's conclusion into the justification or celebration of colonisation, but he did later expound upon the immutability of savages to adapt their ways. He remained throughout his career an adherent of human evolution and of the superiority of his own race.[13] 'The two best races of mankind are the Teutons and the Kelts,' he wrote to his children from Tasmania. 'The English are a mixture of the two and are therefore somewhat of an improvement on either of them.'[14]

Westlake understood his purpose in collecting Tasmanian stone was to demonstrate the antiquity, not the superiority, of European culture. But the assumption of racial superiority underpinned his project. As Lawson observes, the Tasmanians' supposed extinction was part of the British psyche. It was integral to shaping a sense of national identity 'in which Britain was imagined to be at the apex of human development and progress'. Indeed, this imagined superiority 'relied on the memory (and celebration)' of the Tasmanians' destruction.[15]

In the weeks before he left for Tasmania, Westlake returned to the British Museum Library and sought out references for the Tasmanian Aborigines. He had read the 1899 edition of Henry Ling Roth's *The Aborigines of Tasmania*, which had been the first anthropological book on the subject, as well as several papers written by Tylor. Westlake may have been surprised, or perhaps reassured, that his thinking had synchronicity with the most eminent anthropologists of the day. Westlake took notes from one of Tylor's papers, which stated that the

Tasmanians' stone tool culture was 'inferior to that of the … Cave Men of Europe'.[16] Westlake also quoted that their tools should be 'judged' at the same evolutionary stage of development as the 'oldest and rudest sympathized implements' found in Europe, 'the plateau-flints of Kent'.[17] As Westlake would have known, the Kent 'flints' were more commonly known as eoliths. They were the first such find to be made in England, by a storekeeper of the Ightham village in 1885.

It was not until Westlake reached Hobart that he learned from local collector Fritz Noetling that Belgian geologist Aimé Rutot was also comparing Tasmanian Aboriginal stone artefacts to eoliths, in collaboration with German physiologist Max Verworn.[18] By the time he left, Westlake had gained a clear sense of the long-standing significance of the Tasmanian Aborigines in the development of comparative evolutionary theory.

Westlake found it strange that no European scientist had made the decision to go earlier.[19] 'People have been saying for the last 50 years that this ought to be done, but no one does it,' he reflected from Hobart.[20] But had they? For fifty years, scholars had studied the Tasmanian Aboriginal culture from Europe. They had relied upon a network of contacts that relayed artefacts and information from the colony to the metropolitan centres. Westlake had ignored the system of colonial collector and metropolitan anthropologist, which earned kudos and prestige on both sides. He neither deferred his findings to experts and museums, nor did he represent them. 'I asked no one in England whether I should come,' Westlake wrote to his children, 'but just came.'[21]

Why did he go? If the collections of stone implements in the British Museum had struck him as Eolithic the moment he saw them, why did he need to go and form his own collection? Why not carry out 'armchair' anthropology as had been practised for fifty years? The answer was because Westlake had always gone into the field.

His first field had been Hampshire. He had criss-crossed the New Forest hundreds of times and investigated most of the wells, railway and road cuttings. His journeys had extended into neigh-bouring Wiltshire, and across Britain and into France in search of

chalk fossils, palaeoliths and eoliths. It was, for him, a natural extension of that practice to travel to Australia to collect Aboriginal stone
tools. Westlake also held that anthropology should be practised in the
field, observing living societies. In this he seems more influenced by
Australian anthropologist Baldwin Spencer than the American Franz
Boas, who pioneered the participant–observation method of anthropology. Westlake met Spencer in Melbourne in 1908 and in 1910, and
was impressed by his groundbreaking fieldwork with Central Australia
Aboriginal communities. Spencer 'knows how it should be done,'
Westlake reflected.[22] He felt his own efforts in Tasmania were inferior
to Spencer's, because Spencer was 'one of the very few scientists who
have seen the Blacks making and using stone tools'.[23]

There was also his penchant for quantity. Westlake had never been
a collector satisfied with a few stone tools or a representative 'type-set'.
Westlake accumulated stones in the tens of thousands. He believed that
the size of a collection—the range, breadth and repetition—would
more properly realise the reason for collecting it. Westlake collected
around 27,000 stone artefacts throughout his life.

More than sheer volume, Westlake always sought to examine any
artefact in its location. When he learned that Rutot and Verworn
were comparing Tasmanian artefacts sent by Tasmanian collector
Fritz Noetling, he countered: 'They can't do it as well remaining in
Germany, for the thorough study of anything one must see it where
it is in its original state.'[24] When Noetling refused to tell Westlake
where he got his collections, Westlake was frustrated, because it was
important to get things 'at first hand'.[25]

The stones and the landscape from which they came could not,
in Westlake's mind, be easily disconnected and still make sense. In
Europe, Westlake had determined the age of artefacts by studying
the landscape geomorphology, and by sequencing geological strata
exposed in railway or well cuttings or by his own excavations. In
Tasmania, however, he did not dig for stones, partly as he assumed
there was no history to unearth, and partly as he had no need to—the
artefacts lay upon the surface in the thousands, an ironic testimony to
a long Aboriginal occupation.

In this way Westlake's collecting was more like the Australian than the British collectors of his time. They too were rapacious surface collectors who shared Westlake's enthusiasm for going into the field. There are thousands of Aboriginal stone tools in the storerooms of Australian museums.[26] Westlake believed it was essential to see the artefacts' original environments to ascertain if they were fashioned from locally sourced rock, even in the Aboriginal quarries, or exported to different locations to be manufactured.

There is also a far simpler and more encompassing answer to the question why Westlake went to Tasmania. He was a collector. He sought to possess, own, acquire, obtain. Collecting was a cultural pursuit of his generation and class. His comparative project was one part of a popularisation of natural history inspired by evolutionary theory from the mid nineteenth century, but it also had a longer history. Filling cabinets and museums, both public and private, with rare and exotic curiosities—geological, ornithological, zoological, ethnographic—had followed on from and flourished since the early expansion of Empire. 'Collecting was a form of hunting,' writes historian Tom Griffiths. Collectors often mimicked the hunters whose artefacts they sought. They too became nomadic, they travelled far, camped out, brought home their quarry. They were protective of their territory. Noetling refused to tell Westlake his collecting sites; he considered Westlake a rival.[27] Collecting had 'intimations of war, hunting prowess ... and "manly pursuits".' If Westlake was a Quaker and a vegetarian, he was also a cyclist and a camper. He collected as he aspired to live. He joined that 'outdoor school of character formation' from which nineteenth century natural history collecting drew its inspiration, and had among its heroes Robert Baden-Powell and Theodore Roosevelt.[28]

Westlake rarely did what was normal or what he was told. He approached the practice of Tasmanian Aboriginal anthropology with the same disregard for convention that he had for faith, fashion and philosophy. He did not carry out anthropology by correspondence. He did not study stone tools from the comfort of his study. He packed his bags (and his bicycle and tent) and left.

Leaving home

Fordingbridge, late September 1908

Westlake's journey began at Fordingbridge Station, standing near the little brick waiting room and the wooden porter's office. It was a familiar scene: the white picket platform fences and slatted benches, the ivy-clad station master's house on the opposite platform with its curved iron porch, and the square wooden signal box beyond. Autumn yellows had begun to colour the surrounding trees and fields.

Fordingbridge Railway Station, around 1900. The line was closed in 1964. [Hale, 2011]

He had come back to Fordingbridge to pack his camping gear and sort through his French geological notes, which he planned to write up during the two-month sea passage from Liverpool to Hobart. He left a draft of a letter to the White Star Line shipping company amid his descriptions of the Aurillac Valley: 'I do not eat meat + my friends who have been by your line say that your dietary consists so largely of meat that I shall get weak before I reach Australia.' Westlake had sent ahead to the Port of Liverpool forty tins of pineapple and other fruits, 'protein preparations', powdered milk and cheese and bottled lemon juice along with his bicycle.[1]

He turned and scanned the steep bank that rose behind the platform. Some years ago, on this spot, he had noticed an implement while stepping into a train. It had been unearthed when workers shifted gravel to raise the platform. The 'edges were perfectly sharp, showing it had not been derived from higher levels, but been made on or near the spot by Palaeolithic man.'[2] As the railways cut their mark of modern industrialism into England's landscape from the 1860s, so too had they revealed the depths of geological time. The tooth of a woolly mammoth had also been found nearby.[3]

The embankment was now overgrown. He would not miss his train today. He turned back to see the familiar strip of steam etched over the fields heralding the train from West Moors. Here he was, at fifty-three years of age, doing again what he used to do regularly when he was a bachelor: leave Fordingbridge on this branch line to carry out his fieldwork. This time he was crossing half a planet. The engine jerked away under the stone overbridge. As they rounded the bend, Fordingbridge Station was lost from view.[4]

He knew this landscape, this corner of England, so well. He could close his eyes and trace its geological story in his mind—its rises and dips, its ancient rivers and buried ocean floors, even the landscape's smells. The first station, Breamore, had a cattle yard with its own creamery. He listened to the animals lowing, below the sharper sounds of slamming doors and the station master's whistle. His mind travelled away from the station, above the River Avon to Black Bush Plain, 'the highest ground' between Fordingbridge and Southampton.

The 'much battered character of the gravel on the plain' suggested it was left by a retreating sea. He found what he judged were human-worked stone implements among the gravel, which pointed to the presence of humans in Hampshire from before the last Ice Age, 'the ruder flint-work, known as Eolithic (dawn stone)'.[5]

The River Avon captured in its reflection the colours of the changing season as they steamed along the valley floor. Downton church spire showed above the trees. The line had been widened near this point in 1883. He caught the train regularly from Fordingbridge that year to see the new cuttings reveal the layers of chalk.[6] Minute shells had once floated in this landscape, 'more lightly than the motes in a sunbeam'. Some he had measured at '500th of an inch'—'two or three million could go into an ordinary thimble.'[7] Some larger fossils he had painstakingly excavated from the chalk and donated to Salisbury Museum.[8]

Plunged into the darkness of the Downton tunnel, his face was suddenly reflected in the blackened window: keen eyes staring beneath the proud forehead; lids drooping slightly at the edges, suggesting a tinge of sadness; swept-back, greying hair and full beard lending him wisdom and dignity—more than he would have ascribed himself.

Ernest Westlake, around 1910
[Delair, 1985]

There was emphasis on practicality rather than fashion in his dress. He was straight backed and robust in health. There was no pipe and tobacco in his pockets, only the habitual notebook and pencil and a copy of the Gospels.

He was leaving this 'small part of the earth's surface', where he had lived most of his life. Born 'before the age of the railways', by the river, his history, infinitesimally short in geological time, could be plotted across the few miles they had travelled.[9]

The river had run through the centre of his early life. Fordingbridge had offered a safe crossing over the Avon for nearly seven centuries. His first home had stood near that ancient bridge, the river lapping upon the grass at the end of his garden. Southampton House had a name more grandiose than was worthy. It was a cottage, whitewashed and a little crooked, with no more than a step between the gutter and front door.[10] Its name bespoke his father's middle-class Quaker aspirations. It also remembered Thomas Westlake's birthplace on the other side of the New Forest, to where the road and river travel together from the village, through the Avon valley, until they meet the sea.

At a tight bend in the Avon, about a mile from the bridge, churning rapids turned a large waterwheel that charged the machines of East Mills factory. Nearly two hundred hands turned the local flax into sailcloth. Thomas Westlake had left Southampton at age seventeen to join his uncle Samuel Thompson in the business. At night Thomas indulged his passion for astronomy. On his days off he explored the vast wilderness of the New Forest. Protected by William the Conqueror's decree for nearly eight hundred years, the forest had a medieval and mystical spirit, was a place of deep, dark recesses; it was one of England's last wildernesses and bastions of paganism.[11] But Thomas's favourite spot looked out from tall, clean-smelling fir trees to open fields. It had been known for centuries as Sandy Balls.

There was no connotation of impropriety in the name for the sober nineteen year old. He found the landscape reminded him 'of that beauteous country which is in store for those who walk in uprightness in this life'.[12] Thomas modelled uprightness. He continued to work hard at the Mill, 'gradually rising in the estimation of all,' as his brother, Richard Westlake, sympathised.[13] The river made him wealthy. The river brought him his wife, and took her away soon after.

Hannah Neave came from a large Quaker family at Bicton, four kilometres south from Fordingbridge on the Avon, where her father was also a miller.[14] She married in 1854, and had Ernest in 1855. But the river made their cottage damp. Ernest Westlake would always abhor damp houses. He was eighteen months old when Hannah died of tuberculosis. She was twenty-four and pregnant.[15] She died with the wish that her husband should marry her sister Agnes.[16] It was illegal to marry your sister-in-law in England, and so Agnes and Thomas made their vows in Switzerland, when Ernest Westlake was seven years old.[17] Their marriage continued the bonds between two old Quaker families of industry, keeping faith and profit within the fold. But they did not have any other children, nor was the village school considered appropriate for Ernest. He remembered himself as 'a solitary child'. His home was sombre and puritanical. It 'was almost a sin to smile.'[18]

The garden was his escape. It was a long strip that ended at the water where the trees grew tall. He would climb to the tree tops and sit 'high above the earth … swaying over the summery breezes … disdaining the grown-ups … on the ground.' He fell only once; his nose never looked quite as straight again. Jasmine grew on the walls, a rose-covered bridge crossed a small stream, and a waterfall tumbled among flowering osmunda ferns. He 'found peace and contentment'. And pride when he had managed to construct 'an undershot water-wheel' that turned in the waterfall, just 'like the one in his father's mill'. He could see the fields of flax from his treetop retreat.[19]

Going away to Oliver's Mount Quaker School in Scarborough at the age of twelve was one of the happiest periods in his life. Headmaster Thomas Walton offered him freedom and encourage-ment, and fostered in him a deepening love of nature and science.[20] In his second year, he returned to Fordingbridge to find his father had commissioned a new home. It was further from the river, near to the freshly cut railway line, but the house remained hidden from the arriving passengers. It was reached via the old, rutted Marl Lane, so densely lined with trees that it seemed a surprise to find such a large house, square and tall, rising out of expansive gardens. It had white bricks from Fisherton, slate roof tiles with an extra deep lap, windows of plate glass—everything 'solid and of the best'.[21] Oaklands was worthy of its grand name. His father had an observatory built of his own design, with a canvas roof that opened with a system of pulleys.[22] A vastly expensive 32-centimetre Calver reflecting telescope stood as big as a cannon, bolted to the floor, and aimed at the skies.[23] Its mathematical precision revealed to Thomas the perfection of God's universe.[24]

It was Thomas's success and love of science that meant his son's journey from home at the age of seventeen was vastly different from his own. In 1873, Ernest Westlake left the riverside village and travelled to London, to the house of Jabez Hogg—it was most likely Thomas's and Hogg's shared interest in mirrors and lenses brought this about, for there was little else in common between the country Quaker and city Freemason. Hoff was an ophthalmic surgeon who pioneered the use of microscopic pathology and daguerreotype photography, a former journalist at the *Illustrated London News*, and urbane sophisticate.[25] He lived at one of London's best addresses: 1 Bedford Square, Bloomsbury. For years Westlake lodged with Hogg while he studied physics, pure and applied mathematics, chemistry, mineralogy, geology and English at University College.[26]

It was an introduction for Ernest into another world of ideas, cultures and values. The wide double-fronted doors of Hogg's Georgian townhouse offered an entrance hall so expansive it took up almost the entire ground floor. Curved white stone stairs, edged with a fine brass balustrade, swept to a first-floor drawing room lined with ornate plasterwork.[27] Hogg's house was as much a celebration of luxury and beauty as his father's home had been a reflection of financial success and austerity. It was the 'best side' of Bedford Square, as the upstairs bedrooms looked out onto the grounds of Montagu House, then home to the British Museum.[28] That the grounds were still a building site seemed an apt remark on the momentous changes occurring within his life.

Conversion

Westlake was seventeen, living in the intellectual centre of London and among the first generation of students to be taught natural sciences in the wake of the Darwinian revolution. Biology was not one of Westlake's formal subjects, but he chose to travel to the Royal School of Mines in South Kensington to attend laboratory tutorials under Thomas Huxley. Known widely as 'Darwin's Bulldog', Huxley had famously defended biological transmutation against Samuel Wilberforce at the Oxford University Museum in 1860: 'I once dissected a snail in Huxley's laboratory and remember something about it.'[29] Westlake also attended lectures by the Professor of Physics at the Royal Institution of Great Britain, John Tyndall, who spoke prominently on the importance of keeping a clear distinction between scientific rationality and religious faith.[30] One of his essays, written in a stiff but brave voice, captured those early influences:

> [a] dogmatic view of the biblical cosmogony retarded for many years the advance[ment of] the knowledge of nature … investigators of geology and … biology were looked upon as heretics … even at the present day such men as Darwin, Huxley and Tyndall are considered as dangerous and to be shunned by all serious thinking persons.[31]

Westlake returned from university a 'votary' of geology, dedicated to his chosen discipline with the 'zeal of a whole-hearted devotee'. He did some occasional work in his father's office, but it was decided he had 'no aptitude for business'. There would be 'no need for him to make money'; he could 'dedicate himself to the pursuit of science'.[32] Ernest Westlake joined the Geologists' Association in 1877, and was elected a Fellow of the Geological Society of London two years later.[33] In 1885, with four other men, he co-founded the Hampshire Field Club, holding the post of Fordingbridge secretary until 1890.[34] But his membership of societies and clubs was largely formal. Westlake never joined the academy, and he mostly worked and collected alone. The shy child had become a rather introverted adult.[35] He travelled across Britain to Yorkshire and Devon, and on to Ireland, and even to

La Havre to map the ocean that had once covered most of Europe.[36] His 1888 *Tabular Index* of 435 fossil species had been an exacting task that offered a small correction to Charles Barrois's 1876 survey of British chalk.[37] It was his only scholarly citation.

Westlake's first publication, the geological history of Fordingbridge, had been years in the writing and remained little known and hardly cited. It was a work of passion; a conversation of conversion that compelled his fellow residents to see their district in evolutionary and progressive terms, to 'enlarge our thoughts of the world, and so enable us to form a better notion of our place in it'.[38]

His father was enthused by another mission of conversion. When Ernest returned from university in 1875 a lecture hall was standing next to their old house on Bridge Road. A solid, square and red-brick building that made the old cottage seem even more diminutive and crooked. The name, made out in wrought iron, The Victoria Rooms, was nailed above the double wooden doors. They opened upon the 'Mission' Hall, which held up to four hundred people: 'crowds flocked nightly to the services … the people coming in from the villages for miles round, thus evincing the deep interest that was awakened.'[39]

For a faith that had traditionally worshipped in silence the mission meetings, with their hymns and sermons, were 'little short of revolutionary'.[40] Quaker evangelism had begun its rise in England from the 1830s, challenging the Quietist ways of 'partial isolation' and 'Peculiar' dress and speech.[41] It was a cross-denominational phenomenon, brought together by the chief concern of finding salvation from Original Sin.[42] Thomas Westlake sought out links with the Salvation Army and the Bible Society. He preached on the imperative of man 'yielding to Christ'. Once He had 'possession' of his heart, then a man's every action was in 'conformity and union with the Will of God'.[43] It was with such confidence that Thomas Westlake took up his missionary causes: 'Giving up drink is personal work,' he had lectured at the age of twenty-one, 'a real thing which each must do for himself.'[44] He was recorded a Minister in 1888, and led worship in villages through the district. A garden house at Oaklands could hold up to two hundred people for his Sunday afternoon services.[45]

Ernest Westlake thought his father had never read Darwin's *On the Origin of Species* as he 'thought its ideas too awful for anything'.[46] 'His well-balanced mind never allowed him to go astray on the lines of scientific research as opposed to Revelation.' Through his telescope he 'gazed on the wonders of the Universe, as they told how "the Heavens declare the glory of God".'[47] His father's faith and science drew his gaze ever upwards.

Ernest's science drew his gaze ever downwards, earthwards, plumbing the depths of time. When he stood under the fir trees at Sandy Balls, the gently undulating landscape did not remind him 'of that beauteous country', he saw the vestiges of an Eocene river.[48] The landscape bespoke not of man's future paradise, but his deep past.

'Evangelism, Absolutism, Revelation,' he thought, were the causes of so much conflict and pain in the world, and in his own life. Buddha was right in saying 'that worldly people were often better than the religious'. His Uncle Richard wrote that Thomas Westlake always put the interests of others first—'he was nothing, Christ was all'— but it was telling that Richard's 'Memoir' (a pamphlet written for the *Friends Quarterly*) made no mention that Thomas Westlake had married twice, nor even that he had a son.[49] Ernest's father was, admittedly, one of the 'most peaceable of men', but his religion had been doctrinaire.[50] Ernest recalled, 'When I was a child it was forced on me with threats of hell-fire, which greatly terrified me.' As he grew older, 'every serious discussion' he had with his father, 'closed with: "God says so and so, therefore you are wrong".' His attempts to 'point out that God elsewhere said the exact opposite did not tend to help matters.' Westlake never came to agree 'that black was white'.[51] But he did continue to trust that Christ died 'for the love of man and according to the will of God'. He approached the Bible in a 'scientific' way, believing the 'spirit of truth' would guide him, as 'Jesus said he would'.[52] His steadfast faith held to the simple doctrine 'The Saviour says quite simply that the pure in heart will see God.'[53]

Westlake shared his father's house as a bachelor for fifteen years after his return from London but he left it often, travelling far in search of fossils and stone and even further from his father's stern values. By his late twenties, Westlake began to explore some of the more alternative ideas and practices of his age. Under the influence of the unconventional upper-class social set of the New Forest, his introversion began to grow into a self-fashioned eccentricity.

Spiritualism and sandals

Auberon Herbert, the third son of the Earl of Carnarvon of Highclere Castle, Hampshire, and former Liberal Member of Parliament for Nottingham, had taken up farming at Ashley Arnewood in the New Forest from 1874. He operated an esoteric circle in New Forest. His wife, Lady Florence Amabel, was the niece of William Francis Cowper, the first Baron Mount Temple. Cowper and his wife Georgiana offered his large estate Broadlands as a 'haven' for vegetarianism, homeopathy, anti-vaccinationism and spiritualism. Poet and literary critic John Ruskin was a frequent houseguest. Both Cowper and Herbert gave refuge to the ecstatic Christian sect, the 'Girlingite' Shakers, who were evicted from their New Forest home to wide publicity in 1874.[54]

By the 1880s, Herbert was living much of the time in 'Old House', a former charcoal-burner's hut near Ringwood in the New Forest. He had haphazardly added rooms over the years, including a three-storey observatory tower with a bed on each floor. Herbert was said to sleep in a different room each night, and occasionally take off in one of his gipsy caravans. He was also remembered as the first man to ride a bicycle in the New Forest. Herbert also published political philosophy, pioneering the notion of 'voluntaryism': taxation without coercion.[55] Such ideas were shared with Westlake, but their first connection was science. They went collecting stone artefacts in the New Forest together. They also made plans to establish a Hampshire Psychical Society.[56] Nothing formal eventuated, but Westlake remained an active researcher in the paranormal. A founding member of the London-based Society for Psychical Research since 1882, he carried out research for the renowned mathematician Eleanor Balfour Sidgwick, whose husband, Henry Sidgwick, was the Society's President. Eleanor sought information regarding the wreck of the *Asia*, seeking answers to how, when ship went down near Cape Horn in 1852, a relative of a passenger dreamed of the incident as it happened while at home in Manchester.[57]

Westlake followed up other personal stories of spiritual phenomena, visited haunted houses, conducted interviews and received lengthy descriptions of ghostly encounters.[58] He corresponded with eminent physicist William Crookes, and fellow Society member, on the possibility of building a machine that might record the presence of ghosts. Crookes's own experiments using a self-devised 'galvanometer' with DD Home between 1871 and 1873 had been well-known attempts to prove the authenticity of seances. Crookes sent Westlake diagrams and detailed descriptions.[59] Westlake attended a seance in which a boot flew off a man who never untied it and coins magically rained upon the attendees.[60] But he maintained that he was always a detached observer. The Society for Psychical Research was a serious and sceptical organisation, distinct from the many table-rappers and dubious mediums that emerged from mid-nineteenth century society, whom Westlake judged were prone to 'lose their heads, their judgment and their common sense'.[61]

Spiritualism was one aspect of the huge intellectual upheaval of nineteenth century-European society. The Darwinian revolution, the expansion of Empire and the discoveries of primitive cultures led to the questioning and reinterpretation of faith, ritual, belief and tradition. The huge and sustained impact of industrialisation upon Britain's rural environment and class systems inspired a wide-ranging response, from early socialism to romantic utopianism. The political, arts and literature movements called for a return to nature, the restoration of communal land living, and the preservation of Britain's rural crafts and folk traditions.

Herbert gave Westlake an entrée to this movement, and to the ideas and people that had brought him to farming in the New Forest—Cowper, with Ruskin's urging, campaigned to protect the New Forest.[62] Ruskin's utopianism, like that of Shelley, Coleridge and Wordsworth and artist William Morris, later informed the politics of the Guild Socialists and the early Fabian and Labour parties.[63]

Edward Carpenter was a founder of both parties and a prominent figure of alternative politics from the 1880s. His writing questioned orthodox religion, sexuality and politics. Homosexuality was openly accepted at his communal farm near Sheffield. Carpenter was known as the 'Saint in Sandals'; he called himself an 'anarchist at heart'. His socialism inspired a romantic rather than hardline political response, realised in the 'everyday activities' of nature rambles, camping weekends, cycling trips, land colonies and caravan holidays.[64]

Westlake emulated this movement. He professed to being an anarchist ('not a militant one').[65] He took up cycling, became a vegetarian, used alternative health remedies, upheld his Quaker temperance (for reasons of health more than morality) and gave up tea, coffee and all 'alkaloids'.[66] He even wore sandals.

———

The first stage in Westlake's journey was nearly over. As they neared Alderbury Junction the flat fields either side of the line offered the last clear views of rural Wiltshire. Then they were circling Salisbury in a wide arc, cutting through the outer streets, as they made their way to Fisherton Street Station. The Cathedral spire kept appearing through the gaps in the houses in momentary, taunting flashes, like a recurring memory.

It had been months after she'd died, early on the morning of 16 November 1901, that he had had the dream—'she came and kissed me'. Had it really been her? It was only later he realised it had been his birthday. Had Lucy wanted to send her birthday greetings 'before anyone else'?[67] Or was it just that he missed his wife? He had always tried to maintain some reserve over the idea of communing with the dead. His doubt stemmed more from his own lack of intuition than any outright rejection of the possibility. Lucy was the one with the gift.

They pulled into Salisbury Station. It was a sharp, painful, stabbing pain of memory. This was the city where he had last been with her, where Blackmore, who had given her the lethal injections of morphine, still lived. The Cathedral stood, beautiful and steadfast, a constant reminder of his mistakes, of what he might have done differently.

Love and loss

As Westlake entered his thirties he remained, as he euphemistically put it in later life, a man with an 'intellectual turn … fostered by a long course of science'. What he knew about sex he learned from books. He 'gradually accumulated' information 'either for reference, or from some idea that it might be useful later on, as a chart is useful for a sailor.' His prescience proved sensible. Westlake had these early notes forwarded from Fordingbridge to Switzerland when on his honeymoon years later.[68]

His journey to marriage had been slow. At thirty-five his father thought he was 'unlikely to marry', but he had in fact fallen in love. Lucy Rutter was from a large and wealthy Quaker family, of Dewes House in Mere, Wiltshire. Her father operated a soliciting firm.[69] They too were Evangelicals of a kind Westlake 'knew very well'— temperance supporters who 'laid undue stress upon hell-fire'. But he thought that Lucy transformed 'the family Puritanism into an intensely sympathetic' devotion to Christ.[70] She was 'fearless, truthful and sincere'. People would share with her troubles they had told no one else. Her 'name and nature was light'; to be with her 'was like being in the sun'.[71]

For years Lucy 'did not care for' Westlake. 'I can't love thee as thou loves me,' Westlake remembers her telling him, 'and thou knows why'. She had fallen in love with her school music teacher when she was aged about sixteen, and was still in love when Westlake met her nearly seven years later. Miss Jenkins never did 'return her affection', but she was 'flattered by the attention' and kept Lucy as a close friend. It was not until they were on holiday in Cromer that they eventually 'fell out'.[72] Lucy was heartbroken. Westlake believed Jenkins had 'failed in her duty' to Lucy, and was 'stupidly unfit to guide her'. By chance the teacher moved to Tasmania and he agreed to meet her when he was there. He 'wished she had been fathoms deep beneath the earth.' He warned his children, 'it was your mother's misfortune to fall in love with a person of her own sex—so take care you don't.'[73]

His own love unrequited, Westlake sought other ways to be close to Lucy. On the eve of her twenty-fourth birthday, Westlake rode thirty miles to her house, climbed the orchard wall as the clock struck midnight, and by the light of the moon planted bulbs of scilla, snow-drops and daffodil in the corners of the lawn. He returned the same day each month through that winter and lay upon the earth. It was not until after they were married that he told her what he had done. She admitted that the gardener had been perplexed, and that she had noticed 'how bright' the garden had been that spring. Westlake wondered if the flowers had 'breathed in her ears' his name, and while he was 'sowing seeds he had been weaving a web of magic'.[74] For Lucy eventually 'loved' Westlake 'enough to marry' him.

During the months before their spring wedding in 1891, Westlake followed Herbert's lead and bought a wooden caravan. Carved on the doorframe was an image of the first gipsy owner and his wife. Westlake dreamed of evoking their freedom and roaming with Lucy through the forest and countryside. Disapproval was swift. Lucy received a long letter from Westlake's two aunts in Southampton, who seemed to think she and her fiancé 'were going step into a place very nigh to Hades'. But she reflected that 'Ernest and I just suit each other in not liking to bow to conventionalities, and we both dislike to be dictated to.' She sympathised with his life of strict moral censure: 'I expect married life will be like heaven to him.'[75]

They were married in the Friends Meeting House in Mere before taking an eighteen-week honeymoon in Switzerland: 'all day she would walk singing through the myriad of bright flowers.' At night he made them a bed of hay. They walked through mountains bare-foot, if not naked, and slept in caves. It was 'paradise' indeed.[76] On their return they moved to Redhill, London, before settling into Vale Lodge, Hampstead Heath. The caravan remained in New Forest. They enjoyed a life of relative freedom and comfort. 'Neither your mother nor I had extravagant tastes,' Westlake later reflected to his children, but money was not a concern.[77] Westlake was able to research as freely as he wished. He spent much of his first married year in the British Library. The 'Bibliography of the Divining Rod, circa 1100 to 1900 AD', resulted, an enormous manuscript with references to water divining in more than a dozen languages.[78]

Then Thomas Westlake expressed his outright and final disapproval of his son's interest in psychical research. Westlake 'was dishonouring God ... he must give it up.' Westlake countered that he was 'certainly not a Spiritualist'; he was carrying out scientific research. He said that it was 'impossible to abandon what he thought to be a plain duty'. He never heard from his father again.[79]

Thomas Westlake died months later in the influenza pandemic of 1891–92. In the final days of his illness, Thomas saw his first wife and 'other deceased relatives' around his bed.[80] In the final minutes his eyes opened with what his brother Richard thought was 'a look of reverent wonder, a smile of intense joy overspread his countenance. Richard was sure Thomas "saw the glory of God".'[81] 'It might have been real, as He had no more devoted follower.'[82] Westlake did not miss the irony: his father could see dead relatives, the Risen Christ, believe His Spirit had 'possession' of his heart, and call it Salvation not spiritualism.

Thomas's property was bequeathed entirely to Westlake's step-mother, but Westlake was 'comfortably off' and soon absorbed in family life. His son Aubrey was born in 1893 and Margaret three years later. Both of Lucy's pregnancies had been frightening and dif-ficult. After Margaret's birth Westlake and Lucy agreed to 'remain', as Westlake later put it, 'unmarried'. Westlake later reflected 'how absurdly ignorant' they both were. It was not until later, when he researched the topic in the British Museum Library, that he realised how simple birth control might have been. At the time, he had found their 'celibacy relatively depressing'.[83]

It was also in the year of Margaret's birth Westlake's financial problems began. He had invested in gold mining and railway com-panies in Western Australia, America and Brazil, buying the shares on loan. When the market fell sharply, he bought a thousand shares in Pardoe Yates' Royal Carpet Works of Wilton. Yates was reputedly 'a good fellow', married to Lucy's sister, twice the Mayor of Wilton, a friend and a leader in the temperance movement. But when he died suddenly in 1898, the extent of his debts and double life was revealed—the drinking and womanising on business trips to London and Chicago, the company losses and his own misappropriation of funds. Half the population of Wilton was left unemployed.[84] None of the shareholders recovered any of their funds. Many 'lost hundreds' reflected Westlake, but he 'lost thousands'.[85]

The loss began a rift between Westlake and Lucy's family. He discovered that the Rutters had known something of Pardoe's finances, but had done nothing to warn investors. Nor did they come to his and Lucy's aid. In fact, one of her brothers thought their loss 'was a very good thing' and that they had long regarded Westlake an 'idler'. Then Lucy's father had heard she had attended meetings held by a 'spiritualist woman'. Just as Thomas Westlake had done, he 'simply dropped' his daughter and son-in-law.[86]

Lucy began to take in boarders at Vale Lodge, work she was neither trained nor fit enough for. She had been overweight most of her life. His father had not wanted Westlake to marry Lucy due to her weight, 'fearing that she would die and leave me alone—but this did not influence me,' Westlake said. She had suffered from eczema for which the treatment was arsenic, and she never fully recovered her health after childbirth. Within a year of keeping lodgers Lucy 'was worn out with work and worry'.[87] Then, late in 1899, her father became very ill. Despite their differences, she and Westlake went to Mere to live with him. He soon died, and Lucy asked the family whether she and Westlake could stay on in on Dewes House. Her siblings refused them.[88]

They decided to rent a home in Salisbury as Westlake wanted to complete geological research nearby, and they could not afford to keep Vale Lodge anyway. They found a house 'with a beautiful look out on the meadows and the Cathedral'.[89] It was 'the end of January, as damp and wet as possible'. In their economy they lit only one fire downstairs. About a week into their tenancy Lucy came home from church and went to bed early, saying she was tired. She woke early the next morning with intense pain in her side. Westlake's friend Dr Humphrey Purnell Blackmore, physician and director of the Salisbury Museum, came and injected her with morphine. He did so without, Westlake thought, actually knowing 'what was wrong' with her. Lucy spent the day 'half conscious' from the drug. Blackmore returned that night and gave her more. 'He found something wrong with her lungs, but said nothing about danger, and doubtless suspected none—which shows how much he was worth.'

Lucy's breathing became difficult and shallow. Westlake went out to get help, but returned with only an unqualified nurse: 'I might as well have hired a cat.' The woman sat looking at Lucy, repeating, 'she seems very ill'. She didn't even check her pulse. Reluctant to rouse Blackmore from his bed Westlake passed a 'night of nightmare as I can never have again'. The doctor returned in the morning and diagnosed Lucy with pneumonia.[90] Westlake later thought she had had pleurisy.[91] This time Blackmore gave her as much strychnine as he 'dared' to counteract the morphine. He never admitted to making a mistake, but Westlake later wondered if she had been 'poisoned by morphine'.[92]

Westlake went out and bought oxygen from a man who presented 'magic lantern' slide shows—he used the oxygen to light his projection lamp—but it was of no real help. He called in a second doctor but he would only converse with Blackmore if Westlake was out of the room. It was clear, however, that they thought her recovery impossible.

'[T]hou wilt soon be feeling better,' Westlake told Lucy. He wanted to give her 'encouragement and every chance'. But it meant Westlake never got to say goodbye to his wife. 'I feel very sleepy,' Lucy answered.[93] Then, 'she died as I have seen an amoeba die under the microscope when I have added a drop of salt solution to the slide.' She was only thirty-six. 'Vale in Eternum.'[94]

'Faith is an extension of light, and I could see nothing.' Westlake was blinded by grief, guilt and shock. He had done what he thought was right and the result was death, and in her death the bottom had fallen out of the universe.[95] In just a year he had lost his wife, his home and most of his money. Then his family wanted to take his children away from him as well. But, as he wrote to his uncle, Richard Westlake, 'I will not let them go.'[96] Aubrey was eight and Margaret five. They remained with him, schooled by a governess, until they were old enough to board at school. The three lived half the time in Oaklands with Westlake's cousin Sidney Rake, and half the time with Clarence and Aunt Mary Rutter of Wincanton in Somerset. The Rutters' eight children were to become more like brothers and sisters to Aubrey and Margaret than cousins.[97] Clarence had been Lucy's 'favourite brother', and remained Westlake's close friend and confidant. He directed the family law firm, and could keep the rest of the family at bay. Clarence took over Westlake's financial affairs, and supported many of his plans and ideas.[98] He issued him a fortnightly allowance of £4, drawn from his remaining funds. It was enough to continue his research.

Three months after Lucy's death, in the spring following the terrible winter, Westlake was back in the field. He retraced his journeys in the New Forest, 'radiating out in his quest from Fordingbridge in many directions'.[99] The search was his solace.

Surprisingly it was Blackmore, whose two injections of morphine had probably hastened Lucy's death, who instigated and encouraged the fieldwork.[100] Blackmore had discovered what he believed were human stone tools even older than the Palaeolithic epoch in Wiltshire. When Westlake made similar finds he had to adjust his earlier assessment. In 1883 he had stated, '[t]he antiquity of man in Hampshire must be measured in hundreds of centuries.' By 1901 he believed it extended back 'thousands' of centuries.[101] The idea of a human antiquity of that age anywhere in Europe was highly contentious, but the mission seemed imperative.

The same science

Liverpool, 24 September 1908

Westlake jostled through the chaos and heavy rain with the other 350 passengers and their innumerable friends and relatives as he boarded the SS *Afric*. 'Visitors ought not to be allowed on boats,' he later wrote. He edged his way through hot, crammed passageways in a 'fearful squash'. Children howled. The dining room was flooded. 'The people here look 3rd class but better than cheap emigrants.' To his immense relief he found that in his shared cabin he had 'a port-hole exactly' at his head—'fresh air is better than food for my part.' All his baggage was accounted for, 'which is something'—enough clothes without washing for eight weeks, forty tins of food, a tent, an extra box for storage, a deck chair, rubber-soled shoes, and a cloth bag with pockets hung up near his pillow. Hopefully his bicycle, his 'machine', was undamaged in the hold.[1]

The fog had to lift before they could leave the Mersey River. Westlake discovered the ship's reading room, a civilised space lined with wood panelling, glass-fronted bookshelves and hinged portholes. The desks were each supplied with their own blotter and ship's stationery. At one of these he wrote with urgency, hoping to catch the post before they sailed. He had in fact written 'all the way from London', but those were long letters to teachers at Sidcot School,

Winscombe in Somerset.[2] Aubrey was starting his third year there, and Margaret, who was twelve, was beginning her first. Westlake wanted to ensure both children's specific concerns would be met. Did they have to attend the silent meetings? Would Margaret be able to keep up her German? And also her exercises to ensure her feet pointed forward? But Westlake also wanted to write to his children, to bid them farewell once again.

The weather during the first weeks was 'oppressive', but he could walk around the entire ship before breakfast, and have a swim in the canvas pool filled with seawater before spending his day writing. It was the journey that had prompted this voyage that Westlake wanted to document before his arrival at Hobart. 'All day,' he sat in the reading room of the ship, but in his mind he was 'walking in spirit among the hills of Aurillac and understanding them better than when [he] was there'.[3]

Reading room, possibly on the SS *Afric* [vintage brochure, Australian and New Zealand Services 1907, Gjenvick-Gjønvik online archives]

'Antieolithisme'

Westlake was writing an exacting geological survey of the region in central France, where he had excavated his collection of 4000 eoliths from 1905 to 1907. It was, he explained to his children, 'only a preliminary' step before turning to the 'important subject' of the eoliths themselves. He did not want to attempt that second task until he was back in Fordingbridge with the French collection to hand. Moreover, he expected on returning home his interpretation of the eoliths would 'no doubt have to be considerably modified'.[4] Once he learned how the Tasmanian Aborigines made and used their stone tools, he believed he would have a key to interpreting the ancient French artefacts.

When Westlake had gone to France to excavate eoliths in the spring of 1905, he had gone with the 'strongest bicycles', the 'lightest' camping gear, his nine-year-old daughter Margaret and her Estonian governess, Fraulein Saas.[5] Aubrey was at boarding school. His family's disapproval had been clamorous: it was an 'unheard of thing to do'. But Westlake took little heed. He planned to get to Spain by the end of the summer. When they reached the village of Aurillac in the central Auvergne region, he was forced to wait for his fortnightly allowance to arrive.[6] It was not far from the village that he made his discovery.

The deposit of artefacts was undisturbed and large. The tooth of the extinct three-toed horse, the 'Hipparion', as well as a careful study of the stratigraphic correlations, confirmed the artefacts were 'upper' Miocene, from what was then referred to as the Tertiary geological period, dating back at least five million years.[7] Westlake remained in Aurillac for the next two years, digging into the ancient lava flow.[8] Aubrey travelled alone from Fordingbridge at the age of twelve to join him in Aurillac in the summer of 1906.[9] It was in 1907 that French customs forced Westlake to reduced his collection from 100,000 eoliths to 4000. It still weighed over 90 tons and was a challenge to transport and store in Fordingbridge, where he already had around 10,000 English palaeoliths, eoliths and fossils. His stepmother Agnes had died while he was abroad, and his cousin Sidney Rake had full charge of the house. Rake had little sympathy or patience with Westlake's assiduous collecting, nor his financial difficulties.[10]

Westlake's biggest challenge remained convincing the scholarly world his eoliths were genuine tools. During his absence, the debate had reached its zenith with a series of heated volleys between the Belgian geologist Aimé Rutot and his critics. Rutot held that the crude simplicity of eoliths was explained by a lack of intentional design—an idea Westlake shared. This low phase of stone culture had lasted a long time until the onset of the Last Ice Age, when competition for resources forced an evolutionary adaptation, and a more advanced human race emerged, able to craft stone tools with intention and skill.[11]

English geologist S Hazzledine Warren agreed that some kind of primitive culture must have preceded the Palaeolithic phase, but for eoliths to fill that gap 'would be a triumph of science'.[12] Hazzledine Warren found that natural causes—turbulent rivers, abrasive ice—created excellent examples of eoliths. In fact a 'very large proportion of the eoliths' could be imitated by the pressure of a cartwheel, or even 'a sudden stamp with one's heel'.[13]

It was this vein of thought that sent two French sceptics to a concrete-making factory in Mantes near Paris, where they claimed flints knocked together in the large mixer made fine eoliths. Rutot responded that the machine-made tools in fact proved his theory of non-intentional design, and he too began to experiment with concrete mixers to demonstrate the point. But how to prove something made accidentally was once a tool? Rutot resorted to derision, claiming that his critics suffered from 'a new form of mental illness' called 'antieolithisme'.[14] There was indeed madness in the debate. Undeterred, and subsidised by Belgian industrialists, Rutot continued his excavations. By 1907, he claimed to have found eoliths in Boncelle in Oligocene deposits—more than 23 million years old.[15]

Westlake's Miocene finds seem reasonable in contrast. Certainly he did not wish to emulate such ungentlemanly behaviour as that of the continental eolithologists. But Westlake recognised the challenge of finding evidence convincing enough to demonstrate his eolith thesis. This would be the reason for his passage to Australia.

By the time the *Afric* had crossed the equator, where Westlake had seen the Southern Cross and Africa for the first time, and the winds had brought sleet and albatrosses, he had filled '48 quarto [large] sheets' with his geological account of Aurillac. He was filled with optimism for the next stage in the project. Westlake expected that Tasmania would shine 'a good deal of light on the subject' of his French eoliths.

Port Melbourne, 11 November 1908

The 'SS *Marama* was palatial'. He felt an immediate affection for the 'dirt and roughness' of the older single-class *Afric*. There had been cockroaches in his bed there, 'but not large ones'. On '*Marama* the seats are soft, the bread is perfection, the milk is from the cow … Only the passengers are a little rowdy as befits men returning from the annual races'—the Melbourne Cup had just ended.[16]

Westlake had spent two nights in Melbourne before his final leg to Hobart—the first amid the din of stevedores unloading freight from the *Afric*; the second at the Victoria Coffee Palace, a 'temperance' hotel behind the Melbourne Town Hall.[17] Westlake found Melbourne a 'miniature London'. Swanston Street thronged with rushing pedestrians, trams and all manner of horse-drawn vehicles; it was a challenge to cross the road. 'The shops in Collins Street are as fine as those in Regent Street,' but the cost of food and accommodation was far higher. It was 'curious' to travel so far 'to find the same money, and the same English language and the same pointed shoes, and the same religion.'

He also found 'the same science' as in England, 'or even better'.[18]

'they were only made yesterday'

On his second day in Melbourne, Westlake walked up to the National Museum on the corner of Russell and La Trobe streets and entered McCoy Hall. A totem pole of considerable proportions presided over a dense zoo of animals, both skeletal and taxidermal in form, populating several small mountains and a range of glass cabinets. As arranged, Westlake met with the Museum's Director and the Professor of Natural History at the University of Melbourne, Baldwin Spencer, who showed him a collection of Aboriginal stone implements. Westlake thought some were the 'very image' of eoliths he had found in France.

Display of animals and fossils in McCoy Hall, National Museum, Melbourne, around 1910
[State Library Victoria, H12937]

'It was very interesting to talk to him,' Westlake wrote later of
Spencer, 'because he is one of the <u>very</u> few scientists who have seen
the Blacks making and using stone tools.'[19] Westlake had gone to
the Public Library the previous day and read Spencer's 1904 book,
The Northern Tribes of Central Australia. Like Spencer's 1899 book, *The
Native Tribes of Central Australia*, this work was co-written with Francis
James Gillen, the Alice Springs postmaster with whom he had travelled in 1896 and 1901–02 to visit Aboriginal communities. Their
work formed a landmark in anthropological publishing for its detailed
accounts and wealth of photographs of daily and ceremonial life.

Spencer and Gillen's books also set an important precedent for
Westlake before he arrived in Tasmania, both for what he assumed
was authentically Aboriginal—people still in 'their savage state'—and
what he believed a professional anthropologist to be—someone who
studied such people. From the outset, Westlake believed he would

never meet that standard in either regard; he was foremost a geologist without a formal degree and the Tasmanian Aborigines were extinct.

Westlake had first met Spencer the previous day at his home. He had also gone to the home of public engineer and stone tool collector AS Kenyon. Westlake accurately deduced they were 'the two chief stone men' in Victoria. Kenyon and Spencer, with fellow collector SR Mitchell, 'dominated' the interpretation of Aboriginal culture in Victoria for over sixty years. They formed the centre of what Tom Griffiths named the 'stone circle'.[20]

What might Kenyon and Spencer have made of Westlake? They most likely approved of his amateur rank. While Westlake considered Spencer to be professional he was not trained in anthropology and, like Kenyon, carried his amateur status as a 'banner of distinction'. They probably applauded Westlake's enthusiasm to get into the field. It was what distinguished and inspired their anthropological approach.[21] But what did they make of his eolith thesis? 'They think it ridiculous out here for Europeans to hesitate to recognise stones as human work merely because they are rough,' Westlake happily reported to his children. 'On the other hand,' he added, 'they don't like the word Eo-lith for such stones, seeing that out here they were only made yesterday.'[22]

It is an intriguing rebuke that points to a key difference between how the Australians and Westlake interpreted Aboriginal culture. While they agreed with Westlake that the Aboriginal people had no antiquity beyond a few hundred or, at most, a few thousand years earlier ('yesterday' in geological time) they did not agree that Australian stone tools, however 'rough', could be considered Eolithic. This was not because they were opposed to the existence of a pre-Palaeolithic epoch, but because they thought the entire question had no relevance to the study of Aboriginal culture; it did not belong 'out here'.

Spencer and Kenyon loosely accepted the comparative evolutionary framework as established by European scholars. They regarded Aborigines as Stone Age 'survivals'.[23] But they rejected as helpful the extensive questioning as to which particular phase of European culture Aboriginal people represented, and in fact Kenyon was resolutely dismissive of this approach. In his private correspondence he warned against the 'evil of the European archeologist' and denounced descriptions of Aboriginal stone tools as 'Mousterian' or 'Azillian'—typological phases named after European Palaeolithic sites—as mere 'piffle'.[24] Kenyon held that 'genuine, local insights' were gained through 'practical fieldwork and commonsense'. There were strong 'nationalistic overtones' to his opinions. Like Spencer and their circle, Kenyon's opinions demonstrate a determined shift away from the old deferential system of colonial collector and metropolitan anthropologist. Importantly, they were not interested in Aboriginal stone tools foremost as a way to illuminate European antquity, but rather for what they could explain about local culture and, even, local prehistory. In this respect Spencer's circle contrasted with the Tasmanian collectors and students of Aboriginal culture of the time, who largely continued to defer to European experts and comparative classificatory systems to describe stone tools, if with a confident assurance in their own expertise.

The 'Problem of the Tasmanians' was one of the most significant founding debates of Australian anthropology and archaeology, and a seemingly unanswerable question: if the Tasmanians were a separate race from the mainland Aborigines, how had they got to their island, and from where? In 1898, Australian geologist Alfred Howitt proposed the theory that Rhys Jones determined by 1965: people had reached Tasmania by foot before rising seas isolated them at the end of the Pleistocene by creating the Bass Strait.[25] The possibility would give Australian Aboriginal people an antiquity of more than 12,000 years; far deeper than was widely accepted.

Kenyon was at first intrigued by Howitt's theory. He had begun scouring Victoria's coastline for implements to see if he could draw a typological connection with Tasmanian artefacts. Howitt wrote to Tylor in Oxford in 1899 that Kenyon had found Victorian implements that 'completely parallel' Tasmanian stone tools. By the time Westlake met Kenyon, he had been searching the Victorian coastline for a decade, and may have begun to doubt that a typological connection could prove antiquity.[26] Most likely with Spencer's influence, Kenyon ultimately rejected Howitt's thesis as fanciful, and hardened his resolve that Aboriginal people had only a short history.[27]

Kenyon and Spencer may not have approved of Westlake's Eolithic theory, but they did concur on the significance of the Tasmanian Aborigines. Trained in biology, Spencer was an evolutionist who held firmly to culture and biology as being progressive. He had been a student at Oxford and had assisted Tylor transfer Lieutenant-General Pitt-River's ethnographic collection from London to Oxford and, in doing so, learned how to classify artefacts according to their cultural development.[28] He agreed that the Tasmanians offered a unique and important example of early human development. He also impressed upon Westlake the significance of their history as a lesson to science.

Westlake wrote to his children from Melbourne that Spencer had taught him that 'the destruction of the Tasmanians was the most serious and irreparable loss that anthropology had ever sustained'.[29] Significantly, the emphasis was on the loss to anthropology, less to the Tasmanian Aborigines themselves. As Westlake continued in his letter to his children, the Tasmanian Aborigines' 'destruction' was 'our loss'. It occurred before they were studied. 'The last page' of that important 'primitive world' was therefore 'closed unread'.[30]

Historian Russell McGregor observes that 'almost all scientific accounts of the Tasmanians' from the mid nineteenth century 'were tinged with a sentimental regret at their passing'. If colonisation facilitated and informed the emergent discipline of anthropology, it also appeared to jeopardise the survival of its subject matter. 'From the start,' writes Patrick Brantlinger, 'anthropology has been a science of mourning.'[31] The ethos of the nineteenth century collector was melancholic. But for Spencer in early-twentieth-century Australia the rationale of his anthropology was urgency. He took to the field with an impetus to capture Northern and Central Australian Aboriginal culture before it was lost.

Spencer told Westlake that it was the exchange of insulator glass for tool making on the Overland Telegraph Line, on which Gillen worked as operator, that facilitated their communication with the Aranda people. This was apparently offered to Westlake as an example of the 'rapid change' that (somewhat paradoxically) threatened the opportunity to study a race 'that represented early stages of evolutionary development'.[32] Westlake left the museum with the impression that the use of insulator glass did not represent ingenuity and cultural adaptation, but loss. He wrote to his children:

> money is no use to the Black, you can't pay him for your use of the desert. He may take the occasional piece of glass as a set off, but he belongs to those races so primitive that their 'civilisation' is impossible. Take away his desert, and his tribal customs and you leave nothing and he is soon dead.

This thinking also echoes Charles Darwin's in *The Descent of Man*. Darwin concluded that the cultivation of land is 'fatal ... to the savages, for they cannot, or will not, change their habits'.[33]

When Westlake left his meeting with Spencer it was not with melancholic regret, but anger:

> As I came out ... from the Victoria Coffee Palace ... the Town Hall was full of people singing 'tell me the old old story of Jesus and his love'—but ... the words coming from such a quarter jarred on me. The only text I cared to hear expounded was 'Hast thou killed and hast also taken possession!' So I withdrew noticing by the way that the foundation stone of the Hall had been 'laid by the Mayor William Cain Esq' (stones sometimes speak the truth).[34]

Westlake wished that not only foundation stones would speak the truth.

At 10.30 am on 12 November 1908, on the palatial SS *Marama*, Westlake passed by the northeastern coast of Tasmania in a 'smooth sea and bright sunlight'. But he felt heavy of heart. He was 'sorry' to see Tasmania's northern shores 'as I knew I should be', for there were no more Aborigines in Tasmania, thought Westlake, 'only stones now'. How much would he be able to read from these remnants of culture he worried? 'I shall do my best.'[35] It was this determination to find every remnant artefact, and memory of, and all information about, a culture presumably dead that ironically bequeathed a rich record of what had in fact survived.

Collecting stones

Hobart, 22 November 1908

The room was small. Westlake had only just 'enough room to turn around'. But the fireplace was large enough to store his bicycle and a sink had 'water laid on'. It was in fact an old external kitchen in a small and enclosed backyard. The sounds filtering from neighbouring yards were already familiar: chickens, wood chopping, children and calling mothers. The street beyond was quiet, with the occasional soft footfall of horses and pedestrians passing the modest and close-set weatherboard houses. Their front gardens were no more than thin strips of green squeezed between iron lace-worked verandahs and picket fences. The edges of the city began a few blocks south, and ended at the wharf, where the square sandstone Tasmanian Museum overlooked the skiffs and tugboats. He already enjoyed riding his bike down there, the heat of the day pleasantly countered by the sea breeze.

'Mr Ernest Westlake has arrived here from London on a special mission to study the past of the aboriginal race of Tasmania,' the Hobart *Mercury* had reported days earlier.[1] The announcement was unsolicited and, Westlake thought, 'exaggerated'. He was not, he explained in a letter to local collector Fritz Noetling, 'on a "mission" ... he was not sent by anyone'.[2] He had come without institutional standing and no more funding than the Lloyds Bank orders organised by his brother-in-law, Clarence.[3] Money was in fact tighter than ever. Westlake was alarmed to find 'the prices of everything were double what they are in England'. He could not afford even modest lodging. He became 'fairly scared as to what would become of' him. But then Joseph Paxton Moir 'came to the rescue like a good one as he is', and offered him the disused kitchen behind his house at Strahan Street, North Hobart.[4]

Westlake had made contact with Moir after seeing his name among the research papers he read in the British Museum.[5] Until recently, Moir had run the shot tower at Taroona, south of Hobart. His father had built it in 1870 to make lead shots for muzzle-loading guns, but Federation in 1901 had removed the protective tariff and they could not compete with Australia's three other towers. Since 1905 Moir had almost no income, but had found in unemployment more time to dedicate to his collecting.

Moir was 'very unbusiness like, very poor and very happy,' Westlake admired. He had 'neither enough to eat nor teeth to eat it with' but still 'everyone was pleased to meet him—so we see how far a cheerful disposition can go.'[6] The two men were much alike: bearded, in their fifties, inured to relative poverty, and keen collectors. Within days of Westlake's arrival the two were out in the field.

They travelled south from Hobart along the coast. At their furthest destination, North West Bay, overlooking the beautiful D'Entrecasteaux Channel, Westlake asked Moir how he planned to get back—'he had overlooked that point.' But just as he pondered the problem an occasional steamboat came fortuitously by, Westlake, who had plans to stay nearby, mounted his bike and rode through the bush—'The sun had set, but steering by Mt Wellington I made a straight line of it.' He joined the Briggs for tea, 'a family of young fellows', perhaps introduced to Westlake by Moir. Like many in the Channel area, they grew fruit, but the Briggs's orchard was on 'a favourite camping ground of the Blacks'. Blackmans Bay was rich with stone tools, 'very nice ones', Westlake thought, and the Briggs promised to 'look out for more'.

Back in Hobart, Moir went down to the shot tower and picked up several hundred stone tools he had stored there to give to Westlake. 'Being of a rough character' they were just 'what he wanted'. Westlake felt sure that what he had already collected was 'so close to the Aurillac flint as to leave no doubt that both were made by men practically the same stage of culture'—this 'will be obvious to everyone'. Westlake's anxious reflection on seeing Tasmania's northern coast a week earlier had been quickly assuaged. He was confident his 'object in coming out will be accomplished'.[7]

While Moir and Westlake were much alike, they looked to Tasmanian stone implements and culture in very different ways. The only hint of this in Westlake's papers is a note on the manufacture of stone tools: 'P.M. thinks there is intentional design … eg straight edges.'[8] In fact, Moir believed the Aborigines' capabilities were far more advanced than the unintentional design of Westlake's supposed Eolithic French race.

Moir had begun ten years earlier to 'dig over' the Aboriginal 'camping grounds' that surrounded him at Taroona. He came across stone tools that appeared to show Aborigines as 'skilful and ingenious tool makers'. They could 'control the break of the stone so as to make … curves … straight breaks and edges, and … angles … according to the intended use of the tool.'[9] He reported his findings to members of the Royal Society of Tasmania, but received no response.[10] So Moir wrote to Tylor, professor of anthropology at Oxford.[11]

I found Moir's letters to Tylor in an old cigarette box among Westlake's papers in the Pitt Rivers Museum in 2000. I wondered if Henry Balfour, keeper of the Museum, placed Moir's letters among Westlake's papers around the time he was studying Westlake's collection of stone tools in the 1920s and 1930s. Folded into a tight bundle were eight years worth of letters, including some of Tylor's drafted replies, spanning from 1898 to 1906. Moir wrote careful, long letters; some were formal essays. They were filled with drawings of stone tools, illustrating their possible uses and the ways they might have been held. The sketches were at times organised into types with names of Moir's devising, and often corresponded to examples that Moir also sent Tylor for his collections. But the main point of Moir's letters was an argument, politely but persistently put, that the cultural status of Aboriginal Tasmanians should not be regarded as too low. Moir agreed with Tylor that they were representative of the Palaeolithic era, but came late in the culture phase, and were in fact 'on the eve of the Neolithic Age'.[12] Moir observed that it took 'more skill … to break a stone into shape than to grind it.'[13]

Even on the margins of his local scholarly community, Moir was challenging one of the world's most prestigious anthropologists on an idea that he had advanced, an idea that would have significant impact on the direction of early cultural evolutionary theory. How did Tylor receive the letters? With enthusiasm and interest.

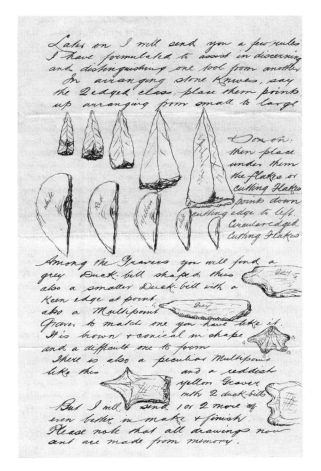

A letter from Joseph Paxton Moir to Edward Burnett Tylor, 14 May 1905 [© Pitt Rivers Museum, University of Oxford Pitt Rivers Museum Manuscript Collections, Westlake Papers, Box 2, Folder 3, folio 81 verso]

The first stone

Tylor had been fascinated by the Tasmanian Aborigines for nearly forty years. It began with just one Tasmanian stone tool, presented to a meeting of the Somerset Archaeological Society in Taunton in about 1860. It was small, and chipped roughly, but effectively, on one side, creating a sharp edge useful for scraping.[14] Tylor immediately thought it looked like French stone tools that only months earlier had been confirmed as dating from the last Ice Age, or Pleistocene. The comparison was a revelation. As Tylor later put it, 'Man of the Lower Stone Age ceases to be a creature of philosophic inference, but becomes a reality.'[15] The European Stone Age was both remote in time and an object of recent discovery. The Tasmanian scraper encapsulated the deep past. It was as if Tylor could hold the beginning of human culture in the palm of his hand. This single tool continued to play an inspiring role throughout Tylor's lifework, shaping his theories of evolutionism. And the reverse is true: Tylor's thinking about the Taunton scraper developed as he continued to research the culture of Tasmanian Aborigines as well as other societies.

In 1862, Tylor attended the Great Exhibition in London and spoke with Joseph Milligan, Commissioner for Tasmania and former superintendent at the Oyster Cove Aboriginal Station. Milligan told Tylor, as Tylor later quoted, that the Aborigines would 'pick up a suitable flat stone, knock off chips from one side, partly or all round the edge, and use it without more ado'. From this one exchange, Tylor deduced that the Taunton Scraper was typical of the Tasmanian Aborigines' stone culture, and so concluded in 1865 that they are 'among the lowest tribes known to ethnology'.[16]

Tylor did not explain the significance of this idea for another twenty-five years. In the Preface to Henry Ling Roth's *The Aborigines of Tasmania*, Tylor wrote about why the Tasmanians were so important to anthropology: of the many 'Stone Age' tribes, the Tasmanians alone illuminated life as it had been in the earliest phase of European culture. If it seemed improbable that men of the 'Drift', as he called the last Ice Age, held their axes rather than hafted them, their 'ignorance' became plausible 'because it prevailed in Tasmania'.[17]

Tylor then sought to expand his collection of stone tools. On his behalf, Henry Ling Roth wrote to James Backhouse Walker of Hobart that, 'we, in England, are badly in want' of Tasmanian stone implements. Roth explained that with the exception of 'the one stone' in the Taunton Museum, and 'half a dozen' in the Pitt Rivers Museum, 'no one at home appears to be the possessor of any'.[18] Tylor soon received 'a number' of stone implements from Alexander Morton, curator of the Royal Society of Tasmania's Museum, and a 'general collection' of about 150 implements from WL Williamson of Browns River, near Hobart. Williamson required exchange for the stone tools he sent to Tylor—Roman and English coins, shells and stamps—which he sold in what was described later to Tylor as a 'higgledy-piggledy museum in a little shed near the beach'.[19]

Tylor then set out his ideas about the Tasmanians across five papers from 1894 to 1900, as well as in the new Preface to Roth's second edition in 1899.[20] The first publication, 'On The Tasmanians as Representatives of Palaeolithic Man', was the most referenced. The title alone assured its impact. It reaffirmed the Tasmanians in the culture phase defined by Lubbock in 1865—the earliest phase of human evolution.

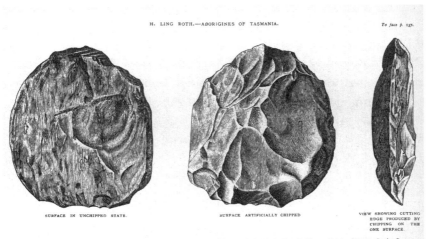

H. LING ROTH.—ABORIGINES OF TASMANIA.

To face p. 137.

SURFACE IN UNCHIPPED STATE.

SURFACE ARTIFICIALLY CHIPPED.

VIEW SHOWING CUTTING EDGE PRODUCED BY CHIPPING ON THE ONE SURFACE.

Tasmanian stone implement in the Museum of the Somersetshire Archæological and Natural History Society, Taunton Castle, Somerset, received some forty years ago from Mr. Thos. Dawson on his return from the Antipodes. Mr Wm. Bidgood, the Curator of the Museum, has described it to me as follows: "It measures 3¼ inches in length by 2⅝ broad. It has a cherty appearance; olive brown in colour; bluish shade in parts; fresh fractures show a deep dull blue lead colour; texture, very fine grain and smooth; but not so glossy as our black flint; perfectly opaque. It weighs just under 6 oz." From drawings by Mr. Alfred Robinson, Oxford.

The 'Taunton Scraper' in Henry Ling Roth's *The Aborigines of Tasmania*, 1899

This was the paper that Moir had read, and it prompted him to write to Tylor. In fact, it was, Moir admitted to Tylor, the only thing he had ever read on Tasmanian stone tools. He explained he had actually avoided reading any more so as to 'prevent' his thinking from being 'warped', and leaving him unable to offer some original thinking on the subject.[21] Moir succeeded in this ambition, pointing to the variation of types and intricate chipping work among the Tasmanian stone culture. In doing so, Moir challenged Tylor's 1894 paper, which had been fundamentally influential in debates over human origins and in defining cultural evolution and racial hierarchy.

In many ways, Tylor's 1894 paper continued the same conclusion he had drawn from seeing the Taunton Scraper in 1860. It was the context of that conclusion that had changed. The former discipline of ethnology had, largely as a result of Tylor's writing, transformed into the science of anthropology. This is evident in Tylor's language to describe the Tasmanians between 1865 and 1894. There was the abandonment of the word 'ethnology', but more significant is that the Tasmanians are no longer 'known', but have become 'representatives' who stand for another time, place and people, and not for themselves. As geologist WJ Sollas famously summarised in his influential 1911 *Ancient Hunters and their Modern Representatives*, 'the real value of what little we know about the Tasmanians lies in the analysis it provides … of the earliest relics of Palaeolithic man'.[22] It was, Sollas admitted, 'a wilfull anachronism', wilful for the vast expanse of time and space that the comparison forced into collapse.

If ethnology had aimed to tell a global story of human diversity across space, then anthropology became a science by 'shedding' this historical vision. It 'defined itself against history' in order to interpret culture according to 'general laws across time'.[23] Tylor's anthropology was unswervingly progressive. It was an improving science that saw promise in the least advanced. It broadened the concept of culture to encompass that 'complex whole' of customs, beliefs and knowledge that determined membership of a society. All societies, however primitive, shared culture, and with it a potential to evolve.[24] When applied to the Tasmanians, this idea of culture went to the heart of a question over human origins.

Shortly before the world-changing year of 1859, British scientists had been moving towards an understanding of racial difference as being explained by different origins—the theory of 'polygeny'.[25] Darwin's *On the Origin of Species* strengthened the argument for shared origins—monogeny—while the concurrent realisation of human antiquity gave sufficient time for global migration and cultural and physical divergence to have taken place.

Tasmanians had a distinct place in this debate. With them understood to be the most isolated race on earth, anatomist Joseph Barnard Davis had argued in 1874 that the only logical explanation for their supposedly unique physical and cultural differences—distinct even from their neighbouring races—was different biological origins. Anatomist William Flower answered that the Tasmanians' differences were the result of isolation and slow transformation and, as such, demonstrated how racial divergence could transpire out of a shared origin.

Tylor interjected that humans shared their descent, but primitivism could not be explained by degeneration. The significance of the Tasmanians for Tylor was their status as cultural beginning, not as an example of historical change. 'In their remote corner of the globe,' he reflected, the Tasmanians, 'may have gone on little changed from early ages.'[26]

Tylor's monogenist stance and inclusive concept of culture should have made his anthropology unifying. But his evolutionary understanding of progress divided rather than unified. It organised societies hierarchically.[27] If European society represented the pinnacle, other societies were reproducing cultural forms it had left behind. They were, as Tylor defined, 'survivals'.

The determined progressiveness of Tylor's evolutionism was at odds with the random nature of Darwin's biological transmutation.[28] But it was Darwin who observed that the demise of the Tasmanians was a 'natural' consequence of 'when civilised nations come into contact with barbarians'.[29] The idea not only vindicated colonisation, it celebrated the superiority of British civilisation.

Nineteenth century belief in racial superiority was a product of the transformation of ethnology into the science of evolutionary anthropology, and the Tasmanian Aborigines were in the centre of that shift. The Taunton Scraper not only inspired such a lasting and influential idea, it also inspired a vast accumulation of stone tools. By the early twentieth century most British museums with an anthropological purpose, and some beyond, had at least a small number of Tasmanian Aboriginal stone implements. Many possessed far more. Stone tools make up the largest part of the overseas Tasmanian Aboriginal collections. Museums in Brighton, Bristol, Belfast, Cambridge, Leeds, Liverpool, London, Manchester, Oxford and Sheffield each house more than a hundred Tasmanian stone tools. There are also collections in Basel, Bern, Brussels, Copenhagen, Geneva, Göteborg, Leipzig, Leiden, Paris, Rome and Stockholm, and further afield in Cape Town and Hawaii. Almost all of these had been collected by Tasmanian colonists and sent either as donations or by request. Institutional exchanges were common, as curators sought to obtain a type-set of implements, or to off-load surfeit collections.

It is both profound as well as accurate to reflect that this vast accumulation of rock was inspired by just one stone. The eagerness to accept large numbers of stone tools was not always so wholehearted. When The Reverend CG Wilkinson sent over sixty artefacts to the British Museum in 1901 they were acknowledged with gratitude, but Keeper Charles Read thought it 'rather illjudged' to claim the Tasmanian Aboriginal people were 'associated with paleolithic man any more than with any other race or similar culture period'.[30] Read did not explain his reasoning further, but it seems he shared Moir's questioning of Tylor's emphatic idea. It was largely due to Tylor that the Tasmanian Aborigines came to be seen as one of the most primitive cultures in the world for nearly a century. So did Moir have no impact at all?

'Justice done to my black brothers'

At first Tylor took Moir's findings into account and seemed convinced by them. He presented one of Moir's letters to the Royal Anthropological Institute in 1900, stating that '[f]or variety of form and purpose and ingenuity of chipping, the Tasmanians hold their own against Australian implements'.[31] Tylor insisted that Roth, who had some doubt about the idea, include four illustrations of Moir's artefacts in his 1899 edition of *The Aborigines of Tasmania*, including a new type of tool Moir coined a 'duck bill' scraper, named after its beak-like nodule.[32] Tylor wrote in the Preface to the second edition that the Tasmanian stone tools showed the 'delicacy ... as seen in neolithic work'.[33]

In the same Preface, Tylor maintained that, 'judged by general character', Tasmanian Aboriginal stone tools were most closely representative of 'those oldest and rudest palaeolithic implements, the plateau-flints of Kent'.[34] While Tylor claimed the 'plateau-flints' as Palaeolithic, their collector, Benjamin Harrison of Kent, said they were Eolithic.[35] Tylor added that the reputed geologist John Prestwich and archaeologist Lieutenant-General Pitt Rivers supported this 'comparison'. Indeed, Pitt Rivers apparently inspired it when he wrote to Tylor in 1898, asking, 'Has it occurred to you that your Tasmanian flints, the flat ones chipped only at the edge that you shewed me at Oxford, are exactly like Mr. Harrisons chalk plateau flints that he considers pre-Palaeolithic and calls Eolithic?'[36]

By 1905 Tylor was working on his final book, *Growth and Spread of Culture*. It was to be his last effort to illustrate his monumental ideas of evolutionary human development. But by this time Tylor was not well. The unfinished manuscript in the Pitt Rivers Museum archives reveals rough notes of the first chapter, entitled 'The Eolithic Age and [the] Tasmanians'.[37]

In the same year, the assistant Secretary and Curator of Taunton Castle Museum, H St George Gray, sent to Charles Read at the British Museum a 'coloured plaster cast of the famous Tasmanian stone implement' from their collection. It had been made at Tylor's request, 'to give to certain museums'. The plaster was painted brown. Its label gave only the name 'Tasmania', as if the hollow object could represent an entire island and its people. But that was precisely its ambition. In an attempt to illustrate the significance of the Taunton Scraper to Read, Gray had added in his letter, 'Dr. Tylor never comes here (and he is often here) without asking to see our Tasmanian implement'.[38]

Forty-five years after he first saw the small scraper, it continued to inspire and inform Tylor's work. If the 'Eolithic Age' was controversial, it was also appealing. Even its name reflected how Tylor had always seen the Taunton Scraper: as the symbol of the dawn of humanity.

After nearly seven years of correspondence Moir wrote with gratitude to Tylor that he had placed the Tasmanian Aborigines:

> in a better light and exhibited their capabilities as clever and ingenious stone-breakers … This result alone is sufficient to repay and qualify me for my interest and work in this Tasmanian phase of the Stone Age (partly perhaps because I am a white Native of Tasmania and wish justice done to my black brothers).[39]

Moir sought reparation in evolutionary science, and he made the designation of Late, rather than Early, Palaeolithic, an act of compassionate

Joseph Paxton Moir sent this photograph of himself to EB Tylor in 1905 after seven years of correspondence [© Pitt Rivers Museum, University of Oxford, 1998.544.1]

reparation. If the colonised society was not so 'low', Moir's logic seemingly followed, and then their destruction could not be so easily vindicated as natural.

Moir understood the stone implements he collected within the spaces where they had been made and used—the old camping grounds, the middens and beaches—but, more, he knew the stories and memories that went with those places. He knew the reasons he was able to pick up that which was once an implement of simple use, and that had been the property of someone else. He sent a photograph taken in JW Beattie's Hobart studio of what is presumably his own hand holding a stone tool. His stiff shirt and jacket cuffs seem incongruous with the stone tool and with the person who once used it. While Moir's hand replaces the original owner's hand, it also remembers it, and its efficacy. Moir hoped to demonstrate that a handle was not essential for a good axe. But the photograph is not only proving a point of anthropological detail; it reflects the justice Moir hoped his science could give his 'black brothers'.

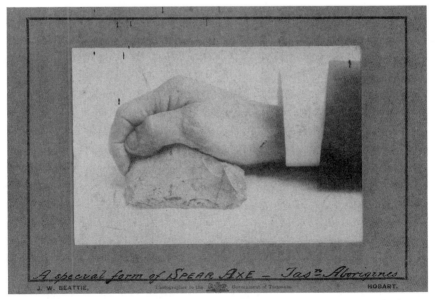

'A special form of Spear Axe', JW Beattie, around 1899. Joseph Paxton Moir had this photograph taken and sent to EB Tylor, who reproduced it in his 1900 paper, 'On Stone Implements from Tasmania'. [© Pitt Rivers Museum, University of Oxford, 1998.466.219]

Australian archaeologist John Mulvaney reflected in 1961 that the idea of Tasmanians as a culture of extreme simplicity, formed upon 'only one Tasmanian flake', remained a 'tradition' difficult to overturn. In reality, Mulvaney explained, 'Tasmanian assemblages included artefacts of specialised type and fine craftsmanship,' in particular the 'variety of scrapers, including nosed and keeled types'. He noted the first publication to demonstrate this was by Henry Balfour, in 1925.[40] Balfour was reiterating precisely what Moir had attempted to relate to Tylor through his correspondence. Balfour's 1925 paper was in fact the result of an extensive study of Westlake's collection of Tasmanian stone tools, which he had acquired for the museum in 1923. He did not agree that the tools were Eolithic. He did not see them as Westlake did, as rough and unintentionally made. Balfour saw them as Moir had, as clever and ingenious. I have always wondered if it was Balfour who put Moir's letters in a cigarette box and left them among Westlake's papers. If so, perhaps he too was touched by Moir's effort to get 'justice' for his 'brothers'.

'They lay about on the surface ... as ... in my dreams'

In early December Westlake left Hobart in a 'cockle-shell of a steam boat' to travel up the east coast. The journey was arduous. They threaded the inner harbours east of the city for hours. At the Denison Canal at Dunalley they got jammed at the swing bridge and had to be hauled through by an engine-powered winch from the shore. Out in the open sea the little boat 'pitched and rolled' so roughly they had to put in at Triabunna for the night. Westlake cycled the next 40 kilometres up the east coast the following morning. He had 'nothing to eat or drink except water so dirty' he was 'afraid of it'. Fires had blackened the trees and the sun was scorching.

Kelvedon station house finally appeared with its welcoming shady garden. A deep second-floor verandah overlooked a lagoon, a beach and the sea. This had long been a meeting place for fellow 'Friends'— Quakers—and home to the Cotton family since 1829.[41] Westlake searched in Edward Cotton's orchard and pastures in the hot sun, his eyes cast down. Sheep wandered through his pickings; 'scraggy, and dead ones lay about in various places'. The crops were 'poor and the grass burnt up', but the effort was rewarded. He picked up around a thousand stones in four days: 'so you will see they are not difficult to get when one finds the right place.'

Westlake took another steamboat down the coast from Kelvedon, arriving at Drake's Farm in Little Swanport just after New Year 1909. It was windy, dry and exciting: 'the Blacks must have lived here either in great numbers or for a long time, as there are acres of oyster shells several feet thick.'[42] He was not interested in investigating them further. He went to a site called 'Banwell', several miles south, to which he had returned three or four days running. Riding through the bush, over rocks and ruts, with more than 15 kilograms of stones upon his bicycle, had been almost comical. Picking up the stone tools from the dried paddocks, though, had been wonderful: 'they lay about on the surface of the dried pastures,' he wrote to his children, 'as I have seen them in my dreams.' He hauled another thousand stones in four days.

Westlake packed his stones carefully in paraffin tins left in the farm shed and began to plan how he would get them back to London. 'I knew the moment I saw the few Tasmanian things in the British Museum that my proper course was to come here,' he reflected, 'and all has turned out as I expected.'[43]

Westlake collected more extensively, swiftly and voraciously than any other collector of Tasmanian stone tools, but his enthusiasm was not unique. The principal of Launceston Grammar School, The Reverend CG Wilkinson, spent the school holidays searching 'more than twenty miles of Coast line along the Western shores of Port Sorell' for stone tools, and had 'ransacked' at least one site of its artefacts.[44] Fritz Noetling lived in Hobart and travelled to the furthest corner of the island's northwest coast, Rocky Cape and Mole Creek, to go collecting. Moir collected hundreds of artefacts and spent years trying to have their workmanship recognised. In Victoria, Mitchell formed one of the largest private collections in Australia; 'every corner' of his Frankston house was filled with artefacts until he constructed his own purpose-built museum. Kenyon was 'continually picking up and bringing home' artefacts as he travelled for his work. Griffiths, the author of *Hunters and Collectors*, estimates there are 100,000 Aboriginal stone tools in the National Museum of Victoria.[45]

The vast bulk of all stones was collected from the surface. Collectors 'relied on their culture's environmental intrusions'—sheep, rabbits, ploughing and erosion—to expose artefacts sufficiently.[46] They did not need to dig, nor did they consider there to be any reason to. They did not think Aboriginal people had a history to unearth. Westlake, in fact, did believe he had found evidence that pointed to a deep occupation of Tasmania, but since he did not need this evidence to prove his Eolithic thesis, he did not gauge its significance.

Near 'Melton Mowbray, in Tasmania's midlands', Westlake found a 'native quarry'. For 'hundreds of yards the ground was strewn with fragments.' The sheer number of stones suggested to Westlake that the 'blacks for ages resorted' in the area. But his chief concern was how he was going to carry away the stones. He wrote to his children from the east coast of Tasmania that there were 'acres' of oyster shells. He thought 'the Blacks' must have lived there 'for a long time'.[47] He was right. By the late 1960s archaeologist Harry Lourandos dated the Swanport middens at close to five thousand years old.[48] Westlake took only a photograph.

It was at Moir's bidding that Westlake spent several days at Adventure Bay on Bruny Island, excavating a 'kitchen-midden of the Blacks'. They revealed what was probably millennia of occupation of the nuenonne clanspeople—'about 13 cubic yards of earth,' including 'a fair lot of stones, bones and shells'. Westlake could not see the significance of the volume, even as it weighed upon his shovel. 'There is not much in it,' he wrote, 'but better than nothing.'[49]

At the other end of Tasmania, Westlake rode the last 20 kilometres from Scottsdale railway station to reach the mouth of Pipers River on the island's northeast coast. He found 'many stones broken by the blacks'. Their position, at the base of exposed, windblown sand dunes, suggests an ancient camping ground. But Westlake left the tools; they showed few 'chipped edges'. He walked past vast 'piles of shells' left by generations of meals. He left feeling he had 'got little for his exertions'.[50]

Shell Bed (midden), Little Swanport, east coast of Tasmania, Ernest Westlake, around December 1908 [© Pitt Rivers Museum, University of Oxford, 1998.466.229]

Even as he dug into it, photographed and walked upon it, Westlake looked past the evidence of Aboriginal antiquity. He did not really see it at all. His treasure was the thousands of stones strewn upon the surface, the stuff of his dreams. Indeed, Westlake was more excited by the several hundred tools Moir gave to him from his store in the shot tower. While he emphasised the importance of studying stones in their 'original state', Westlake's first goal was to demonstrate the authenticity of his eoliths. Shortly before his departure to England in June 1910, Police Inspector JV Cook had allowed Westlake to 'overhaul' his collection of stone tools and 'take anything' he wanted to England. Westlake was delighted. He thought them better comparative material than his artefacts. He took more than 400 and planned to photograph them when he returned home. Westlake believed the illustrations would 'form the basis for the study of archaeolithic stone work for the students everywhere and ... settle for ever the nonsense ... about this work in Europe not being human.'[51]

Westlake had come to Tasmania to discover European, not Aboriginal, antiquity. He was looking for a comparative anachronism. Just as Tylor had seen the early Stone Age encapsulated in the Taunton Scraper, Westlake saw it lying across the dusty paddocks of Tasmania. By drawing the comparison, be it with one or with 13,000 stones, the Tasmanian Aboriginal people were denied their history and their cultural complexity in order to become representatives of an Eolithic age. The act was more than Sollas's 'wilfull anachronism'; it was a wilful invention. Westlake did not just compare Aboriginal stone tools to genuine European palaeoliths, he compared them to naturally broken rocks. All that time, effort and money to move thousands of stones to the other side of the planet just to verify a fiction.

Collecting memories

RECOLLECTIONS OF THE
ABORIGINES.
A Student from England, who is collecting information about the Blacks of Tasmania, desires the addresses of persons
possessing personal recollections, or unpublished manuscript, or rare printed
matter.
Address: E. WESTLAKE, care of Mr.
Moir, 20 Strahan-st., North Hobart.

The Mercury advertisements, 7 December 1908
[National Library of Australia, ISSN: 10399992]

Westlake was seeking memories. His advertisement appeared among
listings for 'Ice – Ice – Ice In Any Quantity', 'Young Reliable Draught
Horse', 'Gent's Bicycle' and 'Pianos – Good, Second-hand'.[1] Where
were the memories of a people who lived before such goods were
available? Everywhere. But how was a new arrival to flush them
out? Place an ad. Use the contacts he had already. Create a network.
'Everyone here is very helpful,' Westlake wrote days after his arrival.
He had 'lots of people to see and places to go to.'[2]

Westlake recorded conversations with ninety-five people in
Tasmania about Aboriginal culture, history and language. They came
from all over the state and from all walks of life: publicans, politicians,
farmers, storekeepers, clergymen, boat builders and fishermen, scientists and teachers. The eldest people had direct memories of the life
on the frontier, or in the former Aboriginal establishments on Flinders

Island and Oyster Cove; others related what they had been told by parents. Many were Aboriginal. Some conversations were noted at length; some were just a few hurried comments. Westlake sought out people recognised for their reputed knowledge, and then was introduced to more along the way.

Westlake did not write down his questions but, gauging from the answers, he was consistent in what he wanted to know: How did Aboriginal peoples use their stone tools? Did they scrape their wooden weapons, and was it towards, or away from, their bodies? Were they right- or left-handed? Did they skin their game? Cut it open? How did they cook it, and how did they catch it? Did they climb trees to hunt possums? Did they catch fish? How did they make fire? What were their languages?

The longest and most detailed of Westlake's interview notes were with Aboriginal people. Westlake filled thirty pages when talking to the children, and one grandchild, of Fanny Smith at Nicholls Rivulet, south of Hobart. When he later met another of her daughters, Sarah Miller, in Hobart, Westlake told his children that he had to write 'hard as I could for three hours', adding another fifteen pages with 'further information'.[3] When Westlake met the Bass Strait Islanders, he filled around seventy dense pages of his notebooks. Journeys to both communities had taken Westlake several days, but he was surprised at and thrilled with the amount of information he received.

Westlake did not want to pass up any opportunity to collect potentially useful information. He gathered memories like he gathered stones—indeed, he often combined the two. But some of his journeys to speak to people, especially older settlers and Aboriginal people, were specifically made, and were no less requiring of good boots and resolve. Westlake crossed beaches and seas to hear a bit more language, note down a little more culture. 'I don't get much for any one person,' he reflected from the Bass Strait Islands, 'but by degrees I get together a considerable amount of information.'[4] It was a gather-all approach to anthropology; a dragnet pulled across Tasmanian memory.

Westlake also sought out archival records with equal determination. He spent nearly a month transcribing the government records

and early newspaper articles relating to Aborigines in the Hobart
library, filling thirteen lined exercise books with notes. He paid Joseph
Paxton Moir to complete some of the task so he could return to the
field.[5] In early 1910, Westlake learned that photographer JW Beattie
had received an offer to buy the journals written by George Augustus
Robinson during his travels across Tasmania to 'conciliate' the
Aboriginal people from 1831 to 1836.[6] Neither Beattie nor Westlake
wanted to pay for, or own, the journals, they just wanted the chance to
read them, but Westlake's concern was that they might leave England
before he had returned home. He wrote to the Mitchell Library in
Sydney, suggesting that they buy the journals, even offering to have
them valued, on the proviso he got to read them first. Westlake
never read Robinson's journals, but the Mitchell Library eventually
purchased them in 1939.[7] When NJB Plomley published the journals in 1966 they transformed what scholars knew of Tasmanian
Aboriginal history.[8]

It was perhaps more perseverance than prescience that led Westlake
to discover sources of such value to future scholars. He attempted to
follow every record and memory of the Tasmanian Aborigines. He
explained his persistence to the Mitchell Librarian in 1910: 'everything that pertains to the Tasmanians' has the potential of 'throwing
light on the early (pre-palaeolithic) history of man in Europe, + hence
proby. on that of the human race.'[9] That Westlake searched the recent
colonial past to try to inform European prehistory was in keeping
with the comparative anthropological practice of his time. But the
way Westlake went about it was radically different.

The 'aftercomer'

When Westlake first arrived in Tasmania, he used Henry Ling Roth's
book *The Aborigines of Tasmania* as a kind of guide. He found it to be
'extremely complete' and planned to present his own research findings
in the same way that Roth had done, with anthropological information organised by subject with referenced sources.[10] One of his first
journeys was to a quarry at Plenty, near Hobart, described at length
in Roth's book by Beattie and James Backhouse Walker, a Hobart

barrister and a member of the Royal Society who had assisted Roth at length with the second edition of his book.[11] Settler descendant GH Rayner had led them to the quarry, insistent that it was 'unknown' outside his family, and that his father had been one of the few people who had seen the Aborigines working stone there.[12]

Westlake then travelled up the eastern coast to visit Edward Cotton. It was a difficult journey, but he went because Roth had quoted Walker's letter that stated Cotton's memories: 'carry us back to ... when the natives were still roaming about the country.'[13] Westlake was excited about meeting Cotton, whom, he wrote to his children, 'knew the Blacks and has collections of their things'. But he was disappointed to find that Cotton seemingly knew little. 'Cotton is only 71, which was not old enough,' Westlake complained. Apart from the thousand stone tools Westlake gathered at Kelvedon, Westlake left Cotton's station dispirited. He wrote to his children: 'Aubrey's hope that I may learn all I want to about the Tasmanians is impossible to be realised—they are dead and their knowledge has died with them.'[14]

Cotton had showed Westlake six Aboriginal skulls in his possession, and he found them 'wonderfully thick—about double the thickness of Europeans—and it must have been a lot of weight to carry about.'[15] Westlake's observations demonstrate how little he understood of anatomy or physical anthropology. He showed no other interest in the subject and made no effort to study or collect human remains in Tasmania.

In contrast, Walker spent over a year trying to access Cotton's skulls on Roth's behalf.[16] Walker thought Cotton's collection of skulls was 'most desirable', because he knew 'the history of each, and they are undoubtedly Tasmanians', but Cotton refused to send them, and Walker was unable to make the journey.[17] Bishop Montgomery finally visited Cotton and extracted a promise to send the skulls down to Hobart. '[I]f only these could be measured in time for publication,' Roth worried, but Cotton did not keep his word.

Walker organised for Roth the study of nineteen Aboriginal skulls housed in the Tasmanian Museum in Hobart.[18] Roth sent instructions on how to determine craniometrical capacity by pouring lead shot into the upturned skulls and then transferring it to a glass gauge, also sent by Roth. Three skulls were rejected from the study as belonging to 'half-castes', and three others because they did not certainly belong to Tasmanian Aborigines. Walker tried to extract from a matted and 'much ochred' lock of hair a few strands long enough to be of 'use' to Roth, which Walker thought had belonged to either Wooreddy or Mannalargenna, Aboriginal leaders who had negotiated with the colonial government on behalf of their people.[19] Roth received the hairs with sanguinity: 'it is really sad to dwell on their fate.'[20] But he was 'extremely obliged' to later receive a piece of Truganini's hair, which Walker had secured from Arthur Clarke. He considered it a 'most interesting relic' that he promised would be 'carefully preserved'.[21]

These disturbing efforts reveal Roth and Walker's research as a kind of morbid relic hunting, a search for the most rare artefacts of what they assumed was a lost race. The hair or bones of the dead 'full-bloods' was deemed more valuable than the knowledge or memories of their living descendants, whom Westlake tenaciously sought out. Indeed, when it came to historical or oral sources, Walker was far choosier than Westlake's grab-all approach. Walker sought out the memories of only a few white settler descendants, such as Cotton and Rayner, and cautioned Roth against the general unreliability of Tasmanian historical sources, from the first explorers' journals to government records and most settlers' memories.[22]

Walker's parameters were rigorous. For him the idea of extinction challenged certainty to the point that his anthropology of the Tasmanian Aborigines was not just salvage, but careful interpretation, sifting and even rejection. Such interpretation required expertise. Like Spencer's 'stone circle' of Melbourne, Walker sat at the centre of his Hobart 'clique', as Moir had termed it, and his influence was considerable.[23] He was a member of the Royal Society of Tasmania and of the Board of Education, and was the University of Tasmania's second vice-chancellor and a trustee of the Public Library. Walker was also an accomplished historian of Tasmania, with several publications to his name. A friend and advisor to pastoralists, politicians and premiers,

Walker's house was an intellectual and literary centre of Hobart. While Walker's circle was more deferential to the British metropole than that of Spencer, he too was confident and self-assured in his local knowledge and expertise. Walker did not seek kudos from his correspondence with Roth; he was his guide and advisor.[24] Roth acknowledged that Walker's 'unsurpassed knowledge', and 'never failing keenness', had been of 'inestimable value' to his new edition. At his own insistence, Walker was listed as assistant in the book's frontispiece.

On more than one occasion Walker invited Roth to Hobart. 'Why not take a six month holiday, and come and study the Tasmanian question on the spot?' he asked in 1897. 'You would learn more in a month here, then in years of correspondence.'[25] But Roth had a business in Halifax, north England, a new family, and was writing another book.[26] But then it was neither expected nor required that the most authoritative anthropologist on Tasmanian Aborigines should actually visit the place. And just as Roth did not leave Halifax, neither did Walker leave Hobart, except for the one journey to Plenty. The small city was his metropole from where they carried out most of Roth's requests by correspondence, by sending others afield, or by researching records in Hobart.

Walker and Roth believed in their thoroughness, tenacity and high scholarly standards. When Walker finally received the second edition of *The Aborigines of Tasmania* he was 'exceedingly pleased'. He congratulated Roth for having 'the final word on our unfortunate Aborigines' and leaving 'very little indeed for any aftercomer to glean'.[27]

Westlake was that aftercomer, and he gleaned a good deal. He travelled to four remote native quarries and over a hundred camping grounds, and spoke to people from Bruny Island to the Bass Strait. While Walker spent a year unsuccessfully trying to get to Cotton's station, Westlake reached it within three weeks of arriving in Tasmania. He did not just read about the Aborigines and the history of settlement, he walked over the places where that history had happened and he listened to it.

It was this listening that marked the greatest difference between Roth and Westlake's anthropological research. Roth read what was in the archives in Britain, or what Walker sent him. Walker was a choosey filter—he gleaned and discarded information before he sent it. Westlake picked up a lot of historical detritus in his anthropological net. He heard what Roth never did: Tasmanian Aborigines reveal their living culture, and white settlers relate not only 'facts' about Aboriginal people, but the way they felt about them personally, collectively and politically.

'The land soaked in blood'

Westlake received a response to his advertisement: Sarah Ann Hughes of Oyster Cove wrote promptly with a promise of memories of the Aborigines.[28] After returning from a month of collecting stone tools on the east coast, Westlake travelled down to the D'Entrecasteaux Channel for the second time.

Oyster Cove was a place of natural beauty with an ugly history. A convict station had been built in 1843, but was closed two years later because it received effluent from the upstream farms. By 1847, it was somehow deemed acceptable to house Aboriginal people, although not without an outcry of disapproval from white Tasmanians who saw it as a misuse of potential farm land or, worse, placing the security of the island once again in jeopardy from dangerous 'savages'.

There were about 300 Aboriginal people who agreed to surrender to conciliator GA Robinson at the close of what was known from the nineteenth century as the 'Black War' of Tasmania, which was waged from about 1826 to 1831. By the time they were moved and incarcerated in Wybalenna Aboriginal Establishment in Flinders Island in 1835, they numbered 112. Twelve years later, when it was decided they should be moved to Oyster Cove, they numbered forty-nine. Nine of their children were taken away to the Hobart Orphan School.[29]

Sarah Hughes, aged sixty-nine in 1908, was the adopted daughter of Sinclair Keith Davey, former Assistant Superintendent at Wybalenna. She had memories of that settlement, strong impressions of being a child in a place where more than sixty people died in twelve years. Following a loss, the Aboriginal clans people would

grieve vociferously ('howl with their dogs'). The departed was sewn
up 'in a blanket' and placed in a 'dead house' on the beach. The clans
people would not pass the house at night; it 'made us children that
nervous—used to shut our eyes.'[30]

Oyster Cove included a chapel, living quarters and land set aside
for the Aborigines to hunt. They cooked over open fires lit outside, and held ceremonious dances and song. It was nuenonne land.
Truganini, who was among the residents, had returned to Country.
But Westlake wanted to know how the residents used stone tools.
Sarah Hughes remembered how they had adapted their technology to
a new resource, using 'broken glass bottles to scrape their spears and
waddies'. She added—no doubt in response to Westlake's questioning—that 'they used to scrape <u>both</u> ways (in both directions)'.[31]

Sarah Hughes was particularly keen to give Westlake what
Aboriginal words she knew, including 'paraway' or 'parrawé', which
she—and others at Oyster Cove—thought meant 'throw it away'.
She tried to capture the original pronunciation, remembering how
'their voice had a crackle in it'. The effort to record the language,
she reflected, 'has been left far too long'. But this word had been
remembered for nearly eighty years. Westlake recorded a somewhat

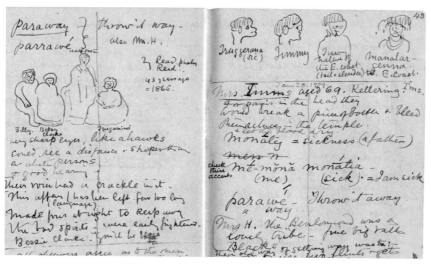

Ernest Westlake's notes from Oyster Cove, January 1909 [© Pitt Rivers Museum,
University of Oxford Pitt Rivers Museum Manuscript Collections, Westlake Papers,
Box 1, Notebook 2, pp. 42–43]

different translation in the British Museum Library when reading John Sherwin's report of an attack on his property in 1830: 'parrawar: "Go away you white man", "what business have you here".'[32] In 2016, I saw a filmed re-enactment of Sherwin's report, which was on constant replay in the Tasmanian Museum and Art Gallery. Jim Everett played the part of the Aboriginal man, stepping out from behind a tree and shouting 'parrawar', a flame captured poetically reflecting in his eye. Jim was with me as I watched it. Then, out of the dark museum space, he mischievously shouted once again: 'parrawar'!

Sarah Hughes introduced Westlake to other locals. Mrs Annie Benbow was four when the Aboriginal people arrived at Oyster Cove. She became 'fond' of them; she used 'to cry when anyone' of them died.[33] Annie Benbow showed Westlake a photograph of the last four residents of the settlement, which he sketched in his notebook (see p. 80): 'Billy' (William Lanne), 'Betsy Clarke' (Bessy Clark, Pangernowidedic), 'half caste' (Mary Ann Arthur) and Truganini, taken by Henry Frith at the Government House in 1864, and later distributed widely.[34] The image contrasts with her childhood

'The last Aboriginal people of Tasmania', Henry Albert Frith, Hobart, around 1864. From left: William Lanne, Bessy Clark (Plangernowidedic), Mary Ann Arthur and Truganini. [National Library of Australia, nla.obj-133844253]

memories of how these people 'Reddened their faces with ochre' to perform their ritual celebrations: they formed 'a string round the beach singing their wild songs'.

Annie Benbow and Sarah Hughes had vivid and emotional recollections: of death (howling, fear, crying) and of life (voices that 'crackle', the scrape of glass upon wood, of fire, ochre, and singing). They are the recollections of children, clear and unadulterated. But Westlake also heard Annie Benbow offer an adult's reasoning, an explanation of a wider history of frontier warfare learned later in life: 'If they had let them alone and not meddled with their young women …' The consequences were explained later: the 'lubras were taken by whites and it was this that led to … the murders' of whites. Sarah Hughes said, 'They burned and committed murder too' of the Aborigines—'wholesale bloodshed … the land soaked in blood.'[35]

The whites' crime was abduction; the blacks', wholesale murder. It is a simplified, unequal version of events acquired from a collective conversation of a generation coming to terms with a history of settlement—an effort to explain away its violence, its creation of absence.

'It was a job to shoot 'em'

The sentiment that the Tasmanian Aborigines were a 'harmless' and 'peaceful' people until they were mistreated was repeated to Westlake like a mantra. Edward Elmer of Westbury thought the Aborigines were, 'a very harmless race if they was let alone'.[36] Mrs Elmer of Huonville told Westlake that 'in their wild state I don't think they would hurt anyone'.[37] Benjamin Joseph of Rokeby thought the 'Blacks at Rokeby quite harmless … till they began to ill-use them'.[38] William Williams of Latrobe thought the Aborigines were a 'harmless race— not spiteful till their gins were taken away'.[39] It was an echo of Annie Benbow's speculation. William Thorne of Sorell offered a little more detail for the same explanation:

> Were very inoffensive … Would never have been dangerous but for convicts. Father said when he was a boy he could go anywhere and they would give you anything—a kind race of people … They were

used very bad—I think what harm the black done it was the fault of the white. The whites who came out were more like savages + would shoot the blacks at night when laying round their fires + that would make anybody bad. Then the blacks took it into their head to kill anything they came across.[40]

Throughout these interviews the settlers admit that 'the whites' mistreated Aborigines, but who the 'whites' are is little more than a vague entity—an amorphous 'they', the abductors of women, the 'savage' convicts.[41] They are never the landed settlers. The settler descendants Westlake spoke to rarely mentioned the massive and swift pastoral expansion that invaded a third of the island and its best arable land. They remembered that the Aborigines committed 'murders' but did not speak of the massive deployment of military and civilian forces in response. They deferred responsibility to a time before the pastoral invasion of the 1820s—they blamed the convicts, the first 'savage whites' to arrive. And they spoke repeatedly about the first massacre to take place in Tasmania.

Risdon Cove on the Derwent River was the first site of British settlement in Tasmania. On 4 May 1804 about three hundred Aborigines came close to the settlement, probably arriving as part of their annual autumn migration to the coast. Armed soldiers were dispatched, and two Aboriginal people were shot. After the Aborigines moved to land above the settlement, orders were given to fire the cannon, rifles, pistols and muskets at them. The inquiry, held twenty-six years later, heard the Aborigines had never threatened or attacked, but reports of their numbers of dead varied: 'five or six', 'thirty bodies were found and burnt or buried' and 'no fewer than fifty of them had been shot down'.[42] Historians have repeated these, and higher, figures since.[43]

On 12 February 1909 Westlake met with Thomas Reibey near Launceston. A former Archdeacon, Premier of Tasmania and Colonial Secretary, Reibey was born into a substantial pastoral family in the north of Tasmania.[44] He thought that Risdon was 'a standing blot to the disgrace of the English nation. Shot 50'.[45] After his meeting,

Westlake wrote to his children and explained in more detail what Reibey told him:

> He said the Blacks were a most harmless and peaceful people and would never have become enemies had they not been cruelly treated and vilely outraged, and he thought their treatment a great shame on the Christian people of England who were responsible for the management of the colony. When the monument commemorating the founding of the colony was opened at Risdon, he 'refused to go near the place', because it had been the scene of the first massacre of the Blacks.[46]

Mrs Charles Smith of Launceston told Westlake that when her father 'came out and took land' the Aborigines were a 'very peaceful people', but they were 'ill treated and took revenge—e.g. Risdon'.[47] The reasoning doesn't follow, as the Risdon massacre occurred before the pastoralists arrived. Still, the event is held up as the cause of 'revenge', rather than settlers who 'took land'.

'I think it was a diabolical thing to have done,' Beattie reflected on Risdon Cove.[48] Seventy-six-year-old William Blyth of Oyster Cove, who thought the Aborigines a 'very harmless innocent race,' told Westlake that they were 'villainously treated, first at Risdon by a cowardly lieutenant. The natives would encircle game and came yelling and shouting, driving kangaroos and wallabies in front to them. Some of them were shot. That yarn is sniggled up but true enough.'[49]

Blyth's final words speak volumes. If the Risdon Cove massacre was 'sniggled up', or exaggerated, then why? Historian Keith Windschuttle argues that contemporary Tasmanian Aborigines and modern historians fabricated the 'massacre' to 'milk the event for maximum political gain'. He does not think that the colonists did this 'milking'. Their response 'for decades afterwards, ranged from regret to repugnance,' Windschuttle explains, but he interprets regret to mean that 'no one urged that shooting Aborigines was an acceptable thing to do'.[50] But Westlake's interviews suggest that if the Risdon Cove massacre was exaggerated, then it was the colonists who did so first for their own 'political gain'.

The Risdon massacre is a foundation story for Tasmanian colonisation that has come to represent many of the injustices to the Tasmanian Aborigines that followed. But its significance is not its primacy alone. It was British soldiers, not colonial settlers, who were responsible for killing Aborigines on 4 May 1804. It was, as Westlake quoted Reibey, a 'great shame on the Christian people of England who were responsible for the management of the colony'. The burden of Tasmania's violent past is thus not carried by the citizens of a newly Federated Australian nation, but by their former colonial rulers. Accordingly, the Tasmanian settler community can talk of a time when the Aborigines were 'harmless'. They can recall their own acts of kindness towards them. Reibey recalled for Westlake how he once took them a basket of apples when he was ten or eleven.[51] Mrs Smith (not related to Fanny Smith) remembered how her father 'used to allow them a gully to have a corroboree' and how an 'old friend' used to give them a 'periodical feast of bread and brown sugar'.[52]

Despite these kindnesses, the settlers had to suffer the consequences of an irrational, murderous people turned 'bad' by others: the British rulers and 'savage whites'. The Aborigines decided to 'kill anything they came across', as Thorne put it, making the land 'soaked in blood'. It is ultimately the Aborigines who are to blame. The fact that settler families, such as the Riebeys, occupied vast tracts of Aboriginal land, which was a primary cause of the frontier conflict, is glossed over. But a few of Westlake's interviewees suggested what lay below the smooth surface. Charles Smith of Launceston told Westlake that he thought:

> The object of all the landholders (including the VDL [Van Dieman's Land Company]) was simply to exterminate them ... they murdered them frightful ... Lewis ... (old hand—only one left) ... used to be with the Archers at Cressy, was an assigned servant, very calm and clear in head—saw the blacks killed many a score ... [At] 'Bone Flat' whole tribe murdered ... left unburied ... Only object of the early colonists was to stamp 'em out. The settlers would surround their camps by night and destroy every man, woman and child.[53]

Here the lower-class Lewis shot the Aborigines not because he was a 'savage white', as in Thorne's narrative, but because he was following the orders of his landholding employers. The Archer family settled at the Norfolk Plains in the 1820s, where they acquired vast tracts of land.

Ninety-year-old Thomas Riley of Carlton, whose grandfather had been one of Carlton's first settlers, offered Westlake a glimpse of what his people did to the Aborigines on the frontier: 'Very smart + active, would whip behind a tree, it was a job to shoot 'em.'[54] It is a piercing echo of the words Westlake had recorded in the British Museum Library, given by James Steel in 1829: 'from their well known cunning added to their extreme quickness of sight ... it was impossible to get sufficiently near to catch them.'[55]

As it did in the quiet enclave of the British Museum Library, the violence of the frontier past again seeps through Westlake's efforts to capture anthropological information from colonial history. Such raw, pitiless memories are less evident in Roth's monograph. Instead the collections of hair, bones, photographs and memories are collected with 'sadness' and 'obliging thanks', and the stories of their acquisition are smoothed away. The violence of the past is more successfully concealed on the published page. In Westlake's handwritten, messy archive it is revealed afresh: Hughes's memory of the word 'paraway' and the swift escape from the armed frontiersman resonates between the British Museum library and Carlton, Tasmania, with more than seventy years of retelling. The handwritten words turn up sharp memories that pierce the illogical justifications for a war over land. The repetition of adjectives, ideas and events reveals these justifications to be a collective effort. This was a voice of 'white' Tasmania in the newly Federated Australian nation at the start of a new century. They wanted to advance with a cleaner rendition of the colonial past. But most of all, they wanted that past to have decisively and irrevocably ended.

Broken promise

When I first saw Truganini she was sitting with her hands clasped round her knees apparently gazing at the open bay ... and just gave me a momentary glance as I rode up such as the animals in the Zoological

Gardens give one—swift but expressionless and without the faintest trace of interest or animation ... I imagined the object before me could hardly be a human being ... it may have been due to her dark sooty brown colour, and partly to the pronounced prognathism of her face.[56]

This memory from The Reverend Henry Dresser Atkinson dates back to when he first arrived in Tasmania in 1868. He had written them for the Anglican *Church News* in 1905, and Westlake transcribed the words carefully into an exercise book in Hobart. Westlake met Atkinson in late November 1908, probably when the retired priest was visiting Hobart from his home in Evandale in the north. It was the first interview Westlake noted at length in Tasmania. Westlake seemingly sought to know what Atkinson knew about traditional Aboriginal cultural practice and language (the responses to such questions feature in sparse outline), but what Atkinson gave him was essentially a reiteration of his first meeting with Truganini. That was, for all its personal and emotional content, a memory distilled by repetition and the preacher's skill of oratory into a structured and pointed homily.

Truganini, photograph by Charles Woolley, around 1866, from the albums of JW Beattie, created around 1882 [National Library of Australia, nla.obj-141200694]

Atkinson repeated his candid racism to Westlake, telling him that Truganini 'looked like an ape, the most repulsive object I had ever seen'. Why make such an admission, and several times over? Atkinson intended to echo what any newly arrived nineteenth century British citizen might also have felt upon meeting Truganini. A scene-setter in other words, offered in order to contrast with what followed: 'that feeling soon wore away when I got to know her better.' Or, as Atkinson put it in his earlier writing, 'There was never any sign of frost during the years that she and I were friends ... learned more from her than I could have learned from any one else, and in some respects, I enjoyed her society more.'[57]

During their nine-year friendship, Atkinson went on excursions with Truganini around Bruny Island, and she pointed out the words for places and things: her own name was the word for 'seaweed'. Once, at reaching a lagoon, Truganini said she did not want to walk around it: 'No, father, me no go'—she called Atkinson 'father,' he explained, 'tho. She was over 60, and I not half that age'. So he picked her up and carried her, 'she screaming with laughter'.[58] Truganini taught Atkinson how to fish for oysters. She picked them up deftly from the shallows with her toes. He 'used to have to go head over heels'. Again she 'would roar with laughter' until 'the tears ran down her face'.[59]

These were not the only tears Atkinson remembered Truganini shedding. This laughter is another preamble, and this time to set up the point of Atkinson's recounted storytelling for over forty years: how a promise, given in the bond of friendship, was unwittingly broken. One day Truganini asked Atkinson to take her out fishing in a boat, to the 'Shepherds', a spot in the D'Entrecasteaux Channel just past the North Point. But they 'never put down a line'. Truganini 'was in very low spirits':

> the tears were rolling down her black cheeks and for some time she
> never spoke a word ... Then she broke down and sobbed afresh.
> She told me they were all dead now excepting herself, and the people
> in Hobart had got all their skulls, and they would get her skull. And
> then, it appeared, she had got me to come with her in order to extract

a promise from me that, when she died, I would see that nobody should get her skull. And then after a lot of weeping and sobbing, she suddenly came and knelt before me, and, clasping me round the knees, exclaimed, 'Oh! Father, father, bury me here, it's the deepest place. Promise me! Promise me!'

Atkinson told Westlake how he 'promised faithfully' that he 'would certainly' have carried this out 'to the letter' if the 'fates had not been dead against' him.[60]

Truganini was the last resident of the Oyster Cove Aboriginal Station. She had moved to Hobart in 1874 after the site was flooded, and into the home of Matilda Dandridge and her husband John Strange Dandridge, former superintendent of the Oyster Cove Aboriginal Station.[61] It was here that she died in May 1876. Atkinson gave instructions to his colleagues to follow Truganini's last wishes, but the Church had by then transferred him to Stanley on Tasmania's northern coast.[62] Truganini, who had been baptised, was given an Anglican funeral Mass; however, she was not buried at sea but in the former Female Factory at Cascades. Two years later her body was disinterred after a successful application by the Royal Society of Tasmania, and stored there in a box. In 1904 the Society sent Truganini's skeleton to Melbourne to be articulated by anatomist RJA Berry. When she returned, she was displayed in the Museum in Hobart.[63] Atkinson was said to be unaware her wishes had not been followed until he saw Truganini's remains at the Tasmanian Exhibit of the Melbourne Exhibition in 1888, although in another account he saw Truganini's skeleton in Hobart and 'never again entered the Museum'.[64]

Atkinson's son, The Archdeacon Henry Brune Atkinson (his middle name an older spelling of the island where Truganini was born; she had nursed him in his final two years of life), said his father 'had been troubled all his life' by Truganini's unfulfilled plea.[65] From 1947 Henry Atkinson lobbied the Museum to have Truganini's final wishes recognised. The Museum's insistence on the scientific significance of her remains was finally upheld, although her skeleton was removed from public display in 1947. Plans to have her skeleton enshrined in a new exhibit from 1970 did not eventuate and, in 1976, the Aboriginal Information Centre (later the Tasmanian Aboriginal Centre) was successful in their bid to have Truganini's remains repatriated to community.[66] A hundred years after her death she was cremated and buried, finally, in the D'Entrecasteaux Channel.

Did Westlake see Truganini's remains in the Museum? Probably. He visited the museum several times between 1908 and 1910. Did he think of Atkinson's story, of Truganini's tearful pleas, as he looked upon her small skeleton? Did it reignite that sense of anger felt in Melbourne over 'the destruction of the Tasmanians as the most serious ... loss that anthropology had ever sustained'? He did not write about seeing her remains. Anatomy and biological anthropology were outside his disciplinary parameters. His driving interest was material culture.

As Westlake explored archives and memories to better know that culture, he encountered history and emotion. He encountered a meeting point between science and feeling. Just as Moir hoped that his recognition of a near-Neolithic stone-breaking skill would give 'justice' to his 'black brothers', Atkinson challenged Tylor's idea of the Tasmanian Aborigines as representatives of the 'lowest' evolution-ary phase, telling Westlake they 'had sympathy, fidelity—traits above lowest'.[67] His friendship with Truganini was testimony to this. As a priest Atkinson did not share the cold detachment of the Royal Society; he could not condone the removal of a buried friend for the auspices of science; he could not tolerate a broken promise. Atkinson told his story over and again not only to assuage or explain his own guilt, but that of the colony, of a promise not merely broken by his community, but one they never truly made.

For Atkinson, that his friend was the 'last' of her people made the wrongdoing against her all the worse. For others in his community it made it irrelevant. What recourse could be made? Was not her 'race' extinct? But not all in the Tasmanian community believed that Truganini was the last. Many believed that title belonged to another: a woman born when Truganini was a young woman, and who lived nearly thirty years after she died. In fact, if Westlake had gone to Tasmania a few years earlier, he would have met her.

Fanny Smith

Port Cygnet, mid May 1910

Westlake mounted his bicycle and pushed down on the pedal. The handlebars gave way suddenly, and he found himself lying face down on the road. The steering column had cracked, and he had careered over the front wheel. It 'might well have been a nasty accident', but he escaped with only a cut thumb. Westlake then walked nearly 10 kilometres in rough weather. It was 'a most awkward point to reach'. He had been 'trying all the week' to get there but, finally, he passed the weatherboard Methodist Wesleyan Church that had been built on land donated by Fanny Smith.[1]

In 1889, Tasmania's government printer, James Barnard, wrote to the prestigious journal *Nature* that Fanny Smith (née Cochrane[2]) of Nicholls Rivulet, southern Tasmania, a 55-year-old mother of eleven, was 'upon her own testimony' a 'full blood' Aboriginal and the 'last survivor' of her 'race'. Fanny had been born on Flinders Island in 1834 or 1835 to parents who were both 'undeniably aboriginals', asserted Barnard, which had been endorsed by Tasmania's parliament. It was also popularly believed in Tasmania that Fanny Smith was the 'last'. When she performed her traditional songs at benefit concerts she was billed as 'the last of the Tasmanian Aboriginals'. A newspaper advertisement proclaimed that 'Mrs. Fanny Smith is the last of her race, but

Fanny Smith (née Cochrane) with her hair adorned with peacock feathers and a string of shells, wallaby furs about her waist and wrist and wearing traditional shell necklaces—description by Clinton Mundy [Allport Library and Museum of Fine Arts, Tasmanian Archives and Heritage Office]

Magic Soap is always first'.[3] Barnard was stirred to write to the journal because many people believed that Fanny Smith was a half-caste and therefore all of Tasmania's Aborigines were extinct.[4]

The idea of extinction relied upon an understanding that blood was both the conveyor of racial distinction and quantifiable. It could be mixed and measured in parts to create new 'hybrids', such as 'half-castes' and 'quarter-castes', but these hybrids could not, in this logic, represent the original, 'pure' race. In the case of Tasmania, extinction, historian Russell McGregor explains, 'referred not to the demise of all persons of … Aboriginal descent, but to the disappearance of a supposed racial entity'.[5] This entity was defined as 'distinct from the Aboriginal race of mainland Australia'. The Tasmanians were thought to have 'woollier' hair, supposedly simpler and fewer tools, and possibly different geographic origins—although this last distinction was a point of much debate.[6] While mainland southeastern colonies marked the passing of the 'last full-blood' Aborigines of certain 'tribes', it was assumed that members of the same Aboriginal race survived in less densely settled parts of Australia. But when Truganini died in Hobart in 1876, she was named the last of her race.

When Henry Ling Roth wrote his book, *The Aborigines of Tasmania*, there was no doubt in his mind that the people about whom he was writing were extinct. While his book was in press in 1890, he saw Barnard's article and it made him wonder. He was fascinated but incredulous. Roth wrote to *Nature* that no such claim could be made unless an expert scientist ascertained a description of Fanny Smith's features, detailed enough to determine her as a 'pure-bred aborigine'.[7] It was too late to establish this fact for his book, but the desire to do so was a key reason Roth began work on a second edition, and why, in 1891, he initially wrote to James Backhouse Walker with a request for help.[8]

Roth asked Walker if he could help him get a 'fairly large portrait' photograph of Fanny Smith—'full face and profile'. He also asked for hair to be taken from her head, from the armpits, 'if it grow there', and 'from the pubes', as well as a 'concise scientific description of her physical characteristics'. The request went further: 'On her death her skeleton should be preserved and sent home to be examined by an expert … it could be consigned … to the agent general in London so as to ensure it's safe return to Tasmania.'[9]

The request was astonishingly insensitive, but it was in keeping with the blatant descriptions and images of Tasmanian Aboriginal ancestral remains stolen from gravesites and reproduced in Roth's book. His presumption this theft was appropriate academic practice resounds in his use of the word 'home'. It is not that he considers England to be Fanny Smith's home—he suggests plans for her body to have a 'safe return'—but that it is the home of 'expert' study and, no less presumptively, the home of Hobart-born Walker. The word bespeaks the condescension of a generation and of an Empire.

Walker's response was politely understated. He advised that the procurement of Fanny Smith's skeleton was 'a rather delicate matter' that would pose 'some difficulty'. He imagined her 'husband might very likely object to allow the dissection of her body in case of her death'. Walker may also have been remembering the notorious episode of 1869, when Hobart hospital surgeons dissected the body of William Lanne.[10] Walker had 'no doubt' Fanny was a half-caste, but he promised Roth he would procure her photograph and hair samples.[11] A year later, however, Fanny Smith remained, as Walker offensively put it to Roth, 'an unattained object'. After another six months Walker delegated the task to a friend, photographer JW Beattie.[12]

Beattie told Roth he was 'intensely' interested in the Tasmanian Aborigines. His large Hobart studios displayed a 'very complete collection' of their historical images. He promised to secure a photograph of Fanny Smith soon—as she was often seen in Hobart.[13] A year later, Beattie sent his brother down to Nicholls Rivulet 'with full instructions' and orders 'to stay till he gets her to sit, if it takes a fortnight'. He went with several photos of 'her people' to use 'as a bait'—if she agreed to be photographed again in Hobart, she would be given more.[14] Fanny Smith was not photographed in his studio, but Beattie's brother successfully procured the images and hair in Nicholls Rivulet. Her family has not forgotten that Beattie also took away many family photos. Clinton Mundy wrote to me that 'Down at Nicholls Rivulet, at old Grandfather Tas Smith's place, they had boxes of photos. Beatties [sic] borrowed them and my family never saw them *again*. They went to Beatties Studios on loan but they never came back.'[15]

When Roth finally received the commissioned photograph of Smith he found he agreed with Walker: 'I do not think she is a pure aborigine.' But as he had not yet received the expert report on her hair sample, he 'would rather this opinion is not yet made public'.[16] In the interim, Roth sought descriptions of Fanny Smith's 'mental' and 'physical' details, including her blood status. Beattie dutifully sent out letters to those who knew her well, requesting this information.[17]

The two friends who responded would not condescend to Roth's terms. The former Wesleyan parson of Port Cygnet, AJ Holden, stated that 'physically' Mrs Fanny Smith was a 'marvel', and 'mentally' she was 'very bright'.[18] Mr A Geeves of Hobart described her as a 'Christian woman' who was 'well respected ... by all who know her'.[19] Both men agreed she was a full-blood Aboriginal. 'She certainly believes herself to be,' wrote Holden. If her own testimony could convince Roth he would not have persisted with his inquiries in the first place. He instead asked Beattie to get a description of Fanny Smith's teeth. Beattie tried but found that her friends 'excuse themselves by telling me it is a rather a delicate matter!'[20]

One of Fanny's friends did tell Beattie how she spoke of her people as 'telepathists': they 'knew when any accident happened to any relative'. Her mother would also 'sit and look at the stars' and 'give them names'. They had 'religious belief': 'good and evil spirits, blessing or hindering'.[21] But Roth reported none of this. When he learned from both Walker and Beattie that Fanny planned to go to England 'to see Queen Victoria'—a visit she never made—he did not express much interest either.[22] In early 1898, he presented to the Anthropological Institute his conclusion on the matter. He compared Fanny Smith's photographs to those of Truganini, 'who was a pure blood aboriginal without any doubt'. Mrs Fanny Smith's facial features in contrast were clearly that of a 'half-caste'.[23] It was, he reflected to Walker, 'a result I must confess a little disappointed at'.[24] To discover the last Tasmanian Aborigine would have been an academic coup.

It was not until after Roth's second edition was published that Walker met with Fanny Smith. With Bishop Montgomery they recorded her Aboriginal songs on a gramophone. 'It seemed to me to be soft and pleasing,' Walker reflected, but he did not expect to gain any more 'that is valuable' from her. He thought the best reason for meeting Fanny was confirming what he had always assumed: 'She has a pink tinge in her cheeks, and is manifestly a half caste,' he wrote to Roth. 'The Bishop said so at once.'[25] Walker wished Roth could have seen her too: 'you might have made your paper much stronger.'

Roth didn't need to see Fanny Smith. His appended essay was received approvingly. Reviewer Andrew Lang agreed that Roth's verdict on Fanny Smith's blood status was 'conclusive, and instantaneous', and that her face 'might pass for a true blue, jolly, British landlady'.

In contrast, Truganini's face was, thought Lang, 'black, hideous', the 'face of a pure Tasmanian savage ... the last of a people who ... still lived ... the life ... of the Palaeolithic age—the mammoth period of Europe.'[26] Roth had seemingly realised that which historian Tom Lawson considered British society 'relied' upon for their supposed superiority: the extinction of the 'lowest' race.

Walker had warned Roth in 1891 that Fanny Smith lived in a 'rather out of the way place', and indeed in their nine years of correspondence he never attempted the journey to Irishtown, or Nicholls Rivulet as it later became known.[27] But during his five years of correspondence with Roth, Beattie never went to see her either. Westlake, though, went to Nicholls Rivulet, and was 'pleased' to have made the effort. Soon after Westlake's arrival there he was listening to Fanny Smith's seventh child. 'Tasman (44)' was a 'very good witness,' in Westlake's

Fanny Smith with her husband William 'Bill' Smith and two of their sons at Nicholls Rivulet between 1885 and 1899. Clinton Mundy has identified the son whose hand is on his mother's shoulder as Tasman Smith and believes the other to be William Smith junior.
[Allport Library and Museum of Fine Arts, Tasmanian Archives and Heritage Office]

estimation. He had to write with determined speed to keep up with him. Tasman told Westlake how stones were used for opening game, spears were made of tea tree, fire was made with wood. Tasman had seen his mother make fire: 'when a baby see her do it'. It was 'just done by rubbing'.[28] After making the effort to reach Nicholls Rivulet, Westlake was 'pleased to have found something worth having'.[29]

Westlake found 'about 8 families discended [*sic*] from Fanny Smith' living in Nicholls Rivulet.[30] He spoke to seven of Fanny Smith's eleven children: Tasman, Walter, William, Frederick, Joseph, Mary Miller and Flora Stanton, and to one of her grandchildren, Augustus Eugene 'Gus' Smith, son of Isabella Smith. He filled nearly thirty pages with notes. In early June, back in Hobart, Westlake spoke a second time to Mary Miller and met her sister Sarah Miller. Then he 'wrote as hard as I could for three hours', 'fifteen pages of further information'.[31]

Fanny (centre) and Bill (seated with cane) and their family at Nicholls Rivulet around 1892–93. Back row (left to right): Joseph Smith, Mary Miller holding her son William 'Bill' Miller, her son Les Miller behind her, Tasman Smith, Frederick Smith, child in background at the far right is William 'Billy' Smith (son of William Smith junior). Next to Fanny is Isabella Smith holding her son Augustus Eugene 'Gus' Smith. [courtesy Clinton Mundy]

Bush food was a vital theme in his conversations. Tasman described 'willila', which had a blue flower and an edible root. He thought they were 'good to eat raw'. Sarah agreed, saying, 'I have many a time gathered them as a youngster, + ate them'.[32] The 'Lúnna-búnna' had a root shaped like a kidney potato, explained Tasman. It was 'like a tater,' agreed Mary, but she didn't 'think the[m] very nice'.[33] The 'native bread', or 'tooreela', grew like 'big mushroom' after a bush fire, said Tasman. 'I've seen mother eat it—we all get it,' agreed Joseph.[34] Sarah spoke of how to 'get the heart out and roast' the 'Láckra', or 'old man fern'; William said he had 'chopped down many' tree ferns, and considered the heart 'not bad tasting stuff at all'.[35] Tasman found it as 'bitter as gall when raw', but fine when roasted, and good 'as a medicine (in our time for stomach ache)'.

They spoke to Westlake about other traditional medicines: snake fat was good for curing sores;[36] a bone of a relative could cure sickness and pain—it was called 'the doctor';[37] steamed stinkwood could help if coughing up blood.[38] They knew which plants to use for traditional crafts: Mary Miller described making the rope used for climbing trees out of 'curry john' bark: 'we youngsters used to … twist it all up to make a regular rope'.[39] Sarah Miller spoke of how the leaves of the 'wild lily' that 'grew on burnt ground' were used to make baskets. 'A "sag" we call it,' explained Tasman; the grass was flat with a white flower: 'steam it and twist it up'.[40] Tasman's great-granddaughter, Colleen Mundy uses this same plant for making her traditional twined baskets.[41] Closely woven baskets varied in size and purpose; large open weave baskets were used to hold abalone and crayfish that the women dived for. Walter Smith told Westlake the story of Truganini, who was carrying some 'crawfish in a basket' when 'a shark came … she popped the basket … of fish in his mouth and while he was eating it she got away'.[42]

Their cultural practices were embedded in Country, in their knowledge of plants, animals and the seasons. This knowledge of the land was informed by, and intricately connected to, the movements and patterns of the stars. It was a connection that was at once practical and deeply spiritual. Each year 'three little stars' would 'first appear in the E.' (east), Gus Smith told Westlake. Flora added they came in 'spring time I'm sure'.[43] Spring was an important season to welcome when winters were cold and long, and it was celebrated by Fanny Smith and her family with song and ceremony. Gus explained:

> them 3 little stars on a level once a year they'd come (in the E.) they used to think a lot about them little … F.S. [Fanny Smith] used to get ashes and go outside and … be sprinkling these ashes very early in the morning when the stars are bright before the sun had risen. Just see 'em blinking like. She'd think it a terrible thing if one didn't welcome these three little stars.[44]

Flora said to Westlake that her mother told 'us in wild days' that her people would 'get up and watch for the morning star … they always did that in the bush.' They would 'get ashes and cinders and all as you can scoop up … and throw towards it to strengthen him.'[45]

'Stars was a great deal to them,' Westlake was later told in Port Cygnet by storekeeper, Robert Harvey, and that they 'had names for stars'. He seemed at first to be speaking generally of the Tasmanian Aboriginal people, but then Harvey spoke directly of Fanny Smith, whom he had known well: 'All through her life stars meant a great deal to her she would sit for hours and watch the stars.' Harvey thought Fanny's people read the stars as portents of good or bad events.[46]

Westlake's interviews reflect the rich panoply of Tasmanian Aboriginal astronomical knowledge. Stars were useful to the traditional people across the island to navigate, map, predict weather and mark seasonal change. The stars were, and continue to be, of immense spiritual significance: fire first came from the stars, so did man and woman, and even creation itself. These powerful stories have direct, geographic connection to places in Country and a deeply significant place within Tasmanian Aboriginal culture.[47] Clinton Mundy explained that he finds it 'disturbing' to read non-Tasmanian-Aboriginal-authored descriptions of his family's spiritual beliefs and practices involving the stars. He also refuses to discuss the 'Pukera', which Westlake had noted in conversation with Tasman Smith (see below). He hopes that scholars today will respect the sensitivity of this subject.[48]

The Smith family brought to life for Westlake clear memories and deep understandings of traditional corroboree rituals passed to them through song and careful explanation. Tasman and Frederick Smith, Flora Stanton and Mary Miller sang to Westlake. Tasman shared with him this song:

Tÿaneé / wíthanúnny péthapókarn
neépokárn tameeán lúnăthĕtlíta[49]

The '<u>us</u> are soft … approaching oo,' explained Frederick. Westlake tried, in his brief notes, to capture its meaning: 'two cats having a corroboree', they hear a 'noise in a stone', which they accuse each other of making. The noise is a 'sign of something wrong', a 'token'. '[I]f anything happened,' Frederick continued, 'if heard a noise … a knock said something wrong.'[50] This explanation is part of an intuitive spiritualism of which Fanny Smith had passed on a close and direct knowledge.

'<u>Knew</u> (about death) or any one bad,' said Frederick.[51] 'If a tribe was fifty miles away they would know if anything was the matter,' explained William Smith. The message, or 'carni', was carried by dead people.[52] William's mother also 'knew some future things by dreams'.[53] Tasman said that if a 'sick person was else where' then 'púkera (a ball of fire) … with a long spike or spear to it' would always be watching for a spirit'. The púkera would 'come and stop on a twig or tree limb where they were sleeping and they'd know by this: if sick person is there. If going to be death.' The púkera would 'watch at both camps + would tell everyone what was the matter'.[54]

'Many a time I've heard mother say that the Blacks (wild) believe that if something was going to happen,' Sarah Miller told Westlake:

Say if travelling along the road (at that time murders was not infrequent from Bushrangers + others) they felt that anyone was coming that would harm them, they would feel that they had a nerve twitching …
in their arm or in their leg and … would go off the road + hide away in the bush.[55]

'Mother has told me', Frederick said to Westlake, 'that when the natives were just walking along the road' that they would, 'talk to their flesh and it would jump—say if a white man coming'. Frederick thought it was the 'outside or <u>back</u> muscle of the upper arm,' while 'Mrs S' (Flora Stanton) explained that it was 'a beating in the muscle in the middle of the upper part of right arm'; she had seen it in her mother's arm. Tasman told Westlake that if a 'muscle twitched, would say "ah! ah-h-h-h"' and then 'they' would ask 'so and so bad?' and their 'flesh would go twitch' in answer. 'They'd be always right according to what I could understand,' Tasman added.[56]

'[A]fter have corroborey [sic] for an hour or 1½ hour then sit down still and wait for "Cráckne Wérowa",' explained Flora. '"Cráckne" means "Coming" and "Werówa" means Spirit in general,' Westlake later explained to his children, 'so that <u>Cráckne Werówa</u> is the Coming of the Spirit'.[57] They would 'listen till they hear a knock'. Then they would ask if someone was ill, and be answered with another knock. '"Very, very ill?" Knock again.' Flora explained that while the knock came 'on a board' or 'anywhere in house' after Aborigines began to live in houses, 'their habits when wild the same'. Gus added that his grandmother, Fanny Smith, would 'sometimes hear a knock,' and she would say 'someone going out,' referring to their imminent death and, he told Westlake, she 'would be right too'.[58]

Westlake was fascinated. His long-standing interest in spiritual phenomena made him open-minded and keen to discover more. Shortly after his arrival in Nicholls Rivulet, Westlake wrote to his children that he had gathered 'about five accounts of how the natives were able to receive information' of the deaths of relatives who were far away, and also 'send information of similar urgent events' without having any 'sensible means of communication'. Westlake thought that because the Tasmanian Aborigines were, or had once been, 'represent- ing the most primitive race of mankind', it suggested such an intuitive 'power was an essential' part of human nature, or 'perhaps of some- thing older than human nature itself'.[59]

Westlake also drew parallels between the Smith family's spir- itualism and his own faith. He wrote to his children that 'after their dances the Blacks sat still and waited—like the disciples at Pentecost, or the Friends in their meeting.' Not only did fellow Quaker James Backhouse miss this but, as Westlake noted, so did his father and his other namesake, George Backhouse:

> I seem to have discovered what was missed by those excellent Friends, Backhouse and Walker in their reports on the Tas. Blacks, ie that the Blacks were themselves Quakers, in that they sought for the guidance of the Spirit, and lived more or less in the light of it. Certain it is that Mrs Smith, who had come under Christian influence, was a Quakeress of excellent quality.[60]

Robert Harvey had heard Fanny Smith say 'hundreds and hundreds of times' how the 'spirit was very near', a spirit for whom her people '[w]aited in silence and great reverence' and whom she spoke of often as 'her Heavenly parent' and her Christian God.[61]

Fanny Smith would speak 'in meetings, sing in concert'. She sang in language often to her family, community and church.[62] She was given top billing at benefits in Hobart. Recordings of her songs, made in 1899 and 1903, can still be heard in the permanent exhibition at the Tasmanian Museum and Art Gallery in Hobart. When The Reverend JG Millard replaced The Reverend AJ Holden in 1889, Fanny Smith helped to organise a large gathering of welcome, and 'attracted much attention by singing in the native Tasmanian language, a tongue she evidently remembers'.[63]

Fanny Smith did not leave her Aboriginal culture at the church door, as many Aboriginal people were forced or chose to do throughout the nineteenth and twentieth centuries in Australia, but brought it into the centre of the worship. In fact, services were held in her kitchen until the church was built on land that she donated.[64] If Fanny's friends remembered her as a Christian, they never failed to add how she also continued her Aboriginal traditions and beliefs. Significantly, her own family remember that what she passed on was, first and foremost, 'tribal beliefs and responsibilities'.[65] Her Christian worship in no way diluted or invalidated her Aboriginal beliefs.

Harvey thought that Fanny Smith '[c]ould express her views in her own way' in church. She had an absolute faith in the afterlife, it was for her 'a great joy to know that she was going to meet … friends and her mother—Especially mother'. Holden found this gift inspiring, and thought that it came from her Aboriginal culture: 'God had given them a light that perhaps he couldn't give to the doubtful and skeptical minds.'[66]

Westlake reflected that the Smith family's spiritual communication 'would have fallen flat on most persons but it did not on me'. He not only made the effort to go, but did not dismiss what he heard as irrelevant or inauthentic. Beattie had written to Roth in 1897 that he had been told how Fanny Smith's mother would 'sit and look at the stars', that she had 'religious belief"' and, as he emphatically and excitedly put it, she and her people were 'telepathists'—they 'knew when any accident happened to any relative'.[67] But Roth expressed no curiosity about this knowledge. Instead he asked persistently and repeatedly about Fanny Smith's body in order to confirm her possible racial status as a half-caste.

The question of Smith's parentage seemingly came up rarely in Westlake's discussions. Mary Miller told Westlake that her mother's 'parents were from the "east way"'.[68] Flora Stanton explained that her maternal grandmother, Sarah, was 'a real black out of the bush', and her grandfather, called 'Eugene', was 'a coxwain at Flinders'. Clinton Mundy said that 'Grandmother Sarah' was from Mussel Roe in the north east, Layrappenthe Country; her 'real' name was Tanganooturra; 'Eugene' was from Robbins Island in the north west, and his real name was Nicermenic, the 'Fire Tail Finch'. He was renamed Eugene at Wybalenna. 'As a girl,' Clinton said,

> Grandmother Sarah was abducted by white sealers and sold among them for four seal skins. She was renamed Sarah at Wybalenna [Aboriginal Establishment on Flinders Island] … Grandfather Eugene was a notorious resistance fighter … To this day, white historians continue to disrespect Fanny by disputing that he [Eugene/Nicermenic] was her biological father. Fanny's grandson Gus was named Augustus Eugene Smith in memory of him.[69]

Westlake appears not to have asked repeatedly after Fanny Smith's genealogy, and perhaps for this reason he found that he was 'favourably regarded by the Smith family'.[70] Flora Stanton reminded him before he left not to 'forget to write'.[71] Beattie's repeated requests for descriptions of Fanny's hair, body and teeth may well have made her friends wary. Robert Harvey 'said at first he had no time to tell' Westlake anything but then, after they had spoken, Harvey told him much about Mrs Smith's 'religious life':

> Everyone I met had a good word for her—and I have no doubt I should like to have known her myself—besides for what she could have told me about the stone implements, about which she seems to have known as much or nearly as much as the natives.[72]

NJB Plomley, who published Westlake's Tasmanian interviews in 1991, did not perceive the clear evidence of Aboriginal cultural continuity in the papers. He considered Fanny Smith's 'one claim to fame' was 'the corroboree songs she used to sing, it seems without an exact knowledge of their meaning'.[73] But Tasman and Frederick Smith, Flora Stanton and Mary Miller were able to explain and translate these songs for Westlake.[74] They spoke of traditional foods and medicines in the present tense: 'we all get it,' said Joseph Smith of the native bread. The heart of the tree fern was good 'in our time for stomach ache', emphasised Tasman. When asked about hunting methods, Flora spoke of her younger self: 'When I went out hunting we had no guns and spears ... we used to catch ringtails.'[75]

William, Gus and Frederick Smith shared with Westlake the phrase 'Neena Toonábri my cárni'—'do you understand what I say?'[76] It is tempting to see the poetry in the question: Did Westlake really understand the cultural information that he was given? Could he see that in the exchange there was continuity? Westlake was not interested in the matter of Fanny Smith's racial status in part because it was not a question for him. Westlake told his children he was talking to the children of 'a half-caste aboriginal' who were giving him 'second hand information about them (the Blacks)'.[77] Westlake considered what the Smith family said to him was information about a former people.

But, reading his notes, it is clear that the Smith family are not only talking about the 'natives', and not solely about their mother; they are also talking about themselves. The Smith family retained their Aboriginal identity, and have always been recognised as such by the wider community. As Clinton Mundy wrote, 'people knew our families were the Blacks from out at Nicholls Rivulet'.[78]

Nicholls Rivulet, 30 August 2016

We want to enter the valley the same way that Westlake had come, from the south, although we admit he had been on foot, walking in bad weather. The little hire car is warm and fast but that is a problem. I want to take it slow and take it all in: the quiet valley, the still-bare apple trees, the sudden yellow of the wattle. But the driver behind us is impatient. When Clinton Mundy points out the old schoolhouse to me I don't dare turn off so suddenly. I take the next dirt road instead.

The little Methodist church is hard to recognise at first. Hidden behind trees, it doesn't appear as clearly from the road as it had for Westlake. But then a happy sense of recognition sinks in. I have reached the same point Westlake had 106 years earlier! For Clinton, what is more important than the church is the fact we are on Fanny's land: 300 acres granted by the Tasmanian parliament in recognition of her Aboriginality in 1889 (this was in addition to an earlier grant made to Fanny in 1858, also at Nicholls Rivulet). It is where Fanny practised her parents' culture, built a home, raised a family and watched them build their homes and raise their own families in turn.

Clinton says, 'I still think of it as "our little valley"'.[79] He wasn't born at Nicholls Rivulet, he explains to me, but he has a deep love for the place and returns there often. Clinton becomes animated as he speaks about his family: 'My grandfather Bert Mundy was born at Nicholls Rivulet in 1919, growing up there in the 1920s and 1930s he was raised to be proud of being Aboriginal. He taught us how to look after the bush and never take more than you need.'[80] Clinton explains that much of Bert's knowledge came from his grandfather, Tasman Smith. Clinton is passionate about remembering how Tasman Smith 'handed down important Aboriginal knowledge and qualities to his family, a culture that he 'so loved and taught so lovingly'. He continues to remember as we stand on Fanny's land:

> Old Grandfather Tas Smith used to take his grandchildren into the hills, dig a hole in the ground and light a fire in it. He would get parrots and roast them. The children would find and cook fern roots and lunna bunna (Blackman's potatoes). He used to teach them to speak the language and tell them things. He cooked porcupines and he took the children to the sea and they cooked mussels in the fire. He used to get the Native bread and pick mulla berries. He hunted a lot and believed in sharing everything, he cared about everybody and he looked after everyone, his living in this way was a continuation of his mother's people's way of life that continues in our family today.[81]

Clinton speaks of his own love of being in the bush, how he grew up hunting and gets 'porcupine', as the 'older people' had called echidna. His mother 'cooks it outside, in a fire'. Suddenly curious, I ask: How does she remove the echidna's spines? How does it taste? Is it rich and fatty? Then I catch myself and joke, 'I feel like Westlake, asking all my questions.' Clinton laughs in response.

We walk up the hill, behind the church, so that we can look out over Fanny's land: 'That was Aunty Mary Miller's house; that one was the old schoolhouse; down there was Aunt Flora's.' I ask if Fanny chose this location for her grant. Clinton says she did; it is close to the Oyster Cove Aboriginal Establishment where her family members lived. Her mother, Tanganooturra, visited often, and lived with Fanny and Bill for some time. But she was back at the Cove when Fanny heard her call, using the old intuition. Tanganooturra was dying; it was time to go. Fanny went as fast as she could; it was not far.

I looked to the hills that lay in the direction that Fanny and Tanganooturra had crossed to see each other. Oyster Cove suddenly feels closer, and different. For so long it has been portrayed as a sad, dismal, dysfunctional place where the 'last' waited out their days, dwindling into extinction. Yet, when Westlake went there in 1908, he heard stories of ceremonies filled with song and dance, ochre and celebration. Oyster Cove never stopped being a place of immense cultural significance for the Tasmanian Aboriginal community. As Clinton's Aunty Cheryl Fulton (née Mundy) put it in 1986, Oyster Cove is 'sacred … it is our home, our place.'[82] Two years earlier the Aboriginal community had re-occupied Oyster Cove and taken it back. In 1995, after more than ten years of struggle, the state government officially handed Oyster Cove back. It is a place that reflects the determination and political struggle of the Tasmanian Aboriginal people. It is also a place that Tasmanian Aboriginal people return to throughout the year for community business and personal reasons.

When Clinton points in the direction of the hills that lay between us and Oyster Cove, it also becomes a place close to family; a family that is loving, growing and keeping culture and language alive; a family that still returns, that still remembers and renews that connection. Standing on that sunny, quiet hill with Clinton, listening to him talk of Fanny and Tanganooturra, I realise the power of place to resolve the distance between the past and the present. Clinton's history feels immediate; it feels alive in the land on which we stand.

We eventually drive away into the dusk. The curved road leads us into the thickening forest at the valley's end. It is dark by the time we passed Oyster Cove, but the little Nissan makes good time. We are back in Hobart within an hour. We have travelled faster than my mind can process the journey. I feel part of me is still back in the Rivulet, back in time. It starts to rain, and as Clinton helps me navigate unfamiliar highway signs, I think of Westlake walking through the cold rain to meet Fanny's children.

When Westlake left the Rivulet, he had walked over 10 kilometres to the most northern point of Bruny Island. He lit a fire on the 'rocks to lure the steamboat in out of darkness'. A comet 'shone pale and ghostly and the wind blew shrill and rather cold across the point'. He drew in close to the fire, hoping the steamer could still see it. It was a relief when it came. He stepped into 'a brightly lighted cabin' with his 'parcels of stones' to find the waiters washing up. He sat in the drawing room, fed and warm. The *Imperial* had 'resplendent furniture' reflected Westlake, 'but no Crackne Werowas'.[83]

The Islanders

Beauty Point, 14 February 1909

Westlake sat on the pier, waiting for a ketch to take him to Flinders Island. He wanted to meet the 'half-castes' who lived there. He had travelled seven hours by train from Hobart to Launceston, and then taken a steamboat journey up the Tamar River. The wait now was long, as he sat in a patch of shade writing a letter. He had 'nowhere else to go'. Westlake unpacked some astonishingly bad and expensive gruyère cheese: 'The people here make such bad cheese no one would buy it unless it was "protected" ... by a heavy duty.' And Tasmanian candles, he wrote, 'fill the rooms with smoke'.[1] But Beauty Point lived up to its name.

The bright Sunday morning sun lit up the calm waters tucked behind the heads. Beyond them Bass Strait waited with its notorious reefs. Westlake had not heard good things about the small ketch he was about to board. The *Linda*'s engine was said to rarely work, and even when it did 'the owner ... hardly ever allows it to be used'. In fact, Westlake had deliberated over making the long journey from Hobart. He worried that the 'half-castes' would 'know very little'.

Police Inspector JV Cook had told him that in about 1895 he had met with a 'well known ... ½ caste' from Cape Barren Island

called 'Mr Billon'. Westlake crossed this out in his notes and replaced
the name with 'Bereton', but it was most likely Henry Beeton. This
man, Cook had said, had 'never seen flints', and he concluded that the
'half castes knew nothing about them'.[2] The former School Master
and Superintendent at Cape Barren Island, Edward Stephens, had also
warned Westlake: 'It would be useless going to the Furneaux Islands
now for information re flint work.' Stephens thought there were no
Islanders with 'a clear idea of the past'. Stephens reminded Westlake
that he was trying to quarry anthropology from a history of warfare,
that after the 'natives ... gave themselves up and were deported', all
their implements were, 'as far as possible, destroyed!!' Instead, Stephens
advised Westlake to read his own history of the islands—'Sir [Philip
Oakley] Fysh said it was intensely interesting.' He also suggested looking up James Backhouse Walker's work and speaking to the former
Bishop Montgomery—'mention my name.'[3]

Stephens's sycophancy contrasted with his derogatory attitude
towards those formerly under his charge on Cape Barren Island.
Westlake may have read his insults as quoted by Roth: 'listless' and
'indifferent' to civilisation.[4] In his correspondence with Walker, Roth
had asked if it was true what he had heard from an English contact:
that there were some 'aborigines' living in the Bass Strait. Walker
responded unequivocally: 'The islanders ... are not aborigines, but
half-castes—a mixed breed of Tasmanian, Australian, and European,
with a dash of Maori.'[5] When Roth requested an Aboriginal shell
necklace, Walker explained they were 'commonly for sale here', but
being made by the Islander 'half castes' they were not 'genuine'.[6] Roth
passed on his wife's gratitude nonetheless; the necklace would make a
nice addition to their drawing room.[7]

Westlake had stopped in Launceston before heading for the islands.
Over the course of a few days he asked the locals who would be good
to talk to on the islands. He was given the names of five so-called
half-castes: John Maynard, Philip Thomas, his sister Nancy Mansell,
Henry Beeton and his sister Jane Everett. These men and women
were all born on the islands in the 1830s in the early years of their
parents' new settlements in the Furneaux Group. The Launceston

locals described these men and women with two contrasting and repeated adjectives. Mrs Charles Smith thought that John Maynard was 'very intelligent and straight'. Journalist and author Henry Button considered John Maynard 'intelligent reliable and not shy', that Henry Beeton 'will talk', but that 'the other' Beetons were 'very shy'. Button suggested Westlake interview Philip Thomas but cautioned that his sister Nancy Mansell was 'very nervous'. Both Button and Police Constable Archer described Jane Everett as 'very intelligent'; while Archer added the 'others' were 'shy'. Edward Stephens said in conversation with Westlake that both Philip Thomas and Henry Beeton were 'reticent'.[8] Westlake concluded that the 'balance of opinion is in favour of my going'. The balance may have been tipped by his usual approach to get things 'at first hand'.

Westlake had decided to take with him a 'box of chipped flints'—a selection of collected Aboriginal stone artefacts from other parts of Tasmania. It was a gesture both naive and condescending. Westlake thought that 'they probably never saw any of them used' but that 'it may be interesting to hear their comments on them'.[9] But it was Westlake who wanted the artefacts explained and translated. He hoped 'that they may remember a little by tradition', and even this 'little should be noted'. His pessimism was countered by determination. He held no real hope of finding much of value.

Westlake was still waiting for the ketch at six that evening. The *Linda* had become stuck on mud 'a second time' and the engine had blown up. It was not until seven the next morning that they finally departed Beauty Point. There followed 'many delays' on the crossing. By the time they neared Cape Barren Island it was night and 'very dark', so that the 'low black reefs' were hard to see. But the 'skipper knew the way well and got us through all right'. They arrived at The Corner, the island's main settlement, at midnight, and disembarked in the morning.

The Corner consisted of around thirty-four cottages, an Anglican church and a schoolhouse, gathered in the relative shelter from the Roaring Forties. It was home to around two hundred people. Cape Barren Island had been the principal settlement for the Islanders since the early 1870s, although they continued to inhabit and use many of the smaller islands in the Furneaux Group, including Preservation, Gun Carriage, Clarke, Woody and Big Dog islands. It wasn't the group's largest island—neighbouring Flinders was bigger. Cape Barren and Flinders are separated by Franklin Sound, and by history. More than a hundred Aboriginal people were enforcedly removed and incarcerated on Flinders by the colonial government from 1835 to 1847, and about sixty of those people died.

Another Aboriginal community had also been growing on the smaller islands. The colonial maritime frontier was opened by the sealing trade that operated in Bass Strait from the late 1790s. European men began to settle on the islands permanently from the 1820s, but by this time seal numbers were diminishing. The largely seasonal populations of hunters, which included Aboriginal women workers, ceased coming and, by around 1830, there were about twenty-five Aboriginal women and twenty European men who had made the islands their homes. While often remembered as the 'sealers', historian Patsy Cameron explains the men among these settlers called themselves the 'Eastern Straitsmen'. Their wives were chiefly from the Coastal Plains and Oyster Bay Nations—the northeastern corner and the eastern coast of Tasmania. Cameron writes that they called themselves the tyereelore, a name for a 'new role and status as island wives'.[10]

They adapted their cultures to live both as small farmers and as entrepreneurs, with the tyereelore expanding their traditional practice of hunting the muttonbirds that roosted seasonally on the islands into an organised trade, with their husbands, selling their eggs, oil, feathers and meat. Birding was the heart and rhythm of the Islanders' economic and social lives. The children of tyereelore and Straitsmen, born in the 1830s, grew up knowing their fathers' languages and traditions, including their skills as boatsmen, as well as those of their mothers' clans. They continued to make regular visits to Country, to sing the songs, speak language, gather or hunt traditional foods and medicines and make traditional artefacts. It was what Elder, and descendant of four tyereelore, Patsy Cameron describes as a 'blending of two cultures': a 'new lifeworld and a new peoples of the islands'.[11]

Cape Barren Islanders, Bishop HH Montgomery, 1892. From left: Henry Beeton, Philip Thomas, Jane Everett, Nancy Mansell and John Maynard. [National Library of Australia, nla.obj-141198721]

To Westlake, and to the white Tasmanian community of 1908, the Islanders were half-castes, and he wasted no time after his arrival seeking them to find out what they remembered of stone tools. After all the pessimism as to what they would know, the arduous journey and the dark night, Westlake was jubilant. 'This is the place for me. This afternoon I met a man who had <u>seen</u> his mother and other blacks <u>use</u> flints for various purposes.' The man was 73-year-old Philip Thomas, the son of Straitsman John Thomas, who had settled on Preservation

Island around 1829, and of Teekolterme (or Nimmeranna), a
tyereelore from the Coastal Plains Nation. He described his mother
as coming from the 'Cape Portland' tribe. He was the grandson of
Mannalargenna.[12] Westlake found Thomas was not shy.

Thomas remembers seeing his mother using a 'fine sharp stone', a
narapa, and bottle glass to sharpen sticks, like a 'spokeshave', with an
action moving away from her body. He remembers how she rolled
grass 'on her thigh … just about above her knee' to make cord. And
how the traditional people climbed trees using rope tied around one
wrist, which they flung around the tree trunk. They cut into the bark
with a stone tool to make notches for their feet as they went up: 'I've
seen 'em going up the big gum trees cutting thro' the thick bark.'[13]

Thomas remembers standing on the beach near Cape Portland at
night, watching the big fires on the water's edge, the spears moving
quickly in the shallow water—'Fire fetches all the fish up, like birds
come to light.' The fish they caught were cooked on the coals when
the fires had died down, and then placed on the grass where the flesh
was peeled from the bones and eaten.

On his second day on Cape Barren Island, Westlake spoke with
75-year-old Henry Beeton, brother of the well-known community
leader Lucy Beeton and son of Thomas Beeton, who settled on Gun
Carriage Island around 1831. Beeton described his mother as being
from the Cape Portland 'tribe', and explained their land ranged from
St Helens Point on the east coast and around the coast to the mouth
of the Tamar River: 'all the North East' of Tasmania. His mother was
Woreterneemmerunnertatteyanne, the sister of Teekolterme. He was
a grandson of Mannarlargenna.

Beeton had seen flints, despite what Cook had said, and told
Westlake, 'I have seen them Break up the flint on Flinders anywhere
and where used to be camping. They would see it in bush and carry
it to camp and, if had no iron tomahawk would smack it up with
another stone.' Beeton said that they 'placed the stone on another flat
stone to get it solid, with a cloth to catch the pieces that came off,
and hit with another stone … till they got the piece they wanted.'
He remembered how the traditional people 'used to carry flint in a

little kangaroo pocket like a little bag'—pocket meaning a female's pouch. This was carried with 'a bit of string made out of rushes', or they might simply 'use their caps'.[14] Glass was also useful for flints—it was 'good for scraping'.[15] Both stone and glass flints were better for scraping spears than a metal knife, as they could quickly be replaced when they got blunt.[16]

Beeton, like Thomas, remembered being on the beach in Coastal Plains lands watching his clans people wade in the shallow water. He recalled the eels kicking up suddenly, and the swift spears, two-pronged—the extra one lashed on with kangaroo sinews—that would stab and kill. Food shaped good and strong memories of childhood.

Thomas seemingly joined Beeton and Westlake as they talked, as his reminiscences appear as marginalia, adding his commentary to the shared memories. The 'woollooly' had 'a little blue flower and one leaf broad just like a leek,' Beeton told Westlake—what Tasman Smith (Fanny Smith's son of Nicholls Rivulet) had called 'willila'. Beeton explained it had '2 little 'taters at the end of it' that were roasted 'in the red hot ashes'.

'Like a yam', added Thomas. Beeton said the 'plondoliva' or 'pondaleepa' also had broad leaf, that it 'grows in sandy ground in the edge of the banks,' and its soft, long roots are 'as sweet as sugar … as a child I have eaten many dozen.'

'Sweet rush,' echoed Thomas. And the 'kani com/cong = the pig face' (which Patsy Cameron calls 'canygong'), a seaside succulent— 'I've eaten many cart loads of it,' said Beeton. The fruit was good: 'give it a squeeze and all the juice will shoot out into your mouth.'

Just as Beeton tried to let Westlake taste the intensity of traditional foods, so too did he try to express the mannerisms, inflections and emotions of language: 'tylarlia woolaria' was 'glad to see old friends'; it was 'spoken to someone coming as a welcoming', while 'shading eyes with hands … an inch or two from the face [or] eyebrows.' But when the same phrase, 'tylarlia wooler-erlia', was drawn out into more of a 'mournful cry' and 'high pitched' it became a 'goodbye'.[17]

Three men gave Westlake the majority of information he gathered on Cape Barren. The third was 76-year-old John Maynard.

He was the son of Richard Maynard, who had settled first on Gun Carriage Island around 1824, and of Wyerlooberer (also known as Pollerwottelterrunne) of the Coastal Plains Nation. Maynard had memories that had held fast: of wombats and kangaroos roasted on open fires, of the 'mutton fish' (abalone) prized off rocks, of oysters opening on fire, hands and feet scaling trees, wooden waddies turning over through the air until they hit a hunted animal. He shared with Westlake a list of language, each word and phrase pronounced and explained with care:

nééna toonabri mee kárni = do you understand [what I say]
lúdawinni = a man
lúbra = woman
tablety múlaga = going out to have a hunt
weetikita = up there, high, up in the sky way
päletha = down
murina = road or path
päningabri = wait
mánámáretha = over yonder
moorgrinni = dog's house
leprinni = man's house
mänenna = 2 or 3 of us
kibli = food[18]

By the end of his second day, Westlake thought he would soon have even more 'native words'. Maynard promised a list 'he has written down', in addition to those he had already spoken. And there was 'another man here is said still able to speak it well!' His decision to come had been sound:

Altogether I am very satisfied to have come here and it shows (what is nearly always the case) that there is much more to be found out than one expects and that if one makes the effort to get things at first hand one is rarely disappointed. One should in this life go forward in the spirit of Ulysses in Tennyson's poem, 'to strive, to seek, to find, and not to yield'.[19]

Westlake wrote that evening in 'Bishop's Court', the little wooden room built onto the school for visiting clergy. No, he had not yielded to bleak advice. He had striven across land and sea, and found! He even considered bringing out his box of stone implements the next day, in order to get some 'details'.

Ballawine

Maynard shared with Westlake the same questioning phrase he had recorded in Nicholls Rivulet: 'nééna toonabri mee kárni: do you understand [what I say]?' This time Beeton seemingly answered: 'pōōtia tūnabri nēēna carnia: you don't understand what I am saying'. The question and answer once again seems true of their exchange. Westlake did not really understand what was being offered to him. He knew he was getting more information than he had expected to, or that anyone else had seemingly been given recently. He was excited to have 'met a man who had <u>seen</u> his mother and other blacks <u>use</u> flints'. But did he really see that man? Or did he look past Thomas, a 'half-caste', and try to see his mother, whom Westlake regarded as the 'real' Aborigine? Westlake could not see Thomas as being whole, as embodying the 'lifeworld' of the island culture, as Patsy Cameron calls it. Instead Westlake tried to catch and collect quotes and facts in his little notebook that he hoped to piece together later under anthropological subjects relating to the lost Aborigines. But in those hurriedly jotted notes there is evidence of a richness of culture respected and remembered.

Perhaps the most potent example is Beeton's description of what Westlake transcribed as 'balla-winni'. To capture Beeton's pronunciation, Westlake wrote it again as 'Baulawinni'. The words 'ballawine' and 'polelerwine', as Patsy Cameron writes them, were 'used by the northern and eastern nations respectively'.[20] Beeton described it as 'a red stone'. Ochre.

'I have broken it myself,' Beeton said. The ballawine was first placed upon a bag, he explained, and broken into powder, then put carefully away until they had some possum fat. Then they 'would take it on their hand and rub it on a flat stone' so that the fine powder 'came off'. Any stray powder was caught in laid-out animal skin. The flat stone was also picked up in their hands, and shaken to get the last remnants of powder 'out of the crevices'. Then the powder was mixed with the animal fat, and rubbed on their heads. They put it on 'thick and plenty of it,' Beeton said. It was used to protect their heads from rain and sun.

Ochre and fat were mixed 'for everyday use', agrees Patsy Cameron, but it was also used 'during ceremonial activities'. In fact, '[o]chre was revered and eagerly sought after'.[21] Beeton tells Westlake that the ballawine was wrapped and carried with care. It was precious. It was, as Patsy Cameron puts it, from 'the body of the earth'. To mix the ballawine with '[g]rease from the bodies of birds and animals' and smear it upon their own bodies was an important traditional practice of spiritual observance.

Beeton had broken the ballawine. He was the grandson of a wise man, a 'bungunna'. Mannalargenna had continued his spiritual tra-ditional practices until his death in 1835, when Henry Beeton was a young child. He was 'passionate about grease and ochre', and he 'painted himself all over with the red pigment, kept his long hair and beard dressed with the polerewine.'

Mannalargenna is 'at the heart' of Patsy Cameron's extended family, as father to one of her four ancestral tyreleeore grandmothers, and at the heart of creating the new lifeworld on the islands. He was a 'wise negotiator' who created tactical alliances with the Straitsmen through trade and through marriage.[22] He 'exchanged at least three of his four daughters and a sister with the eastern Straitsmen,' all of whom became tyreleeore. These exchanges included flour, dogs and meat, and they came with reciprocal expectations. The Straitsmen were 'equally answerable to, and responsible for … kinship ties'. These were traditional marriages, 'governed by clan laws', and formalised by ritual—large gatherings that celebrated 'ceremonial dancing, singing, feasting at the beachhead'.[23]

Such agreements were not recognised in colonial society or law. It was neither understood nor accepted that a white man should live with, or become in some ways like, Aboriginal people, those on

'Manarlargenna'
(Mannalargenna), watercolour
by Thomas Bock, around 1831
[National Library of Australia,
nla-obj-135515260]

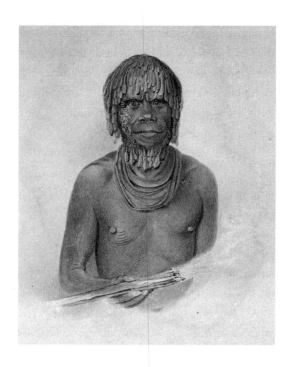

the other side of the frontier, against whom from the early 1820s an intense war was being waged. But as the Tasmanian pastoral settlers fought to retain their control over land from the early 1820s, the Straitsmen made connections with Aboriginal men and women. They became 'creolised' through these links, learning the ways of kinship, trade, language and cultural practices. In the eyes of the official colonists they 'had become actually savages'. And their wives were deemed to be their 'miserable' and 'wretched' slaves. 'Oh, ye friends of the enslaved African,' appealed a writer in the *Hobart Town Gazette* in 1820 to his supposed fellow emancipists, 'ye advocates of freedom, of humanity, extent your benevolent exertions to the most unhappy creatures, who, if comparatively few in numbers, and proportionally more wretched than the wretched negro.'[24]

The reports of the island communities presented to colonial leaders and community were judgements shaped by geography, space and politics. The Straitsmen, as seen from Hobart Town, appeared beyond the laws and morality that were understood to define civilised settlement. Criminality and savagery thrived in remoteness. It was a useful idea when the expansion of pastoral settlement was provoking the most severe conflict. It was just as Annie Benbow and others had said to Westlake in 1908: it was the demand for women by convicts, bushrangers and other less civilised whites that had caused the Aborigines' ferocity, not the invasion of their lands.

The idea of a violent and destructive relationship between the Straitsmen and his 'slaves' found a place in more authoritative histories. John West, in his 1852 *The History of Tasmania*, lists the reasons for the 'extinction' of the Tasmanian Aborigines. The 'sealers' are number five. As escapees or ex-convicts, they 'indulged the boundless licenses of their passions' in the remote islands, 'blending the profession of the petty pirate and the fisherman'.[25]

This picture continues in writing throughout the twentieth century. For Manning Clark the sealers 'pursued a life as savage and elemental as the never-ending roar of the sea'.[26] For Geoffrey Blainey the Bass Strait was a 'Barbary Coast', where 'villains' would 'slaughter or mutilate native women and fellow sealers'.[27] John Molony echoes that the sealers are 'villains', who treated their 'abducted' women 'barbarously'.[28] For Robert Hughes the sealers are 'raparees and bolters' who 'kidnapped hundreds of women' to form 'bloody, troglodytic island colonies'.[29]

The depiction intensified in the twenty-first century. West's fifth reason is elevated to number one by Windschuttle, who states that the 'real tragedy of the [Tasmanian] Aborigines was not British colonization *per se* but that their society was … so internally dysfunctional.' They were morally regressed: they bartered the women with sealers for dogs and flour and thus lost the mothers of future children. So that it is 'therefore not surprising that when the British arrived, this small, precarious society quickly collapsed.'[30]

'What evolved in the Bass Strait was a genuine slave trade,' asserts Nicholas Clements. The 'slave owners also prostituted' the women and even took 'sadistic pleasure in torturing them'. Clements claims they were also paedophiles, 'fond of little girls' and even 'infants'.[31] He also insists that the life of the tyreloore was one of almost tireless suffering, with only 'moments of respite', out of which they established at best a 'functioning community'. The pastoral and the sea frontiers are 'two fronts of the same War, the sealers and the stockmen two faces of the same enemy.'[32]

Clinton Mundy holds to the belief that his ancestor, Tanganooturra, was 'abducted by white sealers' and became a 'slave' hunting kangaroo for her 'white master who sold the skins'. Formerly named Ploorernelle, her name was changed to Tanganooturra, which means 'Weeping Very Much', 'Weeping Bitterly', 'To Cry'. Clinton wrote to me that Tanganooturra was 'sold a second time and badly beaten'. He said 'the sealers tied the women to trees and flogged them and mutilated them with knives and tomahawks. Some were shot and murdered. Many drowned trying to escape':

> These young girls and women, kidnapped from their families, suffered years of abuse of every kind imaginable. The horrors they suffered is heartbreaking. The agonising tortures they endured defy belief. Some survived. Tanganooturra ended up at Wybalenna and then Oyster Cove, North West Bay and Nicholls Rivulet. She saw her first grandchild and was very pleased with him. But it would be so wrong to forget or deny what happened to her and the other women. What a cruel injustice that would be.[33]

When Lyndall Ryan made the pioneering assertion in 1981 that 'The Tasmanian Aborigines have survived,' she recognised that sealing as an industry was instrumental to this fact.[34] Two conflicting historiographical perspectives have since existed in parallel for over three decades. While the sealers were in Ryan's view destructive, they also 'saved Aboriginal society from extinction because their economic activity enabled some of its traditions to continue'.[35] Clinton Mundy finds it imperative to remember the horrors endured by Tanganooturra, but he also wants to remember that she survived and that her family continued. Patsy Cameron notes that in her community the Aboriginal wives are credited with sustaining their traditional languages and cultural practices, but she sees the effort as mutual. The Straitsmen are her community's 'founding fathers'.[36]

She acknowledges the influence of James Boyce, who places the 'sealers' at the centre of Tasmanian history. They made their homes in the middle of a maritime highway that connected Europe, the Pacific and India through trade. They founded a new way of life, forged out a new environment and a fusion of cultures and economies: the cradle of a new Van Diemen's Land identity.[37] But where Ryan, Boyce and Patsy Cameron find collaboration and creation, Clements finds only war and destruction. It's interesting that both Patsy Cameron's and Clements's books began as dissertations supervised by eminent historian Henry Reynolds and were published less than three years apart. They were also informed by many of the same historical sources, including the journals of GA Robinson.

The sea frontier had a short and intense history of contact, conflict and exchange. Its three decades, and its small and disparate population, cannot be characterised in any singular way. Patsy Cameron identifies three separate 'cohorts' of European frontiersmen: the seasonal; the legally employed seal hunters who forged the way for the escapees and 'desperate types'; and the final, smaller group of permanent settlers. These were the fathers of children who were baptised, learned to read and write and to also return to their traditional Country. If Robinson was at first outraged and saddened by the treatment of the Aboriginal women, by 1830 he found almost all were happy, their husbands 'civil' and 'most honorable'. The germs of that peaceful settlement were there at the beginning; some of the early violence resonated into the later period. But that violence was not sustainable.

To try to understand the nature of domestic relationships is, as historian Lynette Russell reflects, difficult terrain. Questions of uncertainty resound.[38] Clinton Mundy believes his ancestor, Tanganooturra, *was* a 'slave', but Patsy Cameron confidently states that 'reciprocity was at the heart' of the relationships between the Straitsmen and their wives.[39] The tyereelore were never 'slaves'; their self-devised title bespoke a new identity as 'equal partners'. Cameron decisively concludes the historiographical shift instigated by Lyndall Ryan, that her ancestors, white and black, founded a 'distinctive and complex' new culture.

Westlake's conversations with Beeton, Maynard and Thomas underpin Patsy Cameron's picture. As children they returned to their traditional Country. They made the seasonal visits that Patsy explains were arranged by smoke signal, when the Aboriginal clans men would hunt with the Straitsmen and trade their skins on the river-town markets. It was when families bonded again.[40] These are not memories of community merely 'functioning', nor ruled by lifelong suffering. There are memories of standing upon beaches where their people had lived for millennia watching fish come to light, spears fly, fire being made, the arc of a spinning waddy; the sweetness of berries, the sounds of stone breaking upon stone, cutting into bark, scraping upon wood; the cries of greeting and mournful goodbyes. They are memories rich with sensory and emotional experience. These are the memories of those who had broken the ballawine.

For Patsy Cameron, Mannalargenna's ancestral granddaughter, the mix of grease and ochre is 'profoundly symbolic'. It is like the 'two cultural groups' from which she was born. And like the 'blended elements that paint [her] being' they are 'warm and vibrant'. Patsy understands that she is 'the product of the contact history', of 'blending' and 'mixing'. But this mixture does not dilute. It has 'trans-formative power'. It turns a destructive history into a regenerative narrative. It turns a supposed end into a beginning. And, like the ballawine, this beginning has the power to endure.

The naivety and condescension in Westlake's ambition to show his box of flints is exposed by this. It is less problematic than Walker's, who didn't go to the islands at all. He wrote from Hobart to Roth in Halifax that he knew 'the genealogy of the whole clan' of Islanders and concluded that they were 'mixed breed'. For Walker this mixture is not something new, but something lost. Within the logic of blood quota the 'parts' of a person identified as 'Aboriginal' reduce incrementally, halved at each new generation until they are supposedly gone. Even in that first generation, when the Islanders are 'halved'—what JW Beattie referred to curiously as the 'pure' half-castes—they are dismissed by Walker and Roth as irrelevant.[41] They are made to disappear.

This disappearance is crucial to their project, and to the construction of a new, 'white' Tasmanian identity. The evidence of the Tasmanian Aborigines' continued existence and endurance must be dismissed and extinction confirmed as total. For extinction is useful. It gives a shameful history an end. The science and history as practised by Walker and Roth underpin this ending. They construct the pure, authentic Aborigine, and then make it disappear.

The dreadlock of ochred hair that Walker thinks was cut from Mannalargenna's head is deemed to be of higher value than a conversation with his grandson. Rather than hear how Beeton broke the ochre, instead of hearing him translate the word ballawine, Walker tries to extract from his grandfather's head a strand of hair long enough to be 'of use' to Roth. There is a prosaic element of farce in this effort. That which was entangled and mixed for spiritual observance, the ballawine and grease, cannot be extricated for scientific practice. In the same way, the blending of the cultures between the Straitsmen and the tyereelore cannot be reduced, scrutinised or halved. They cannot be made to disappear.

It is not really that remarkable that the Islanders knew so much of their traditional culture when it was presumed to have died out. What is remarkable is that they offered it to Westlake. If they were thought to be 'shy' or 'reticent', or even to know 'nothing', it was because they chose to be silent. That which they did not share, they were assumed not to know.

Their silence was renowned because it was encountered repeatedly. Walker's lack of interest in the Islanders was not universal. There were many researchers, from the late nineteenth century, and throughout the twentieth century, who, like Westlake, attempted to get cultural information from the Islanders. One research party, possibly in 1908, offered 'great sums' of money to the Islanders in exchange for Aboriginal language—up to five shillings a word—but had no success.

Islander Cliff Everett recalled this fact to Norman Tindale, an anthropologist at the South Australian Museum, in 1949.

Tindale had first met Cliff on Cape Barren with Harvard physical anthropology student Joseph Birdsell, as part of their Australia–wide study of 'hybrid' Aboriginal peoples. On Cape Barren Island they attempted to study every Islander, record their genealogies, measure their bodies, and take their blood, photographs and hair samples.[42] The Islanders resisted such intrusive research. 'Nine of the islanders refuse to come and be examined,' Tindale wrote in his journal, 'a few are stubborn, a few shy and one is in active opposition to us.'[43] Tindale was keen to record any remembered traditional culture and language; physical anthropology was Birdsell's primary expertise.[44] Tindale's first impression was that while 'the Tasmanian ancestry of some is patent' they were 'not dealing with a group of halfcastes but with an isolated island group of white people'.[45] While his enquiries had been 'exhaustive', Tindale felt 'certain that not one word of native origin or any scrap of a song survives from the past'.[46]

Four days later, Tindale added a question mark above his word 'exhaustive' and a note to 'see p 119'. On that page Tindale recorded the 'Wallaby Song', sung by Cliff Everett, as taught to him by his grandmother, Wottecowwidyer,[47] from the Coast Plains Nation:

tarkja ta:ja parana li: pa: jata
ni:man naratapa naratapa

Cliff translated the song as 'little wallaby went into the water, as hunted there by whiteman, whiteman'. He explained that 'jata ni:man = wallaby' and 'naratapa = whiteman'. The song was created when white men 'first hunted the wallabies which the natives felt were their own "property" and that the white man were taking them away'. Tindale was told 'the song was a lament'.[48] It is telling that Cliff chose to break the pact of silence with a story of white men taking Aboriginal property.

When Tindale and Cliff Everett met again ten years later, he asked Cliff to sing the wallaby song into his tape recorder. Cliff refused, but oversaw Tindale speaking the words as Cliff had given them to him. Tindale prefaced the wallaby song with the following note:

> In a burst of confidence today Cliff Everett said that, under the influence of Captain [Philip] Thomas who was bitter about the treatment meted out to his mother's people, not one word of the Tasmanian languages was given to whites although much was known. Although the people were offered money to reveal the secret side of their life not one word was ever spoken.[49]

Cliff Everett then told Tindale about the 'party' of researchers who had offered money for language. Wondering who the expedition leader had been, Tindale wrote in his journal, 'Mattingley?' Arthur HE Mattingley, ornithologist and pioneer bird photographer, led an expedition to the Bass Strait in 1908, the year before Westlake arrived. But he may not have been the one who asked the Islanders for words; there were other scientists in the group.[50] Tindale reflected that Cliff Everett's 'confidences ... show how secretive the halfcastes were about their native culture'. He also concluded, despite Cliff's assurances, that 'little else is known', that 'I am not sure that we have heard everything'.[51]

Why did Westlake get information about stone tool making when Cook met only silence? Why was Westlake given phrases and words a year after Mattingley's expedition was apparently refused, even with the former's inducements of money? Why did Philip Thomas break his self-imposed decree?

Muttonbirds

In 2003 I go to Cape Barren Island as Jim Everett's guest. I take with me the transcribed interview notes Westlake had made on the island in 1908. Jim introduces me to some of the residents, who thumb through the notes. I ask them if the information Westlake gathered looks familiar. It does. I ask if there is anything else they want to add. There is a collective, and polite, 'no'. I ask how it is that Westlake is given this information when no other researcher of his era was.

Most do not want to guess. But Buck (Brendan) Brown suggests to me it was simply 'his personality'. Jim Everett agrees.[52]

What was distinct about Westlake's personality? His grandchildren remember him as 'shy', 'introverted' and 'eccentric'. The Cape Barren Islanders were also known as 'shy'. Perhaps they found his reserve unassuming and unthreatening.

Why *would* the Islanders share their knowledge with Birdsell and Tindale who came with callipers and needles? Why would they share it with Edward Stephens whom they had for years complained was a drunkard, who had locked children out of the school and had fired shots at two men returning to harbour?[53] Why share it with JV Cook, a police officer, a representative of the government who inspected and reported on their community?[54] While Westlake also came without authority, he represented neither institution nor establishment. He came because he had ignored the opinions of others. He came alone, with his little notebooks and a relatively open mind.

Another Cape Barren Islander, Morton Summers, explains to me that the people who talked to Westlake were most probably nominated 'spokespeople'. According to Buck Brown and Jim Everett, Westlake was given only 'everyday stuff'"—food, cooking, hunting. Summers says the people Westlake met 'didn't say anything <u>secret</u>, but were not <u>really</u> open,' they were 'just answering questions'.[55] Tindale referred to all traditional language on Cape Barren as 'the secret side of life', and it seems that within the traditional there are distinctions that are drawn between the mundane and the secret, and Westlake got none of the latter.

There was a moment when Westlake met with the 'reticence' of which he had been repeatedly warned but, more than that, an explanation for it. After he met Nancy Mansell he wrote in his notebook, 'Mrs M thinks it's no concern of mine what the natives did out here + all her remarks refer to practices of the half casts.'[56] The distinction Nancy Mansell drew between the practices of her mother Teekolterme, her grandfather Mannalargenna and the Coastal Plains traditional people and those of her own generation was a recognition of change, but also of continuity. Nancy Mansell knew what the

'natives did out here', but she was not going to share it with an out-
sider: it was the 'concern' of her community; they are the keepers of
that knowledge. More than just keepers of memories, however, this
community has its own 'practices'.

When I visit Cape Barren Island I believe myself to be an intrepid
historian. I am off to a distant island (albeit by plane), following in
Westlake's footsteps, echoing his questions. I too am trying to seek,
strive and find! But I also have some woolly notion that in bringing
in Westlake's notes I am somehow different: I am bringing something to *them* rather than taking something away! I have a hope that I
will be the bearer of something lost and found, something revelatory.
Of course the revelation is all mine.

If I am following Westlake, it is to emulate his naivety and condescension. My notes are like his box of flints; I am bringing their
culture to 'get details'. I too want them to explain and translate my
collection. I too want to fill notebooks with ideas and facts. But this is
not a research laboratory, it is a lifeworld, a beautiful place, and one I
could barely fathom. As with Westlake, my hosts try to show me. They
explain that this 'everyday stuff' is still 'every day'. The fish still came
to light, I am told. 'Canygong' is still eaten.

Jim and Buck have organised several spits of muttonbirds to be
brought to Jim's house. He has improvised a plucking shed out of Jim's
woodshed. Feathers pile up on the floor. Then they are handed to me.
My job is to scald and gut the birds. I first dip them in a simmering
pot. Then I clean out their guts in a bucket of icy cold water, my
hands going numb, while trying to take care to remove the livers as
instructed (the 'lights', they are called). I think of how Henry Beeton
told Westlake he too had eaten the 'lights' from the muttonbirds. Jim
roasts them over a fire on a piece of wire. I think of how Beeton said
to Westlake he had roasted them on red-hot coals.

'Stop being a researcher,' Jim tells me. 'Put your notebook away.'
So I eat the 'lights'. I eat the birds' fatty, fishy flesh. On another evening I eat the wallaby Jim has trapped. During the day we walk to the
beach and look out to sea. I taste, imbibe, breathe in the lifeworld.
There are moments when I get a glimpse of understanding. Then I

Rebe Taylor scalding a
muttonbird at Modda River,
Cape Barren Island,
Jim Everett, 2003.

realise it is a world that is complete, without needing to be proved, documented or categorised by me or by any researcher. That seems so obvious now, but still it is hard to put the idea into words. It cannot be captured in notebooks, on a page, in words. It lives in the people, on the islands and in Country: 'nééna toonábri mee kárni?'

Marshall Beach, Flinders Island, 28 February 1909

By 28 February, Westlake had travelled from Cape Barren Island, spent time at Settlement Point, and was now leaving, travelling by bike along Marshall Beach. The sand pressed white as his bicycle wheels turned over it. It was 'firm enough'. The heavy rain had lifted, and a sharp and brilliant light pierced through the dark grey clouds, picking out the sparkling tips of cobalt waves. The bright orange lichen almost glowed on the granite boulders. The gusty wind made heavy going of it, but the wild beauty of the place was exhilarating.

It was good to get away from Settlement Point—it had been like 'a place with a curse on it' and, Westlake had reflected, 'as ¾ of the Blacks died [t]here perhaps it has'.[57] At the nearby remains of

Wybalenna settlement Westlake found about '1 doz. Govt houses' and 'about 20 huts'. They were all in ruins or fast falling into decay. In the huts, where the Aboriginal residents had been housed, Westlake saw only one window, which he noted was not designed to open. For a man who believed in the benefits of fresh air this was anathema. He began to measure the still-standing walls and his foot nearly landed upon a black snake. It glided away into fallen beams and sheep's skulls. Westlake calculated that the air space of each hut was about '1800 cubic feet', which would have given each person only ⅕₅ of the amount of fresh air required. This explained for Westlake how it was the Aborigines had died off fast from consumption and other chest diseases.[58] Wybalenna brought to mind for Westlake the Old Testament Book of Isaiah: 'It shall never be inhabited, neither shall it be dwelt in from generation to generation … But wild beasts of the desert shall lie there, and their houses shall be full of doleful creatures…and the wild beasts of the islands shall cry in their desolate houses.'[59]

Westlake had been forced to wait out the rain and mist in the Settlement Point Post Office. When it lifted, the hard, wet sand of Marshall Beach offered escape. The wind was cleansing. He was leaving the desolate past, to continue the search for what was remembered.

Tanners Bay, Flinders Island, early March 1909

John Maynard had promised a longer 'list of words'. So Westlake had caught another boat from Cape Barren to his home at North West River, Flinders Island. But for some reason they never met there. Instead Westlake spoke once again to Henry Beeton and met his son-in-law and daughter, Harry and Victoria Armstrong, at nearby Killiecrankie Bay.[60]

By day Westlake heard descriptions that extended and echoed what he had heard on Cape Barren Island: of 'cod picked out of the water' by torch light; the 'slightly sweet' taste of the 'grass tree' pith; of eating raw seaweed that hung 'like beads on a string'.[61] By night he had to 'rough it' in an empty old house at nearby Tanners Bay. The bedding was so filthy that for about three nights he 'slept (or did not sleep)' in his clothes. 'The fleas on Flinders if placed end to end might reach to the nearest fixed star.'[62] Local farmer William R Allison brought him two blankets, some oatmeal, rice, bread and jam and a few onions.[63]

Westlake stayed nearly ten days at Flinders Island, talking to Beeton and the Armstrongs, and possibly waiting for Maynard to return. Then he got word that the ketches *Dawn* and *Linda* were soon leaving, and would not return for another three weeks. He 'hastened' to Flinders Island's main town, White Mark, on his bike, but he missed the *Linda* 'by 5 minutes!'

The next day Westlake caught a small boat to Cape Barren Island, and 'as fortune would have it found a cruiser in the Sound.' The warship the HMS *Psyche* agreed to take Westlake on board.[64] So he returned to Launceston without his 'list of words'.

Four months later Maynard promised to meet Westlake at George Town, north of Launceston, and give him the list of Aboriginal words. Westlake travelled up the Tamar on the appointed day, but found that Maynard had sailed away before he could reach him, 'tho. he knew I was coming,' he reflected with frustration.[65] Perhaps Maynard had needed to sail with the tide or to beat bad weather. Whatever the reason, Westlake's effort to acquire Maynard's list is testimony to his tenacity. But even that effort is made to seem comparatively minor when compared with the determination Westlake showed to complete his next Tasmanian undertaking.

Photographing stones

Launceston, late September 1909

Westlake had been in Launceston for four months. He had planned to be there for just a 'week or two'. After he returned from the Bass Strait Islands in mid March, Westlake decided to photograph The Reverend CG Wilkinson's collection of about 250 stone tools.[1] Westlake thought Wilkinson 'has made a better study of the native flint implements than anyone in the colony'. He had been collecting for years and he promised to tell Westlake 'all he knows about it'.[2] Westlake had really wanted to take Wilkinson's collection to England on loan, but he 'did not like to ask' since he felt he 'was a stranger'. Moreover, since he had a camera with him he thought that he 'could soon "polish them off"'.[3]

Westlake began the project in a studio in Launceston. He soon found his camera's extension could not capture the actual size of the stone tools. When he borrowed an extension he found he could not focus the lens. He hoped to improvise an extension with a tin box. He had a 'firm mounting' made by a carpenter under his direction, on to which he placed the 'flints on a flat sheet of glass' and photographed them vertically. He also used 'moveable mirrors' and even hung some stone artefacts by string in order to catch their underside in the reflection. Still, he found the light 'diffused'. Some of the negatives were 'perfect', but 'most were not'.[4] Westlake had found the project 'a decided bore'. It was far more difficult than he had supposed. He needed to manipulate light so that it realised the stones' worked edges. Thus Westlake came to realise that stone artefacts 'can only be photographed by a <u>student</u> of the subject'.[5] Without an understanding of the artefact as a tool, that knowledge could not be transmitted in the photographed image.

This is what Tylor had also realised with the drawings of Tasmanian Aboriginal stone implements he had wanted to be included in Roth's second edition of *The Aborigines of Tasmania*. When Roth sent Tylor the illustrations in early 1899, Tylor responded that he and Balfour 'agree that though your artist may be good for drawing pictures he had no idea of a stone implement as a tool'. Tylor explained that that it 'would never do' to show the public images that 'they would not understand'. It was not clear how the implements were actual tools, because the artist did not know how they had been made or used, and it was not clear which part of the tool had been held, or which part had been used to chop, scrape or cut. He ordered Roth to send the tools back so that they could be drawn again.[6]

With similar persistence, Westlake decided that, after working for more than a month in the studio, he would start his photographic project over in the Launceston Electric Lighting Station (or Duck Reach Power Station) near Cataract Gorge. He was given his own room there 'gratis' and the use of an arc light (a beam created between two carbon rods), and he worked from eight in the morning until ten at night.[7] He wrote to his children that he had 'no idea' when he would be back; 'the things that remain to do were so various' that he had 'no means of reckoning up the time'.[8]

By late May Westlake had moved his project to the basement of the Queen Victoria Museum and Art Gallery where he could use a 'condensing lens to get a parallel beam of light' to better capture the implements' edges. He could also print catalogue cards in the Museum. Onto these Westlake mounted 164 photographs.[9]

By September 1909, Westlake was back working in the Power Station. But he found the arc light exasperating; it altered in intensity

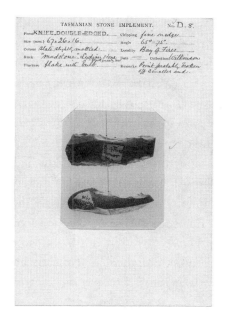

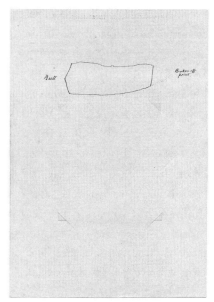

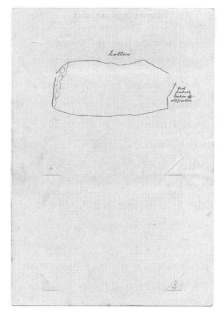

Tasmanian Aboriginal stone tools from the collection of The Reverend Wilkinson, Ernest Westlake, 1909. Westlake traced the tools on the reverse side of the cards. [© Pitt Rivers Museum, University of Oxford, 1998.466.27 and 1998.466.37, and reverse sides]

every few seconds. In 'London or in Paris ... one could get continuous current'. Launceston was one of the first Australian towns to generate its own electricity, using the water flow in the Cataract Gorge from 1895, but the power was not suitable for Westlake's technical needs. He had to expose the camera for up to a minute in order to get sharp contrasts. In some cases Westlake had to superimpose half a dozen successive exposures in order to get the desired result.

It was at this time that Westlake was arrested and gaoled. He had taken his 'eye off' his bicycle lamp for a mere 'six seconds' when 'a bobby came up and said it had been out'. The fine was eight shillings and sixpence. He had been fined for the same offence five months earlier, and had refused to pay. He was arrested, but Wilkinson paid his fine, which Westlake considered a 'nuisance' as it meant he would 'have to pay him back'.[10] Westlake refused to pay again, and was placed in the Launceston Goal. He was given only 'a piece of dry bread' to eat, and was in a solitary cell overnight without light and with bedding so filthy he dared not use it. He was surprised to learn in the morning that he had to serve another twenty-four hours. Westlake decided to call on a friend to pay his fine, but struggled to get any responses. William Frederick Petterd, a boot importer and scientist, was supposedly away in Hobart. Geologist WH Twelvetrees and Museum Curator Herbert Hedley Scott were both said to be 'out'. Westlake 'began to doubt whether' he was 'getting the truth'. But Thompson, a carpenter from the Power Station, came and paid his fine.[11] On their return to the Power Station, the workers explained to him that Constable Alford, who had made his arrest, was well known as a 'bankrupt greengrocer' and did all sorts of 'mean tricks' to raise revenue. They were impressed with Westlake's refusal, and he found he had 'risen in the folks' estimation'.

Westlake had been resident in Launceston long enough to acquire a community of friends. He was asked to give a lecture on eoliths to a small 'local society' in Launceston.[12] Bishop Mercer had stopped him in the street and asked him to tea.[13] But Westlake longed to get away. He missed the open air and 'found the confinement trying'. By November he had gained weight from so much inactivity and was advised by a doctor to give up fat, sugar and starch. In order to save money he moved into lodgings without board, which meant arranging his own meals. He boiled eggs on a Primus stove and found 'junket à la Metchnikoff', a cultured milk pudding, kept well for several days.[14]

Westlake wished he had been 'able to pay a professional photographer'. It was not just a 'presumption of ignorance' to think he could do it himself quickly; it was 'rash'. He had tried to achieve the 'technical results that photographers in Europe have been unable to reach', and in 'an out of the way place'. If doing the job himself had cost less money it had 'meant the expenditure of a great deal more time than' he dared consider.[15]

It was such a long time to be away from his children. 'Aubrey says that letters are not the same as being with a person—indeed they are not!' These words reveal how much Aubrey missed his father. 'When I get back I shall take care not to go away again,' Westlake promised, 'I should have been back before this except for this photography.'[16]

It is hard to fathom how Westlake could justify being away from his children months longer than he had anticipated so he could capture images of stone tools. Certainly he missed them. 'You don't know how much I look forward to your letters,' he wrote in July 1909.[17] His weekly letters during these months are longer, filled with reflections on his reading about world history, war and the divining rod. He transcribed part of a letter to the Bishop, himself 'an outspoken social reformer', about his unusual theological approach to Christianity.[18] Westlake wrote that women should 'be regarded as an incarnation of God … to be worshipped in the spirit and in truth.'

Westlake offered his children more advice, consideration and concern than when he was collecting in the field. Aubrey and Margaret were to take care with their posture, with their bicycles, to attend to their schoolwork, and tell him if they had suitable shoes. At one stage he wished 'we could write across the world so some people can occasionally do—my mind writing with your hand and your writings with mine.' He suggested a few times when they might all try for about ten minutes to sit, pencil in hand, and 'think of each other'.[19]

Writing at the Cataract Gorge on a beautiful day he told Aubrey and Margaret: 'I would sooner have a dull winter's day in England so that I was spending it with you.'[20]

Westlake dreamed of a better future together. One day he and Aubrey would be like 'the De Mortillets in France'—Gabriel de Mortillet, eolith advocate and archaeologist, had passed on his work to his son, Adrien. Westlake thought Aubrey's 'abilities' would prove equal to the 'Sherlock–Holmesian task of reconstructing the life of a vanished race of whom it is doubted whether they ever existed!'

For Westlake the French Miocene race was as real as the Tasmanian Aboriginal people, but both were 'vanished'. Even weeks after he had been in the Bass Strait and met those who knew how those tools were broken and used, Westlake assumed he was photographing the remnants of an extinct people. But Westlake's belief that their stones brought to life the French race gave him the perseverance and patience to deal with a task so challenging and so boring.

Westlake completed his photography by Christmas 1909. He had 'done it, as most things can be done by sticking at it.' He thought 'near all are better than the plates published by Max Verworn,' the German physiologist. Indeed, he thought they were better than any of the published European efforts.[21] But Westlake never published his photographs. The fourteen-hour days, the cold lodging, the boiled eggs and junket pudding, it was all for 218 photographs that almost no one would see and to bring to life a people who had never lived.

Such sweepings

Westlake's last six months in Tasmania were peripatetic and fatiguing. He had no intention of missing the next English summer holidays, and knew he had to leave Tasmania no later than early June to avoid this. His letters became marked by brevity rather than boredom. During this time he went to Nicholls Rivulet and spent a month reading government records, among many other trips to collect stones and memories. It was within the government records relating to the Aborigines that Westlake found a connection between the archive and his collecting. He had read a report to the colonial government written during 'the "war" times' that mentioned a 'flint quarry'.[1] With little more than a conversation in Ross and a handwritten map he had decided to try to find it. To do so, was to retrace a history of invasion.

Kearney Bogs, 9 June 1910
It was 'cold underfoot', but it was easier going in the boggy ground without shoes. This was no terrain for riding. He was more than 600 metres above sea level, in the Tasmanian midlands. There was a 'cold roaring wind' and, when it rained, it poured. Winter had set in.

Westlake had travelled from Hobart to Ross, cycled to Campbell Town and then caught a horse-drawn coach to Lake Leake, which was in fact a dam constructed at Kearney Bogs in 1883. He spent a night in a stock-keeper's hut before starting out on foot in the morning. The wetlands were like a labyrinth; '"2" Tasmanian miles are, as usual, more like 4 English'.[2]

Eighty years before, this had been a 'war zone'.[3] It was Oyster Bay Nation Country, but ran close to the eastern boundary of the North Midlands Nation. Their land ran down the centre of Tasmania, bordered on the west by the Big River Nation.[4] From 1826, these three Nations 'made their intentions clear'. They wanted their hunting grounds back. The recent invasion of their lands had been quick and harmful; thousands of sheep had taken over their kangaroo hunting grounds and trampled the shores of their rivers. Houses, walls and fences were erected as settlers, their convict workers and their military overseers arrived in the hundreds.

By early 1828, around forty-three male colonists had been killed. The reprisals had been swift: 350 Aboriginal people were reported dead. When spring arrived 'all hell broke loose'. The Oyster Bay and Big River people razed a stock hut about every two days. For the first time white women were killed, reportedly as they begged for their lives.[5] On 1 November 1828, Lieutenant-Governor George Arthur proclaimed martial law. All civilians were not only granted the power, they were encouraged, to capture any Aboriginal people found in the 'Settled Districts'. This included the midlands and the eastern coast: all the land between Hobart and Launceston, about a third of Tasmania. By March 1829, there were 200 soldiers in twenty-three parties touring the Settled Districts. By May, there were also six small civilian 'roving parties', each lead by a constable with four or five ex-convicts and an Aboriginal guide, centred in the midlands. Their method was stealth: lie in wait at night and capture Aborigines at dawn. In this they were not always successful. Those they ambushed were sometimes shot dead. These were the 'days of terror'.[6]

On 13 August 1829, William Grant, the leader of one of the roving parties under the direction of Gilbert Robertson, had reached Kearney Bogs. He had found what he described it as 'a large hole dug in the ground by the Natives'. This, he knew, was a place 'to which they resort in great numbers for the purpose of trimming the flint-stones wherewith to shape and make their spears'. Grant had been there a month earlier with Robertson. He noted that 'innumerable fires and huts' had since been made and left by the Aborigines. Moreover, his Aboriginal guide, Jack (Jack Allen, or 'Batman's Jack'),[7] had told him that 'two or three mobs' visited the quarry 'very frequently'. It was, as Grant worded the euphemism, a 'favourable opportunity'. He sent Jack and two others for provisions, and 'planted' himself with the remainder of his party above the quarry, where they were afforded a good view of the surrounding country. They waited nine days. Grant went to get further provisions. When he returned three days later, his men had nothing to report. Grant ended his report on 2 September, twenty days after arriving at Kearney Bogs. Their wait had been in vain.[8]

It had started to rain again. The road had become stony and hard to traverse. Westlake was trying to make a connection between archive, anthropology and warfare in the boggy highlands. He had read Grant's report to the colonial government months earlier, in the Records Office in Hobart.[9] But out in the field the place was 'not easy to find', and he found himself trudging barefoot through the swampy land far longer than he had first expected. Then he saw it.

It covered such a lot of ground. This was much larger than any quarry that Westlake had 'hitherto seen ... probably the largest in the island'. There were millions of stones spread across several acres:

> This is the historic flint quarry where in the 'war' times the whites resorted in the hopes that the blacks would come for flint, and also with the idea that if they could not get flint they could not make spears.
>
> But when the cat is about the mice keep in hiding, and to think that they had only one place to get stone was a great delusion. However, it is certainly the only flint quarry that was ever 'occupied' by a white army.[10]

Westlake spent the rest of the day collecting, leaving without enough time to walk the two hours back in full light. He almost got lost in a 'maze of bogs and drains' as night drew in and was 'jolly glad to get in and get tea!' But he returned to the Kearney Bogs quarry next day, and the morning of the day after, each time making the difficult tramp through the bogs to collect 'fine flakes', and some 'worked edges'.

The evidence of years-long mining and stonework was obvious to Westlake. He was surprised when he spoke to the local people and they told him, 'the stones you see there have been broken by the wind uprooting trees' or, 'those stones have been broken by fires passing thro. the bush'. Westlake reflected ruefully that it 'takes only 80 years for a tradition to be lost about a subject in which no one is interested'.[11] It may be that the midlands farming community's loss of memory stemmed less from a lack of interest in Aboriginal stonework than from a willingness to forget the first owners of their land, and the war they waged to ensure their removal.

If there was private memory, the collective, popular language of remembrance rarely extended beyond a broad elegiac sweep of events with an emphasis on the conclusion: absence and extinction. The Black War was one without public rituals and commemoration, or shared discussions of battles, tactics and numbers of those fallen.

Henry Reynolds, as a university student, remembers telling his history lecturer about the 'appeal' of Tasmania's landscape. 'No', he was reprimanded, 'it's a bloody sad place. You can still hear the Aborigines crying in the wind.'[12] His lecturer's family still owned the land where Aborigines had been killed, and where a shepherd was buried with spear wounds.[13] Here is a private, family memory retained in the land and continuity in its ownership. Reynolds also notes that beyond the colloquial memory, there is a 'rich tradition of historical literature' in Tasmania. Nineteenth century writers 'took up the subject of the Black War' and wrote about it assiduously and about the Aboriginal peoples with 'sympathy', as 'patriots and martyrs'. It was a 'distinctly Tasmanian' view.[14]

Those settlers, or children of settlers, that Westlake spoke to, though, talked of 'shame', but also deferred the blame. Their shame was rarely for the invasion of the lands from which they profited, or for the roving parties and military patrols. It was over a largely unnamed 'they', hinted to be of another class, or even another part of the island: the convicts, the bushrangers and the sealers. If extinction bred a candid shame, it was because it emphasised an absence and an end. A once busy quarry—evidence of an industrious, large population, and evidence of a people dispossessed, murdered and removed—was dismissed as never having been used. Instead, Truganini's sad pleas for a sea burial were repeated over and again. It was, at a popular level, a shame spoken in order to silence. It was a remembering in order to forget.

There is an uncanny echo of the justification Westlake heard for the presence of so many stones at Kearney Bogs quarry. When Walker went to see an Aboriginal quarry near Plenty, northwest of Hobart, Beattie and geologist RM Johnston, and their guide George Rayner, insisted the quarry, while unknown to most people, had once been a place where large groups of Aborigines broke stones and crafted tools.[15] But Walker could see 'no quarry or excavation', only 'two or three small and shallow holes, which might well have been caused by the uprooting of gum-trees'. He reflected how a few months earlier 'a heavy bush fire had swept over the place', obliterating many of the 'natural features'. Finally he admitted that the holes were 'probably' caused by the 'removal of pieces of rock eighty years before'.[16]

Westlake was acquainted with Tasmanian quarries. He visited the quarry in Plenty and had met Rayner in early 1909.[17] Perhaps as he picked up stones there, he imagined the quarry as it had been when Rayner's father had walked past, unnoticed by the Aborigines nearly a century earlier: 'there were twenty or thirty of them, men, women and children. Noisily chattering ... breaking the stones into fragments ... One old fellow [was] leaping up and spreading his legs out at the same time, to avoid ... being struck by the splinters.'[18] This was the busy industry that Westlake imagined, but in Kearney Bogs he could also see Grant's men hiding, watching and waiting. He knew the reason that there was no noisy chatter, no flying splinters of rock.

The last ride: Syndal Quarry, 12 June 1910

Westlake left Kearney Bogs, caught the coach back to Campbell Town and that same evening rode his bicycle to Ross, 16 kilometres away, in an hour—the fastest he had ever travelled on Tasmanian roads 'and in the dark too!' Before daybreak the following morning, he rode another 5 kilometres to 'Tom Fiddler's Ground', 'alias the Syndal Quarry'. It was the same place he had collected from in December 1908, when it had been dusty and windblown. This time it was wet and the wind had strewn so many fallen branches that he had had to leave his bicycle and walk the 2 kilometres. The quarry was a stony terrace, way up a hill—an edge broken by years of mining. Westlake was inspired to pose a mathematical question to his children: 'If you can look at 50 stones in a minute, how many can you look at in 6 hours?'[19] Westlake took away '50 pieces more or less chipped' as well as a 'few very finely so'. This 'settled the question' that had brought him back to Syndal Quarry: 'the stones <u>were</u> sometimes really worked and finished in the quarries.'

He knew he had to finish at three o'clock in order to have enough light to get back; it would be 'dangerous otherwise'. Westlake collected 'to the minute'. Then, 'as if it had waited for me to be done, it began to rain, a heavy soaking rain'. The wind was powerful and the terrace 'caught the full force'. Westlake did not mind. He was 'well wrapped up' and his work 'was done'. This was his final collecting trip in Tasmania. He 'was bound for Canaan's happy shore, otherwise England's.' Westlake walked 2 kilometres with 14 kilograms of stones, loaded it onto his bicycle and, in the 'driving rain', took his last ride in Tasmania.[20]

'such sweepings': Melbourne, 16 June 1910

Westlake was back in the reading room of the SS *Afric*. It smelled: 'Why everything on a ship smells is a subject worthy of physical research.' He had more reason for complaint. His rubber shoes had been stolen out of his 'leather portmanteau' on either the railway to Launceston or the steamboat to Port Dalrymple. The next day he would discover his Jaeger jacket had also been taken.[21] In fact, during his time in Tasmania, all his tools had been stolen from his bag one by one. When he paid for a box of stones to be sent from the North Coast to Hobart, the stones were thrown away and the box stolen. The 'box was worth perhaps 2d' (2 pennies), but the stones were two days' journey away. It was the 'loss of about a month's work and of specimens' that he could not replace. The 'state of morality is low in Tasmania.' It was not due to poverty, Westlake thought, for 'there are few persons here ... in want'. Rather they 'steal because it is natural to them to do so, as descendants of the convicts.'[22] He was leaving 'the hemisphere of thieves'.[23]

It had been a busy day in Melbourne. Westlake visited the National Museum to see a Tasmanian waddy (Aboriginal club) and the East Melbourne home of Thomas Welton Stanford, co-founder of the Victorian Association of Progressive Spiritualists, to see his collection of 'apports'—articles transferred by paranormal activities—and bought a case of apples for the journey home. He had also gone to The University of Melbourne to visit Spencer again. It was an interesting mirror to their first meeting. This time Westlake thought Spencer considered him 'the authority on Tasmanian stone'. Spencer asked Westlake to survey the Museum's Tasmanian collection, but the store keeper had gone to lunch. Westlake did not mind, for he felt that he did not 'yet know my own mind about the subject'.[24] Eighteen months earlier Westlake had concluded with confidence that stone implements he saw were the 'very image' of eoliths he had found in France.

Westlake wanted Spencer to look over his Tasmanian interviews for 'criticism'. It was because, he reflected to his children, 'I am not a professional anthropologist and he is and knows how it should be done.' A week before leaving Tasmania he learned of his successful application to be a Fellow in the Royal Anthropological Institute of Great Britain.[25] He retained, however, the outward appearance of an 'artizan travelling in search of employment'. Shopkeepers offered him 'cheaper things' since he didn't 'look like a learned professor'.[26] Westlake was surprised when Spencer considered the Royal Anthropological Institute would publish a paper on his Tasmanian interviews notes and 'be glad to get it'. Westlake had felt 'some doubt whether he would approve of such sweepings'.[27]

Such sweepings included the memories of Truganini laughing, of a 'land soaked in blood', and waiting in silence for the coming of spirit. Westlake had often been pleased, even excited, by such information. But he had always looked beyond what he was given to try to see something he thought was gone: the living 'Blacks'. Thus, despite the new letters after his name, FRAI, and despite the promise of publication, he did not consider what he had done was truly as valid as that of Spencer, who was 'one of the very few scientists who have seen the Blacks making and using stone tools'.[28]

Instead, Westlake had stood in empty quarries where the silence of absence rang loud in his ears. He collected among grazing sheep, not living Aborigines. The longing to practise anthropology as Spencer did was amplified by a deeper understanding as why he could 'see the Blacks': the months of 'depressing reading' in the archives, the mantra of 'shame' from settlers, and the stories of massacres and murders. There was also the sheer effort to gather the stones and the information: the long and difficult journeys on boats, trains, coaches, by bicycle and foot. And the repeated frustration of finding the informant was not old enough, or did not know enough, and even when they were able to tell him more, it was, he thought, always 'second hand'. So his excitement at collecting was often countered with rueful feelings: if he had come only three years earlier he could have met Fanny Smith, and a larger number of older settlers. If only the colonists had been less destructive, then he might even have met living 'Blacks'. After nearly a year and a half in Tasmania, Westlake wrote the only reflective note in his notebooks:

> It apparently never entered into any white man's head that the few Blacks in Tasmania were more important to human progress than the whole white population + that the reason they were important to progress was because they had not progressed. So this incomparable opportunity of studying this stage of human progress arrested a hundred thousand years ago was lost.[29]

Westlake took his frustration home. When I met Westlake's grandson Chris Charman, he told me his grandfather always spoke of having gone to Tasmania 'too late', that he had found only 'a handful' of descendants. He remembers his mother talking about what Westlake had told her of 'how terrible it was', that all the Aborigines were all 'herded to a cave or something and pepper shot over them'.[30] Jean Westlake told me that despite her grandfather's great pride and trust in British civilisation, he considered Tasmania the most shameful chapter in its history.[31]

Westlake was blinded by what he wanted to see. The Aboriginal people of Tasmania were not missing. If the quarries were empty, it was because they had changed their economies, adapted their tools, and were no longer living in those traditional lands. But the specificity of Westlake's research question could not encompass adaptation and change. Even if Westlake had 'seen the Blacks making and using stones' would he have seen them as a people with a history, beyond a metaphor for a European past? He walked past the stone tools at the base of the wind-swept Pipers River sand dunes. He hardly saw the point of digging into the middens on Bruny Island. He called the corroboree songs gathered at Nicholls Rivulet and the description of breaking the ballawinne on the Bass Strait Islands 'such sweepings'. His search for an Eolithic anachronism meant he could not see what he had unwittingly found: both the Tasmanian Aboriginal peoples' deep past and their continued endurance.

Going home

Westlake had always kept 'the greater part' of his collections in his father's large house, Oaklands. He did not own the house; it had been left in trust to Aubrey and Margaret. Westlake had only some shares in family investments and properties. The 'home' that was his alone was his gipsy caravan.[1] His cousin Sidney Rake lived in Oaklands on the 'understanding', wrote Westlake to his brother-in-law 'that my things remained'.[2]

For four of the nine years since Lucy's death, Westlake had been abroad. His children continued to live between Oaklands (their father paying rent to Rake), Wincanton (where they were welcomed by the Rutters) and Sidcot School. When Westlake returned from Tasmania in August 1910, he decided it was time they had 'a home, or at least some place we can call our own'. His first thought was to try to make Oaklands their home, and to utilise the surrounding lands more profitably. But Westlake soon found he had an irreconcilable 'incompatibility' with his cousin. However large the house, Westlake and Rake could not share it. He had negotiated with Rake before his departure the use of his stepmother's room for his best collections. But while Westlake was in Tasmania, Rake had 'instructed the servants to tidy' both rooms. Westlake's collections had been moved into his caravan and the summerhouse. There was a 'box of Thames Valley Stones', Westlake complained to Clarence Rutter, from '[t]he most important deposit in Britain for the student of the Palaeolithic Age. They were now worthless without their identifying labels.' Westlake faced weeks of work to sort them. He photographed the jumbled box as proof and sent it to Rutter. He implored, 'I must have what the poorest man of independence has, a room I can really call my own.'[3]

Westlake also had to find a place to store the hundreds of Tasmanian stone tools he had shipped before his departure from Hobart; the eleven boxes of his own artefacts, as well as the 400 stones he had taken from JV Cook's collection. Westlake planned to photograph Cook's stones in England and then return them. Despite the months spent photographing Wilkinson's collection in Launceston, Westlake thought Cook's implements would most successfully authenticate his eoliths.[4] Further, Westlake paid Joseph Paxton Moir over the following five years to continue collecting stones and interviewing people. Among Moir's first tasks was to go to the north coast to find the stone tools tossed out by the thief who had stolen the box in which they had been stored. Three weeks after Westlake had arrived home, Moir was 'glad to say' that the manager of the property where Westlake had packed the box had been able to 'collect nearly all the stones thrown away'. Moir agreed they were 'well worth all the trouble of getting'.[5]

In January 1911, Moir reported that he had been 'to the various places and persons according to your instructions'. He had visited over twelve sites and spoken to several residents on the south east coast, been up to the north coast and had made three trips to Oyster Cove.[6] Moir wrote that he had seen 'more of Tasmania than I had ever seen in my whole life'.[7] By August 1911 he had packed and shipped about 70 kilograms of stones to Westlake.[8]

By this time Westlake was renting a room in Market Place, Salisbury, where he both lodged and began work on the Cook collection. But there were record high temperatures that summer. The room became 'intolerable by day and uninhabitable by night'. Westlake sought relief in the ramparts of the ancient Salisbury settlement, Old Sarum, sleeping on a bed of beech leaves: 'this cools me down a bit,' he wrote to

Rutter.[9] By August he was asked to leave his room; he was the only tenant who had not vacated due to the heat and the landlady could not afford to keep the property open for one.

Two months later, Westlake finally settled an agreement on another room in Salisbury. There was considerable work to be done to make the room habitable and to access a power supply suitable for photographing the stones. Then, after he moved in, Westlake was told he was not allowed to sleep there. Westlake wrote to Rutter that he would 'sleep on the floor and hide the clothes by day'. But he soon leased 'the side of a ploughed field close to a road', on Harnham Hill, parked his caravan there, and walked the mile into his room each morning to continue photographing. His aunt Eliza Westlake wrote from Southampton to Rutter, expressing concern that it was an 'unwarrantable risk' for Westlake to commute by foot 'though frost and snow' and to 'sleep through cold and wet under such a very insufficient covering'. She admonished that 'he can afford to have a House or Rooms in Salisbury if would spend less on Science'.[10] Westlake continued to spend his money on science.

In early 1912, he received a heavy consignment of stones from Moir. When they arrived in London, Westlake faced extra customs charges for the fact the stones had been mistakenly marked as 'curios'. Moir promised that in future he would ensure the customs papers indicated they were 'Of no commercial value'.[11]

By July 1912, Moir had shipped four more cases of stones weighing about 500 kilograms, over half a cubic metre. They included almost the remainder of Cook's collection that had come by train from Launceston. Moir had 'examined every stone' in the collection and rejected 'fully 5 cwts' (230 kilograms) 'as being of no use except for road metal, although it was the refuse of stuff handled by the Tas. Natives'.[12]

It may be that Moir also wrote Cook's initials as he studied and packed each stone individually, for many of the stones in the Westlake Collection in the Pitt Rivers Museum have the letters 'J.V.C.' written upon them. Or perhaps these were some of the 404 artefacts that Westlake had packed in Hobart in 1910, with the hope to photograph and return them. The images may never have been finished; certainly they did not go into Westlake's archive in the Pitt Rivers Museum.

By the time the four cases of Tasmanian stone that Moir had packed arrived in late 1912, Westlake still had no permanent home in which to store or study them. He came up with a plan to finance a new house: establish a sanatorium. He outlined his plan to Rutter while he was living in a tent during the holidays. Westlake had had 'nowhere else to go to'.[13] Westlake did not want to consider Oaklands as a place to stay during the holidays. Relations with Rake had not improved.

Westlake's chosen location for his plan was in Woldingham, Surrey, on the outskirts of London, where his family had, for about twenty years, owned nearly 2 hectares of land.[14] There was only one such resort in England, Linford at Ringwood, and this may have offered Westlake a model.[15] The sanatorium would offer healing with the simple cures of 'water, sun and air', and a vegetarian diet from a home-grown garden. It would offer Aubrey future employment—he had recently begun a degree in medicine at St John's College, Cambridge—and, while Westlake hoped Margaret would finish school, attend university and find work, he also thought the sanatorium would offer her the opportunity to learn how to keep a home. But, no less important for Westlake, the sanatorium would allow him the space 'something equivalent to a Museum', so he could store, display and study his French and Tasmanian stone collections.

The plans never eventuated. Westlake admitted in the spring of 1913 that there had been 'too much delay'.[16] He had been home from Tasmania for nearly three years and was seemingly no closer to publishing his findings. It had been around eight years since the French authorities had 'reluctantly' allowed Westlake to take such a large number of stones out of the country on the understanding he would 'work them up in a scientific manner'.

By June 1914, there was a promise of progress. Westlake bought 17 hectares of land at Godshill, about 6 kilometres east of Fordingbridge, a 'wild and windswept landscape' of valley and forest. He parked the caravan there and lived in it while a house was built. Meals were cooked over a Primus stove and the bedclothes 'froze to the walls' of the caravan as autumn turned to winter but, as Jean Westlake put it, 'it <u>was</u> home'.[17]

A 'Heath Robinson' style of wooden bungalow finally emerged. A separate, boxy room perched on crossed stilts with an external staircase—too steep for 'Old Tatsy', their maid, to bring tea—offering 'a magnificent view of the valley' became Westlake's study. It was a 'private place', where he could work 'undisturbed'.[18]

The final two cases of Tasmanian stone tools arrived in London in the summer of 1915. One of the cases had been opened by customs and the stones were reportedly in 'loose conditions'.[19] Westlake suspected some of the stones had been stolen.[20] Since the weight measurements by the Hobart shippers and Moir had not been specific enough to compare, the only way to be certain was to send the case back to Moir.[21] It is here, in June 1916, five years after Westlake had returned from England, that the letters regarding the transport of Tasmanian Aboriginal stones end without resolution.

Westlake had spent more than £30 on paying Moir to carry out research work, and as much on shipping. His comparative project, which had begun in front of a cabinet of Tasmanian stone artefacts in the British Museum, had become a massive task. But after all the effort of travelling, collecting, note taking, photographing, shipping and finding a place to work, Westlake never published any of his findings from Tasmania, or from France. The planned paper for the Royal Anthropological Institute was never sent, nor even drafted. Why? 'Destiny had other things in store for him.'[22]

A new order

War was declared in July 1914 and it eclipsed Westlake's interest in his collections completely. He retreated to his Godshill eyrie and entered a 'profound meditation' for much of the first year of the war. 'With him, as for so many others of the Victorians,' Aubrey reflected, 'the whole civilisation and culture of the 19th century, which had looked so stable and so lasting was crashing around him.'[1]

What Westlake feared was not the 'collapse' of the conservative pillars of Victorian culture, but rather that they were being underpinned. This war, which would be known as the First World War, ushered in a resurgence of Empire and a call-out to nationalism. Westlake was a pacifist through his Quaker upbringing and through its association with Auberon Herbert's circle, and opposed to government coercion and militarism. Like the progressivists of the time, Westlake was deeply concerned about the social cost of corporate greed and industrialism. Foremost, Westlake was an evolutionist. He believed that racial strength was achieved not just through breeding, but also through grappling and being in tune with the natural environment. It was this contact with the natural world that made 'primitive' peoples capable of living in simple bush shelters. Recent generations of Europeans had been led further away from their origins to become, as Aubrey phrased his father's thoughts, 'too refined, too dependent on machines, too cut off from the primary elements of earth, air, fire and water'.[2] The capacity of modern nations to mobilise and kill en masse was not a triumph of human achievement, but its threat. It was 'civilisation' gone too far.

Westlake spent much of his time in retreat, reading and thinking. He may have returned to the ideas that had long shaped his thinking, including John Ruskin's utopian romanticism and Edward Carpenter's early socialism. Certainly he read Carpenter's 1889 book *Civilisation: Its Cause and Cure*, and agreed intensely with the thesis that civilisation was a 'disease', for no society had entered the phase of being 'civilised' and emerged in a 'healthy condition'.[3] He may have also encountered recent additions to these ideas, such as Hilaire Belloc's 1912 book *The Servile State*, which addressed the risk of decline by calling for a return to the free association of the medieaval age.[4] The writing in Alfred Orage's *The New Age* magazine extended the older guild movement into a contemporary socialism that challenged the financial systems backing capitalism and war.

In the autumn of 1914, Aubrey returned to St John's College at Cambridge to begin the second year of his medical degree. He did not want to join up; his father had long impressed a Quaker pacifism upon him.[5] But Aubrey did want to 'engage in some activity of national significance'.[6] The Scouts had lost many leaders to the military, and Aubrey joined them to help fill the gap. He soon became disheartened by what he, and others, found to be the Scouts' overly nationalistic militarism.

Returning to Godshill during term break, Aubrey told his father about the growing disenchantment with Robert Baden-Powell, and how a group of Scouts were turning with enthusiasm to the ideas of Ernest Thompson Seton. Seton was a North American who, in 1902, had established the 'Woodcraft Indians', a movement that drew on First Nation cultures and practices to teach urban children to respect and survive in nature.[7] The Woodcraft Indians had inspired the establishment of the Scouts in 1908, and Baden-Powell and Seton had worked together, but the outbreak of the First World War fractured their alliance—Seton did not think Woodcraft should be used for the promotion of nationalism or military purposes.[8]

Aubrey and his father sat talking in the Godshill eyrie for 'hours and hours', going over ideas and making plans.[9] Westlake emerged from his 'meditation' with a decision. He and Aubrey would establish a new, alternative 'scouts' movement. By 1916, the Order of Woodcraft Chivalry was born. This new Order was for girls as well as boys, women and men. It had a merit system with deeds and trials, uniforms and banners, but none of the fervent patriotism, parades or marches. Like the Scouts, the Order was Christian, but articulated its beliefs more clearly: God was worshipped in Nature.[10] It had a Native American semblance as well—'packs' held 'pow-wows'; adult leaders adopted names like 'Red Buffalo' and 'Wind-in-the-Pines'; members would greet each other with the call 'blue sky!'—but the Order remained more faithful to the original vision for Woodcraft,[11] and Seton was invited to assume the role of Grand Master.[12] The Order drew heavily on English traditions too. While the Scouts claimed to exemplify the bygone chivalry of the knights, the Order took the idea further. Its ruling body was a *Witanagemot*, an Old English term for a council of wise men, and its emblem was two crossed axes beneath a shield bearing the Cross of St George.[13] More than an effort to emulate Ruskin's 1871 Guild of St George, it was a direct response to Ruskin's appeal, voiced in his 1865 book, *Sesame and Lilies*:

> I wish there were a true order of chivalry instituted for our English youth … in which both boys and girls should receive … their knighthood and ladyhood by true title; attainable only by … trial of character and accomplishment.[14]

In 1916 Aubrey's old school headmaster invited him to establish the Order's first Lodge at Sidcot. Aubrey set up a second group in the working-class East End suburb of Hoxton, while studying at Barts Medical School in London. During 1918, Aubrey went to the Le Glandier School in the South of France and created a Woodcraft Lodge with the 500 Belgian refugee children housed there. The following year, when established in General Practice in Bermondsey in

London, Aubrey established the Smoke Tribe Woodcraft group with local youths he took camping in his annual holidays.[15]

The Order publicised its plans in the newsletters of the Society of Friends, who were enthused by a pacifist scouting movement. Other Sunday schools as well as Quaker and Theosophical educationalists sought to apply the Order's educational theories to their teaching.[16] Westlake sought support and inspiration from a wide range of forward-thinking people of the time. Orage's *The New Age* magazine promoted the Order. Toynbee Hall, the London East End home of social reformist charity work, became their meeting place.[17] Westlake joined the 1917 Club in London's Soho district, established by Virginia Woolf's husband Leonard. Its members included the Bloomsbury set and the Fabians, whom Westlake engaged in the activities and ideas of the Order.[18]

By 1919 the Order published its substantial *The Adventurer's Handbook*. It included the practical steps in setting up a lodge, the deeds' system, ritual scripts and uniform patterns. But Westlake's introduction offered a more philosophical outline of the Order's 'educational expression'. Each child should explore a 'self-realisation' of their 'ancestral instincts' and the discovery of the 'infolded God'. Many from the Sunday school and more traditional scouting side left the Order.[19] But this was, Aubrey, reflects, 'how it should have been', for the Order was realising a new 'spiritual inspiration' of post-war England.[20]

Westlake's aspirations for the Order had always extended beyond founding 'an alternative movement to the Scouts with a more woodcrafty and pacifist outlook'. He wanted to establish a school. His conceptual model, which he named 'The Forest School', would offer children a place to explore the natural world and gain the wisdom and skills of the ancient crafts and industries.[21] Its emphasis would be less on the 'three Rs' than on the 'three Hs': 'Heart, Hand and Head'.[22] His ideas were influenced closely by British sociologists Victor Branford and Patrick Geddes, whose 1917 book, *The Coming Polity*, saw the scouting movement as playing a central role in creating a much-needed 'wider mental and cultural renaissance'. Both men accepted Westlake's invitation to join the Order's Council of Guidance.[23]

Westlake found what he believed would make the perfect home for his school in 1919.[24] It was in the Sandy Balls Forest, and it included the same spot his father had pronounced such 'beauteous country'.[25] The land was part of the Breamore Estate, which was subdivided into allotments for sale after the Seventh Baronet Hulse died in the war and the duties could not be paid.[26] 'To the surprise and dismay' of his family, Westlake bought the parcel of land with a loan secured against a mortgage. There was no money to pay back the advance. The only solution, as Westlake proposed, was to sell Oaklands. Rake refused. Westlake took him to court and won a settlement, but Rake would not move out. Rake ultimately bought Oaklands at what was later considered to have been half its estimated value.[27]

The Order held its first children's camp at Sandy Balls for the boys from Aubrey's Bermondsey Smoke Tribe in 1920.[28] A year later, on the eve of the Feast of Lammas (the pagan festival of the harvest), the Order gathered at Sandy Balls to celebrate their first 'Folkmoot'. Dressed in cloaks of the colours of the seasons, seventy members gathered in the 'Festive Circle', a natural clearing in the fir trees, and lit their sacred ceremonial fire.[29] Westlake led the opening invocation, calling for 'beauty in the inward soul'. He had decided upon a new Woodcraft name for himself, 'Jack-in-the-Green', after the traditional English May Day figure who represented new life and spring. But another name and role was bestowed upon Westlake on that Lammas Eve: the new 'British Chieftain of the Order'.[30]

The metamorphosis

Aubrey reflected that the Declaration of War meant for his father, 'a rethinking of all his ideas'.[31] It resulted in a 'transformation of the anthropologist into the humanist and educationalist—a true metamorphosis'.[32] The change from collector to chieftain—from studying stone tools alone to founding a social movement—does indeed seem stark. But as with any metamorphosis, what entered the chrysalis of Westlake's 'profound meditation' in July 1914 were his original, long-standing beliefs and ideas. What emerged was their culmination and realisation in perhaps their truest and most genuine form: a love of nature and outdoor adventure, the belief in the freedom of intellectual and spiritual expression and, most fundamentally, evolutionism.

The Order of Woodcraft Chivalry was the 'application of the evolutionary theory to education'.[33] Seton understood Woodcraft to be that which 'first took the four-legged, hairy brute, set it up on its hind legs and gave it a bigger brain'.[34] It was how Westlake understood his eoliths: as being from the culture that first distinguished the first humans from their evolutionary predecessors. If woodcraft 'made us human', then it was imperative that education should teach those natural skills in their 'historic order'. Children's learning should begin by exploring the simple culture of the early Stone Age and, by late adolescence, engage with the philosophical sophistication of Classical Greece.[35] To do so was to follow their natural inclinations and development. Westlake reflected upon his own childhood. He first began to play in his parents' garden in the treetop platforms, like the hominids. He came down to explore caves and fashion tools of glass. His educational model would allow children to follow this natural course. Such 'going back' or 'recapitulation' in each generation would generate social 'renewal' and thus safeguard against the 'disease' of civilisation.[36]

The Order's merit system followed an evolutionary course, and included trials of 'quick sight', 'keen hearing' and 'noiseless tread'. Children had to find their way through the New Forest using markers or, at night, the moon.[37] They had to try to cross the Avon River swimming with a lighted candle, not letting the flame go out. While these trials remember Seton's adoption of Native American culture, they were also influenced by what Westlake had learned in Tasmania between 1908–1910. William Blyth had told Westlake that the Tasmanian Aborigines' 'eyesight and hearing mighty keen', while William Thorne said that their 'eye sight splendid—better than white' and 'hearing very good'.[38] The Reverend Atkinson said Truganini could see a hawk coming long before he did, and could hear a snake when he heard nothing. Annie Benbow said the Aborigines had 'very sharp eyes, like hawks could see at a distance—sharper than a white person's'. John Maynard agreed that the Aborigines 'could see better than white people'.[39]

Westlake had written to Margaret from Tasmania that she should practise her diving skills, telling her that 'the natives here were like fishes in this respect, and could pick up anything from the bottom of the sea'.[40] In a 1918 article published in *The Woodcraft Way*, Margaret wonders if one day a child brought up in the Forest School, 'may acquire the expertness of the native Tasmanians in their swimming'.[41] 'Where I want all the complication of a tent,' Westlake wrote to his children in 1908, 'a Tasmanian would sleep naked on the ground.' He later confessed, 'I envy the Natives, and I can't think how they did it.'[42] In a 1921 paper promoting the importance of camping for children, Westlake wrote that sleeping outdoors not only remembers the Neolithic wigwams of North America, but also the older Palaeolithic epoch in which people sheltered in 'caves, or behind wind screens of boughs and bark, like the modern Tasmanians'.[43]

The idea of 'chivalry' also stemmed from the notion of 'recapitulation'. In the 'chivalric system,' Westlake explained, the ruling classes reverted to 'aboriginal occupations of war and hunting that *preceded* industrialism'. The natural competition of chivalry allowed for industrial and disciplined pursuits to evolve freely, outside any enforced hierarchy.[44]

The journey towards faith was also evolutionary. Westlake understood Woodcraft to be a naturally Christian movement: Jesus was born in a stable, he questioned the conventional laws, and was resurrected like the seasons. But the discovery of Christ should also be a 'recapitulatory' theological journey.[45] '[O]ne must be a good pagan,' Westlake believed, 'before one can become a good Christian.'[46] He researched the idea extensively and wrote about it passionately. He was deeply influenced by Oxford-based classicist Jane Ellen Harrison's work on Hellenistic worship, especially her reading of the cult of Dionysos.[47] In *The Bacchae* by Euripides, the Bacchants 'leave their human homes, their human work and ordered life' to return to 'the wild things upon the mountains'.[48] It was, Westlake thought, precisely the spiritual awakening that the Order should emulate. To this end he proposed a progressive worship of three woodcraft gods: Pan, the 'spirit of the Wild'; Artemis, the goddess of the civilised; and finally Dionysos, the 'spirit of the Return to Nature'. Westlake saw 'a very close parallel between Dionysos and Jesus', for both represented life born again. He pronounced the Order 'a Dionysos movement', and in the most abstemious sense, prescribed for a wartime England a Bacchanalian 'Worship of Joy'. To the memory of his mother's 'chief wish' that he should become a missionary, he answered, 'very well, here I am, then'.[49]

There was a very personal and heartfelt impetus behind Westlake's religious expression for the Order. He had been devastated by Lucy's death in 1901. She had been his joy but, more, he believed she had an innate connection with the spirit world, which, following her death, he believed was real. Westlake called it 'insight' after Wordsworth's 'Intimations of Immortality'.[50] Usually lost to 'civilised' adults, the gift was natural in children (it was what enabled Samuel to hear the Lord call his name) and to 'primitive' peoples. It was just such a gift that Fanny Smith's children evoked in describing the Tasmanian Aboriginal peoples' abilities to intuit warnings through their bodies, and wait for the spirit in corroborree. Such insight was 'essential' to human nature, Westlake concluded, or 'perhaps of something older than human nature itself'.[51]

Westlake's understanding of primitive religion followed less the categorical systems of anthropologists Tylor and James George Frazer, than Harrison's recognition that via the 'savage's' beliefs it became possible for modernised Europeans to understand that their survival was based upon 'instincts kindred to his'.[52] Westlake had wished for a copy of Carpenter's *Civilisation* while he was in Tasmania; he had a strong intimation that it would echo his own conclusions.[53] By 1909, the idea of civilisation as a 'disease' began to permeate Westlake's thinking in a personal and almost literal way.[54] He spent most of his return voyage from Tasmania writing a biography of his marriage for his children, called 'About Snakes'.[55] The 'snakes' were the causes of Lucy's death. There were thirty-three. More than pleurisy and a dangerously timed dose of morphine they included 'Absolutism', 'Bigotry', 'Clothes', 'Drugs', 'Evangelism', 'Legal Marriage', 'Public companies', 'Riches', 'Selfishness', 'Unbrotherliness', 'War'.[56] It's a 103-page indictment upon middle-class Victorian society, a warning to his children to avoid the narrow-minded conventions of his childhood. What Westlake took away from Tasmania was more than stone tools, but a sense of how the culture of the Aborigines could address the 'disease' of 'civilisation'. '[T]he sooner we go back to the ways of the aborigines the better,' he wrote to his children.[57]

When Westlake left Tasmania in June 1910, he did so with increasing momentum towards a change in his life. He wrote that on his return he should look for work that would keep him in Europe.[58] He was tired of travelling and having no real home, and he had always wanted to work with Aubrey. These had been the motivations behind his plans for a sanatorium.

Nonetheless, founding a social movement did seem if not a 'transformation' of Westlake's thinking, than at least of his personality. Aubrey considered his father to be a 'recluse'. His grandson Chris Charman less charitably described him as 'pathologically shy'. So how did a 'recluse' join the fashionable 1917 Club, or address a large gathering dressed in a cloak? Westlake had always overcome introversion in order to advance his ideas. He had crossed seas, rivers and beaches to talk to people about Tasmanian Aboriginal culture. He was also never shy in the face of authority. He had gone to gaol in Launceston on a matter of principle. He had told the Bishop of Tasmania to find God through the worship of women. Westlake was less an introvert than an eccentric. He lacked 'social niceties', as Jean Westlake put it. He had always flouted those conventions he considered unnecessary, unnatural or even unhealthy. Moreover, the collaboration with Aubrey allowed Westlake to continue spending much of his time reading and writing on his own.[59] It was Aubrey who 'attended to matters of organization and practical detail'. Meanwhile Westlake, through a number of pieces published in their serial *The Woodcraft Way*, gave the Order 'its philosophy and inspiration'.[60]

Founding the Order was Westlake's best-known achievement. While few scholars have connected Westlake's science and collecting to the ideas that shaped the Order, they have recognised the influence the Order has had in shaping post-war social movements. In 1920, John Hargrave, or 'White Fox', left the Order to establish

The Kindred of the Kibbo Kift (Old English for 'Brotherhood of the Strong'). Hargrave described his movement as a 'natural impulse of youth against the totally unnatural environment of our civilisation', and England's only genuine national movement.[61] His call for a new elite world government inspired HG Wells's samurai in *A Modern Utopia*.[62] Among the Kindred members was the pioneer of British youth culture, Rolf Gardiner, who took inspiration from Germany to encourage a local folk revivalism, naturism and traditional land practices.[63] In 1924, Leslie Paul established the Woodcraft Folk, which promoted anti-industrialism and adventuring along revolutionary lines. It flew the 'red and green banner' and ran the by-line 'the Movement of the Workers' Children'.[64]

These were relatively small movements. Baden-Powell's Scouts had 100,000 members by the end of its first year, 1908. The Kindred had 236 members in 1924; the Order grew to 1200 members by 1926; the Woodcraft Folk to about 1000 by the 1930s.[65] But they are recognised for sharing 'a significant place in the British culture and ideas'.[66] The Order of Woodcraft Chivalry is distinct again. It not only preceded the other movements and pioneered many of their ideas, it found inspiration less in socialism or nationalism, but more in a unique mix of Darwin, Dionysos and Jesus. It was, like its founder, both a product of and an exception to its time.

'a mere collector'

By 1920, the 'formative period' of establishing the Order was, Aubrey reflected, 'largely at an end'.[67] Westlake wrote to Aubrey that he planned to finish a paper for the Geological Society outlining the geology of the Aurillac beds and the French eoliths. The first part had already been drafted en route to Australia. He thought it was written 'carefully in proper form, so that I shall prove that I know my geology, and am exact, and not a mere collector'. Echoing his letter from Melbourne a decade earlier, Westlake reflected 'it only remains to go ahead'.[68]

Westlake spent the following year writing and submitted a manuscript for publication, but it was not about French geology. He had

reworked 'About Snakes' into a four-part, 250-page manuscript entitled 'The Bacchic Eros: Being first steps in love's mysteries'. It was
inspired by HG Wells's *The Passionate Friends*, which calls for a 'time
when fathers and mothers will prepare frank and intimate records of
their thoughts and their feelings' for their children. But 'The Bacchic
Eros' went further, to include lengthy reflections on religion and love
and quotations from Sappho's poems, which Westlake had translated
from the ancient Greek.[69]

One reader found the manuscript 'difficult to describe in a word
or phrase', but endeavoured to with the adjective 'unsatisfactory'.
Westlake had achieved 'not first rate, or ... a second or even third-rate
piece of literature ... none but a benevolent publisher would take the
risk'.[70] Westlake tried again, but under the prescient nom de plume
'Roy Me Fail'. The publisher found it 'impossible' to consider the
manuscript. The writer had a 'turn for unconscious humour ... his
powers should have some outlet—though precisely in what direction
it is difficult to determine.'[71]

Westlake returned once again to his Tasmanian and French collections. He hoped that Margaret, who had graduated in anthropology
from St Hugh's College at Oxford would help him.[72] Perhaps the
falling out between them was the reason for further delay. During the
formative years of the Order, Margaret had been an active supporter,
living with her father at Godshill, writing for and participating in the
Order.[73] During this time Westlake had made friends with 55-year-
old Tom Charman, a talented local woodcarver. Despite very different
personalities and backgrounds, they discovered shared interests in
spiritual phenomena, woodcraft and education.

When Westlake discovered Tom and Margaret planned to move
in together at Godshill, he was, as Chris Charman put it, 'appalled'. A
'battle royal of wills went on for weeks'. There was the age difference,
the fact that Tom was an 'improvident artist', but what supposedly
angered Westlake most of all was that Tom and Margaret refused
to marry. Margaret considered civil law had no place in a loving
union.[74] It seems strange this should have offended her father when
'legal marriage' had been listed as the '9th snake' in 'About Snakes'.[75]

Jean Westlake thought her grandfather had 'brought Margaret up to be independent, and when she turned out to be, he couldn't take it.'[76] According to Derek Edgell, the author of a history of the Order, Westlake believed that Tom Charman was racially of the 'lowest grade', and if Margaret had a child by him it would either render her sterile, or throw 'back her children to an extent that probably a thousand years of racial selection would not restore'. Chris Charman laughed out loud when I read this idea to him. He had never heard it before, but did not think it out of character for his grandfather.

Unwilling to share his house, Westlake returned in the early winter of 1921 to the old gipsy caravan.[77] It was parked next to the summer-house at Oaklands. Rake enjoyed the comfort of the large house nearby and Margaret and Tom lived in the Godshill house that Westlake had built. He did not want to talk to any of them. He had little money. He dressed in spartan clothing and, too frugal to see an optometrist, balanced two pairs of cheap Woolworths glasses on his nose to read by the light of the fish-wick lamps. Chris Charman thought he was a 'sad, lonely man'. 'He was,' Chris's partner Jane agreed.[78]

By the summer, Westlake was living with his new private secretary, Paddy O'Leary from Bermondsey in his caravan, and compiling several pamphlets for the Order. In October 1922, Westlake was visiting some friends in a house in Fordingbridge. By coincidence Tom Charman and Margaret were also there. 'He was about to back out of the room in confusion,' Chris says, but Tom 'held out his hand and said "Can't we be friends? Come live with us up here".' Westlake 'hesitated a moment' and then took Tom's hand.[79]

It was a provident amnesty. The next day, 30 October, Westlake went to London with Aubrey. He was riding in the sidecar of Aubrey's motorbike. When they came out of a tunnel in Holborn, a car squeezed them to the side of the road and Aubrey hit a kerb. It was not a violent collision—the sidecar had gently tipped over. But Westlake hit his head and never recovered.[80]

Westlake's unpolished pine coffin with leather handles and his name carved on the lid was transported by cart to 'Woodling's Point' in Sandy Balls. It was covered with an orange flag, a life-giving colour for the Order. The crossed axes and shield emblem was the only other adornment. Westlake was lowered into a traditional chieftain's tumulus, a Celtic burial mound, in the shelter of fir trees.

A wooden monument remembers Westlake as the 'First British Chieftain' and the 'Father of the Order'.[81] The letters after his name also recall his fellowships with the Royal Anthropological Institute and the Geological Society. But these connections seem strangely out of context with the forest burial mound. How would the academic community remember this self-made Chieftain? Would it be, just as he feared, as a 'mere collector'?

In his wake

Westlake died without a will, making his son his automatic heir.[1] Aubrey was left not only with Sandy Balls and a large mortgage, but tens of thousands of stones and many boxes of papers. With them were also the unrealised aspirations to establish a 'Forest School' and to demonstrate that European human antiquity dated back at least 100,000 years. To all these responsibilities Aubrey gave his diligent service, some for the remainder of his life.

Aubrey became the new Chieftain of the Order, supported closely by his wife, Marjorie Harrod. But it was an energetic young Londoner named Henry Byngham who would become one of the Order's most influential figures.[2] Byngham answered Westlake's call to follow Dionysos 'to the full', changing his first name to 'Dion' and launching the Order's new magazine *Pine Cone*, which recalled Dionysos's pine cone-tipped staff.[3] Byngham, an enthusiastic naturist, appeared in a 1924 edition of *Pine Cone* naked and reclining, his girlfriend posing above with one breast bared. The magazine was modelled directly on Gardiner's *Youth*. They shared masculine and sexualised imagery and a message that drew inspiration directly from Germany. Aubrey, who believed the German Youth Movement was 'more alive and virile than [anything] anywhere else', was enthused by the changes.

From 1923 the Order's numbers had grown, especially among its adult membership. But some Christian members of the Order now found it hard to reconcile the increasingly explicit sexual messages with a children's educational movement. They called for Byngham's resignation as editor and council member. Byngham's calls for mixed nude bathing by all ages at the 1924 Folkmoot also met the objections of Fordingbridge villagers.[4] It made for a challenging beginning for the establishment of a school. But with his cousin Cuthbert Rutter as headmaster,[5] and psychiatrist Norman Glaister as advisor, Aubrey opened the Forest School at Sandy Balls in 1928. Students were to follow the recapitulation method and join in with activities and camps run by the Order. But concerns over the Order's morality continued to alienate members and prospective parents.

After Aubrey condoned a 'troth-plighting' ceremony between senior members in the Festive Circle in 1930, and later wrote in support of premarital sex,[6] membership dropped to around four hundred. One furious member announced it to be 'The Order of Witchcraft Devilry'.[7] Aubrey regained some support when, in response to the Great Depression, he established the Grith Fyrd (Anglo-Saxon for 'Peace Army') in 1932. Twenty-five unemployed men camped at Sandy Balls for about eighteen months and built their own accommodation and canoes and wove cloth, in return for benefits.[8] But at the 1933 Folkmoot, Aubrey was asked to stand down as Chieftain.

Aubrey's support had been undermined not only by the perceived sexualisation of the Order, but by questions over his political radicalism. The Grith Fyrd drew its inspiration from the older social credit movement, which by 1932 had reorganised under the banner of New Britain, a broad span of 'Third Way' political enthusiasts, including TS Eliot, Harold Macmillan and Alfred Orage. Aubrey contributed to the movement's publications. When it split, he formed closer links with Hargrave.[9] By this time the Kibbo Kift had transformed into a para-military expression called the Green Shirt Movement for Social Credit.[10] It was a 'militant pacifiism' that stemmed from what one critic called 'a survivalist fantasy embedded in the German and British youth movements'. Indeed, during the seemingly apocalyptic Great Strike of 1926, Hargrave and Aubrey had made a pact to meet at Sandy Balls when civilisation collapsed.[11]

Aubrey's eventual retreat to the New Forest was a far quieter affair. After standing down as Chieftain, he closed Sandy Balls to the Order. The Forest School remained—Aubrey's children boarded there—until it moved to Norfolk in 1938. Then he and his family moved into the converted schoolhouse. From 1934, Marjorie's parents managed the growing Sandy Balls 'Beauty Spot' holiday huts and camping sites. Aubrey remained in practice, incorporating Bach Flower Remedies, pioneering 'Psionic Medicine' (the use of a pendulum and chart to diagnose disorders), defending the cause of local gipsies and researching soil fertility.[12] By the 1960s, Aubrey's two of five children, Jean and Martin, lived on the estate with their families, practising organic gardening and managing the Holiday Camp. Their brother Richard oversaw the instalment of the contemporary recreation facilities. And the Order survived.

For historian Ronald Hutton, the fact that the Order survived is '[p]erhaps, most impressive of all'. It lost its unrestrained Dionysian vigour, but retained its 'ideals of kindness of humanity and kinship with nature'.[13] Aubrey returned as Chieftain in 1976, but stepped down five years later due to age. He passed away at the age of ninety-two in 1985. Ten years later the Order would return to Sandy Balls to celebrate their Folkmoot. Jean Westlake was honoured with the ceremonial name 'Greensleeves'. She was 'completely overwhelmed' by the poignancy of the moment.[14]

By the time I meet Jean in 2000 she is living in her childhood home, which had also been her school, and before that her grandfather's aspiration. She sees the continuity and evolution of his ideals in her own surroundings. Jean has taken over from Aubrey as keeper of Westlake's vision, and has become the family archivist and historian. When she shows me the Festive Circle, her biodynamic garden, Oaklands and Fordingbridge, Jean retraces a story from Quaker Puritanism to Woodcraft Chivalry. It is the story of a Chieftain. But, the question echoes, what of the collector? What has happened to his ambition to prove the depth of human antiquity? What happened to the myriad Tasmanians' memories? What has happened to all those stones?

'Get rid of those rocks'

Before the academic year had begun in the autumn of 1923, Geology Professor WJ Sollas of the Oxford University Museum of Natural History met with Henry Balfour, Curator of the Pitt Rivers Museum, and agreed to put in a joint request to Aubrey Westlake. Sollas wanted to study Westlake's French eolith collection, and Balfour the Tasmanian stone artefacts. They would organise to move the vast collections from Fordingbridge to their respective and adjacent museums—the Pitt Rivers Museum is reached through a door at the rear of the University Museum.[15] Aubrey agreed. He wrote that he was 'profoundly thankful' to both the professors for their commitment to 'the completion' of his father's work. 'I can only say that I trust the interest of the work and its scientific value will be its own reward.'[16]

Ernest Westlake had corresponded with Sollas and met him at least once. In 1920, Westlake had written to Aubrey that Sollas's scepticism regarding eoliths had been swayed by his French flints.[17] Two years later, Sollas wrote to Westlake that he hoped to visit him in Fordingbridge and encouraged him to keep working towards publication.[18]

In August 1923 Sollas presented a paper to the British Association in Liverpool that 'gave an account' of Westlake's French 'discoveries'. He also promised Aubrey he would include Westlake's eoliths in the third edition of his successful book *Ancient Hunters and their Modern Representatives*.[19] The promise came true in 1924. Alongside plates of some of Westlake's Miocene flints, Sollas stated, 'I have … hesitated for long before arriving at a conclusion, but … these eoliths are the work of an intelligent being.' Sollas nonetheless added the caution 'the question is still open and calls for closer and more minute research.'[20]

Sollas planned to study the eoliths in more detail, but did little more than employ an assistant to make plaster casts of some of the stones.[21] He died in 1936 without having published anything further on the collection. The successive geological curator of the University Museum, JA Douglas, then wrote to Aubrey, saying he was 'anxious' that Westlake's vast collection of eoliths 'be removed as soon as possible' for reasons of space and a lack of interest among his staff. Douglas suggested J Reid Moir, President of the Museum of Natural

History, Ethnology and Archaeology in Ipswich, might be interested in studying the collection.[22] He was right.

Moir soon wrote to Aubrey to ask if he could study Westlake's French eoliths.[23] He was a recognised eolith advocate and had seen Westlake's collection some years previously in Fordingbridge.[24] Moir considered it 'most unfortunate' that the collection had ever gone to Sollas, since he 'was not really an archaeologist'.[25] From mid February, the vast collection made its way to Ipswich, with parts still being transported in September, at a cost of £8.[26] A year later Moir prepared a paper on the eoliths for the Royal Society. It included plates of eighty-six professionally drawn illustrations of eoliths for which Aubrey had paid £15.[27]

By early 1939, Moir reported that it would cost £70 to publish the paper with the Royal Society. By November the price had gone up to £75, but the Society promised to contribute £25. Moir then found a benefactor, in a friend who would pay the other £50.[28] Then this friend decided to join the war. Moir promised Aubrey he would finish the project but that 'Hitler and his gang must be eliminated first'.[29]

Aubrey 'lost touch' with Moir during the war. When hostilities were over he discovered Moir had died.[30] His house was bombed and, although Moir had lived another three years, he had suffered from shock. The drawings of the eighty-six eoliths were also lost. So too was Westlake's draft paper on the geology of the Aurillac beds, which he had written en route to Tasmania.[31] The only known copy had been on loan to Moir.

In 1947 the Ipswich Museum Curator, G Maynard, began looking for Westlake's paper, even placing an advertisement in *Nature* asking if anyone had borrowed it from Moir.[32] It was not until mid 1950 that Aubrey recalled Moir had mentioned keeping some of his papers in a box in his linen cupboard. Maynard admitted the 'horrid possibility' that a housewife or second-hand linen dealer had tossed Westlake's geology paper away.[33] It was never found.

Aubrey was given new cause for hope, though. In 1952 Donald Baden-Powell of the Geology Department at Oxford asked if Westlake's collection could be sent, at his expense, from Ipswich back to Oxford. He wrote, 'I cannot help thinking with regret that neither Professor Sollas nor Mr. Moir were able to finish their work on the specimens ... I only hope I will be more fortunate than they were.'[34]

The collection did not arrive in Oxford until mid 1953, and by early 1955 Baden-Powell reported having unpacked just over half of the ninety-five boxes of stones.[35] Six months later he submitted for publication a paper comparing Westlake's French eoliths with others found at the Crag deposit of Suffolk. He wrote that Westlake's eoliths 'leave me in no doubt that they represent a Pre-Palaeolithic flake industry of the Pliocene age'. The Pliocene followed the Miocene, which was the age that Westlake had nominated for the eoliths, but it still predated the more widely accepted date for European human antiquity. The Suffolk eoliths, Baden-Powell assessed, were 'early Pleistocene' and more 'advanced' in technique. He hoped the paper would be published within a month.[36]

Four years later Aubrey heard from Baden-Powell that the soonest he could get his paper published was another five to six years. He complained: 'This is a curious fact, but academic circles in Britain at present seem to be opposed as a body to evidence of ancient man from Europe, although they will accept almost any chipped stone from South Africa as absolutely marvellous!'[37]

Over the next two years Aubrey kept asking if there was any progress with his father's collection, only to be told by Baden-Powell that he could not find a publisher.[38] By June 1963 new hopes arose when Baden-Powell attempted to 'radio-active' (or radiocarbon) date the eoliths using plants or mammal teeth found at the same levels. He was also hoping to compare them to Ugandan stone implements.[39] But another four years passed before he wrote again. After retiring from teaching, sorting forty years of papers and battling bad rheumatism, Baden-Powell was 'starting a new lease of life!' He was hoping to finally complete his work on the Westlake collection.[40] He never did, and died in 1972.

In 1977, Derek Roe of the Donald Baden-Powell Quaternary Research Centre responded to a letter of enquiry from Aubrey. He wrote, 'I am not myself very impressed with the artificial character of such pieces from Aurillac.' If they were 'Upper Miocene', as claimed by Westlake, Moir and Sollas, then 'they remain well beyond the time-range of stone stools anywhere in the world'. If they were 'late Pliocene,' as Baden-Powell assessed, 'then they lie within that range in certain parts of the world,' but not anywhere in Europe. Roe was not 'dismissing' Westlake's collection 'out of hand', he was 'simply recording the present general situation'.[41]

Roe passed Aubrey's letter to Ray Inskeep, Senior Assistant Curator of the Pitt Rivers Museum, who was now responsible for the French collection. Inskeep also wrote to Aubrey a few days after Roe, complaining that the eolith collection 'is bulky and extremely heavy: we are desperately short of space and would really like to see the back of it.' He also suggested that since the French were beginning to look more closely at 'these uncertain early collections', perhaps Aubrey could send the collection there.[42]

Aubrey replied to Roe that Henri Delporte of France had some interest in examining his father's collection.[43] Roe forwarded the letter to Inskeep with the note 'we might contrive to get rid of those rocks if we are careful'.[44] Inskeep then wrote a memo to the University Museum to see if they were interested in the stones.[45] He got a reply from the Department of Geology and Mineralogy: 'The custody of ninety boxes of heavy pieces of flint does not immediately appeal to me, and I have consulted Jim Kennedy … our Curator of the Geological Collections. I have a very brief note from him saying "No! Dispose!"'[46]

Three years later, in 1980, Aubrey finally organised the transport of the heavy flint back to Fordingbridge.[47] 'I am still mystified about this whole problem of Eoliths,' he wrote to Roe. After years of corresponding with reputably academic men Aubrey was astounded to hear that 'the whole of my father's collection is due to natural causes'.[48] Derek Roe responded, 'you might well be puzzled …!' More was now known about the 'processes of natural flaking,' Roe explained, and the 'whole European Palaeolithic sequence is better understood'. The eolith debate had been 'essential' to make this progress and thanks to the work of men like Westlake 'proper solutions' could be found. For this reason Roe thought 'the Aurillac flints retain considerable historical interest ... but I fear that they will not find many proponents in the future.'[49]

I go to Sandy Balls in 2000 and learn that Martin, Westlake's grandson and resident manager of Sandy Balls Caravan Park, has used the eoliths as ballast for his driveway. In August 2000 geologist Justin Delair writes to me that he has been to Sandy Balls to investigate the buried eoliths.[50] It was not his first visit there. In 1961, Southampton University, where Delair taught, had been successful in its submission to house Westlake's English collection of eoliths, palaeoliths and fossils.[51] Delair began to study the huge collection in the early 1980s, and, impressively, read through all of Westlake's English notebooks.[52] In 1984 Delair wrote to Aubrey that, while he recognised they no longer generated much interest, he was just beginning to realise their importance. He had heard of Egyptian peasants using Eolithic-type implements to make fire. Perhaps that explained the prolific and different type of flaking on the French eoliths at the time of the Pleistocene.[53] But Aubrey would die the following year, before any further investigation was carried out.[54]

During his visit to Sandy Balls in 2000, Delair tells me, he found one of Westlake's eoliths 'lying by the side of a nearby gravel path' and was attempting to excavate the rest.[55] A year later Delair tells me he had dug up a 'hundred or so'. They are marked with catalogue numbers and he judges the stones are in fact 'palaeolithic types, and nondescript stones conceivably but not certainly eoliths'.[56] Perhaps Delair hopes to become the first to successfully publish a paper on Westlake's eolith collection.

'a pure myth'

Henry Balfour's contact with Westlake had been indirect. He had taught Margaret while she was studying anthropology at Oxford and had worked in the Pitt Rivers Museum since 1885, when he assisted in setting up the first displays. From 1890 he was Curator, and lectured in anthropology and published widely on aspects of art, music and artefacts of many cultures. Balfour worked with Tylor until the older man retired as Museum Keeper in 1902.[57] He understood the significance of and wide interest in the Tasmanian Aboriginal stone implements within cultural evolutionary theory.

In October 1923, Balfour had organised a truck and an assistant to transport the Tasmanian stone artefacts from Fordingbridge to Oxford. He planned to organise the collection into their original localities and study them geographically as well as typologically. It was something he would only be able to do 'as time permits'—in the few hours he had spare from running the Pitt Rivers Museum and teaching, but he was inspired. 'Working over this collection will be very absorbing,' he considered. 'I never thought that I would have the chance of handling so much Tasmanian material.'[58]

'A Complete List of the Sites Represented in the Westlake Collection of Stone Implements of the Natives of Tasmania', p. 4 [© Pitt Rivers Museum, University of Oxford, Related Documents File 1934.83–86]

```
65.  Half Moon Bay, South Arm
66.  Ralph's Bay
67.  Rokeby
68.  Clarendon Farm, Ralph Bay, near Rokeby
69.  Bellerive
70.  Rosny, Bellerive
71.  Harrison's, Wentworth, Bellerive
72.  Geilston?
73.  Kangaroo Point
74.  Clarence
75.  Howrah, Clarence
76.  Sandford, Clarence
77.  Beltana
78.  Lindisfarne
79.  Risdon
80.  Smelting Works Bay
81.  Old Beach, Baskerville
82.  Woolpack Inn
Jordan River
83.  Jordan River
84.  Brighton
85.  Broadmarsh
86.  Melton Mowbray
87.  Coal Hill (native) Quarry, Melton Mowbray
88.  Kelvingrove Quarry, Melton Mowbray (becomes 86A)
89.  Apsley
90.  Oatlands
```

Over the next year the laborious task of sorting the stones was slowed further by the fact he had to have a finger amputated, and his mother passed away after a long illness and his museum work took him to Canada for seven weeks.[59] But in autumn 1924, Balfour gave his presidential address to the Prehistoric Society of East Anglia: 'The Status of the Tasmanians Among the Stone-age Peoples'. He reported having examined 'some 5,000 specimens' from forty of the localities in the Westlake Collection.[60] The conclusion Balfour drew, though, was not at all what had inspired Westlake to form the collection.

Balfour declared that 'the so-called "Eolithic Tasmanian" is a pure myth'. He thought that the Tasmanians' 'stone technique ... has been marked too low'. To 'do justice to the native potentialities,' it was important to 'draw conclusions from their highest attainments'. From such samples, Balfour 'put forward a plea for a correlation with a post-Mousterian culture-phase, to wit the *Aurignacian*'.[61] While Balfour's ideas were based in evolutionary comparative systems, Australian archaeologist John Mulvaney agreed with his recognition of the 'fine craftsmenship', an idea that had been foreshadowed by Joseph Paxton Moir in his correspondence with EB Tylor.[62]

Balfour reiterated his findings in a paper read on his behalf to the Hobart Meeting of the Australasian Association for the Advancement of Science in 1928. He explained that his Middle Palaeolithic assessment, and the idea of an 'Eolithic' Tasmanian culture, was 'separated in time ... by at least 100,000 years, and possibly by a much greater period!'[63]

Aubrey had been troubled by this contradiction of his father's original thesis. 'It would seem there is a pretty little problem to be solved in the question of Mousterian and Aurignacian technique occurring together in the Tasmanian flints,' he wrote to Balfour, 'perhaps further work on the collection may throw additional light on the matter.'[64] Balfour responded tactfully, explaining that 'each of the 10,000 or so stones has to be examined individually, and very carefully'; it was slow and exacting work.[65] Just over a week later Aubrey wrote again and asked of Balfour's 1924 presidential address: 'does that represent the present stage of your researches?'[66]

Balfour, who had already told Aubrey he was working on a more extensive paper, responded that he had curated a display of Westlake's Tasmanian stones for the British Association meeting, had been abroad, and had undergone a foot operation.[67] He couldn't access the collection, which was held in a building that had been 'like an ice-house' during the recent coal strike. 'I can only spare a certain amount of time for this research,' Balfour reiterated, 'but I am very anxious to get it completed and any delays are very troublesome to me.'[68]

Three years later, in October 1931, Balfour reported to Aubrey that he was drawing the last of the plates for a paper on the Tasmanian stone implements for the Royal Society. The progress had been slow since his right hand was 'partly crippled' and while he was in British East Africa the ceiling of his office had fallen down.[69] Another three years passed before Balfour wrote he had 'broken the back of my "Tasmanian" paper'. He had only to produce a final draft and one last drawing. 'I feel ashamed at having been so long,' he admitted, 'but being practically single-handed in running a very exacting museum leaves me very little leisure.'[70]

In 1939 Balfour died, his 'Tasmanian' paper unpublished. TK Penniman, his successor at the Pitt Rivers Museum, with colleague Beatrice Blackwood, edited Balfour's substantial paper. In their introduction to 'Stone Implements of the Natives of Tasmania', the editors wrote that Balfour had drawn 5,000 of Westlake's implements by 1925, and by the time he died had drawn and described almost twelve thousand across four acquisition books. Each had been catalogued and numbered according to the twenty-eight localities into which Balfour divided the 124 sites from which Westlake collected stone tools in Tasmania.[71] In October 1939 Penniman wrote with confidence to Aubrey that Clarendon Press 'will, of course, [publish it] at some time. The only doubt is whether the publication date may be held up by present conditions.'[72]

It may have been partly due to the outbreak of the Second World War that Balfour's extensive paper, and the proposed series, was never published. Aubrey ultimately received £150 for his father's Tasmanian collection, but he did not receive what he had really hoped for: the fulfilment of his father's dream of proving that European human antiquity began in the Miocene epoch, an idea to which Aubrey, and his daughter Jean after him, remained assiduously faithful.

Westlake had gone to Tasmania with such certainty: 'I knew the moment I saw the few Tasmanian things in the British Museum that my proper course was to come here,' he had reflected to his children from Tasmania's east coast in 1908, 'and all has turned out as I expected.'[73]

What Westlake had really expected was more than to acquire thousands of stones that he knew looked Eolithic. He expected to demonstrate his certainty in a published paper, illustrated with photographic plates, and enhanced by anthropological notes. He expected, foremost, to determine the 'real' beginning of human history. But then came the war, and the urgency of realising the depth of human history diminished before the more imperative task of safeguarding its future.

Westlake worked hard all his life. While he was honoured as a Chieftain, he was almost forgotten as a collector. Few scientists who followed were prepared to accept his ideas; even most of his family did not support his efforts. It was effectively obstacles of his own making that prevented Westlake meeting his expectations. His interests were too ambitious, colossal and multifarious. If they overlapped, influenced by their own progression and the wide mix of ideas of his generation, they also vied and competed with each other for his attention. As The Order of Woodcraft Chivalry eclipsed his geological interests, so they remained incomplete at his death.

The Tasmanian artefacts did not become ballast for a driveway nor were they dropped into a pond; they remained in the Pitt Rivers Museum. But following Balfour it seemed unlikely any scholar would attempt to realise their Eolithic status. Indeed, there seemed little promise that there would be much interest in the collection at all, until an aerogramme arrived from Sydney.

Below the surface

A young student carrying out a PhD in Tasmanian archaeology at the University of Sydney, Rhys Jones, wrote to the Pitt Rivers Museum in 1966, asking to acquire copies of Balfour's unpublished drawings of the Westlake Collection and a list of the 142 sites Westlake had visited.[1] Two years later Jones visited the Pitt Rivers Museum and examined the collection and read through Westlake's six little notebooks of interviews. The breadth of the fieldwork impressed him, and he thought the artefacts had been 'meticulously collected'.[2] Jones concluded that Westlake had helped lay 'the foundations for Tasmanian field archaeology'.[3]

Jones was interested in all collectors and scientists who had preceded his research, and was keenly aware of the intense interest the Tasmanian Aborigines had invoked. In his 1971 PhD thesis, Jones recalls an afternoon in 1968 when he was in one of the off-site storerooms of the Pitt Rivers Museum: 'In my hand was the plaster cast of the "Taunton Scraper" ... and surrounding me, dusty cases filled with loot dug from caves a century ago ... The contents of that cellar seemed to symbolise the fascination of the Tasmanians.'[4] As he held the Taunton Scraper he thought about how Tylor had seen it and later recalled his revelation: 'Man of the Lower Stone Age ceases to be a creature of philosophic inference, but becomes a reality.'[5]

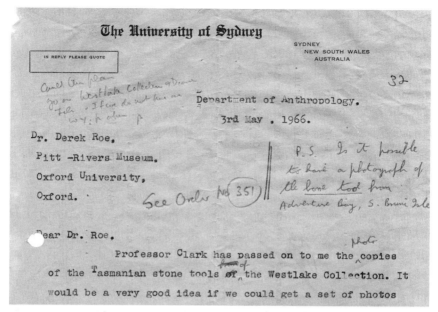

Aerogramme from Rhys Jones to Derek Roe, 3 May 1966 [© Pitt Rivers Museum, University of Oxford, Related Documents File 1934.83–86]

Jones found the concept extraordinarily archaic. He was among the new vanguard of Australian archaeologists who looked upon the older 'evolutionists' in much the same way those scholars had once regarded the Aborigines—as living fossils. Sollas's 'wilful anachronism' had itself become an anachronism. The 'real value' of the Tasmanians was no longer their ability to illuminate the European Palaeolithic, it was their potential to realise the depth of Australia's Aboriginal past.

The 'decades of discovery'

In 1961 Australian archaeologist John Mulvaney reviewed the accomplishments of his discipline and proposed a new direction: it was time to determine the depth of the continent's human occupation and 'fill' a temporal map that was 'for the most part profoundly empty'.[6] It was time to look below the surface.

The following thirty or more years became Australian archaeology's 'decades of discovery'.[7] The known occupation of Aboriginal Australia increased six-fold: from less than 9000 years in 1961 to a proposed 60,000 in 1990.[8] The young Welsh-born archaeologist Rhys Jones was integral to these discoveries; he was part of the team that, in 1969, excavated 'Mungo Woman' from the dry Willandra Lakes district of New South Wales, the oldest cremation rite in the world.[9] In 1981 Jones found evidence in Tasmania of 'the southernmost ... humans ... during the height of the last Ice Age', confirmed to be 35,000 years old.[10] From the late 1980s Jones co-pioneered the use of thermoluminesence (TL) dating, which resulted in a potential date of 60,000 years for the Malakunanja II rock shelter in Kakadu, in northern Australia.[11]

Jones called himself a 'cowboy archaeologist'. His rugged manners and dress were renowned, but the moniker also recalls Jones as a frontiersman on the boundaries of time, extending the depth of Aboriginal occupancy and the science of his discipline.[12] Jones reached beyond the limits of the academy to a wider audience. His 1969 paper 'Firestick farming' coined an internationally recognised term.[13] By the late 1970s his ease with popular media and charismatic appeal had made him a well-known and much-liked Australian figure. Jones translated

Rhys Jones at Nauwalabila, Northern Territory, Mike Smith, August 1989 [courtesy Mike Smith]

the significance of Aboriginal deep time in appealing and vital terms, playing an important role as ambassador to his discipline. In Nicholas Jose's novel *The Custodians*, the character Ralph Kincaid, modelled closely on Jones, enlightens a Canberra bureaucrat that Australian archaeological 'treasure' is not 'gold or silver, but time itself'.[14] Deep time offered new grounds for national pride. It gave to Australians 'our own natural and cultural vestiges and relics to compete with those of the Old World.'[15]

The promoter of this Australian national treasure was born in Bangor, north Wales, in 1941. Rhys Maengwyn Jones was a bright schoolboy with an interest in prehistory. In 1959 he was awarded the prestigious Trevelyan scholarship to Emmanuel College, Cambridge. Archaeology was key among his subjects, and his teachers, Grahame Clark and Eric Higgs, were unusual in having an interest in pre-history that went beyond Africa and Europe. They encouraged their students to take up research posts across the world, and to use the new radiocarbon dating technique. '[P]robably nowhere else did this new technique have so much immediate impact,' Jones reflected, than in 'Australia and its neighbouring regions.'[16] Jones thought of Clark as the 'foster father' of contemporary Australian archaeology. Mulvaney is its well-recognised 'father'.[17] Mulvaney encouraged and fostered Clark's goal to realise the origins of indigenous peoples, eschew older hierarchical models of race, and apply professional and precise dating methods within the Australian region. Mulvaney had studied prehistory under Clark at Cambridge nearly a decade earlier than Jones. After his return to Australia, enough fellow alumni followed that they would become known as the 'Cambridge connection', or, less flatteringly, the 'Cambridge mafia'. Many of the discoveries that contributed to Australian archaeology's 'golden years' of the 1960s were made by its dynamic members.[18]

Jones was twenty-two when he arrived in Sydney in 1963. He took up a teaching post and PhD candidature in the Department of Anthropology at the University of Sydney.[19] After a 'brief formal application' to the Australian Institute of Aboriginal Studies, the grant awarded to Jones 'exceeded his request', as John Mulvaney put it: 'an entire State was given as his research oyster.'[20]

The charge came with a considerable legacy. The 'Problem of the Tasmanians'—the question over their origins—had been a longstanding and formative debate for early Australian archaeology. In 1889, Alfred Howitt had suggested the Tasmanians had reached their island before the creation of the Bass Strait, which had inspired AS Kenyon to search for similarities between Victorian and Tasmanian stone tools.[21] While European 'evolutionists' had looked to Tasmania to explain their own history, Australian scholars had looked down to the island to try to explore the Aboriginal past. But Kenyon finally dismissed Howitt's theory as fancy.

Well into the twentieth century, collectors remained resolute in the idea that Aboriginal people were without antiquity.[22] The Tasmanian Aborgines' supposed racial difference was often explained by migratory sea journeys from the Melanesian region, among other places.[23] When in 1923 TW Edgeworth David returned to Howitt's suggestion and proposed that the 'simplicity' of the Tasmanian culture, including the absence of the dingo, pointed to a Pleistocene link with mainland Australia, Robert Pulleine countered that the Tasmanians were originally 'Papuans', whom he described, famously, as 'an unchanging people in an unchanging environment'. Pulliene did concede, however, that if there was any evidence of connection with mainland Australia or of cultural change, then Rocky Cape, on Tasmania's north-west corner, would offer 'the best deposit' in Tasmania to excavate. Stone tool collectors had known the site for decades.[24] JV Cook had shown Westlake a bone awl found in Rocky Cape cave by Mr Mollison in 1892.[25] Westlake had written to his children that he had a 'mind to dig in' the cave.[26]

AL Meston dug two large trenches at Rocky Cape in 1936 and 1938. His unearthed stone implements interested Norman Tindale, then Australia's leading prehistorian. Tindale deemed the lower strata tools part of a wider 'Kartan' culture first identified on Kangaroo Island, South Australia, and which he nominated as the first phase of five Australian Aboriginal phases of cultural development dating from the late Pleistocene. Tindale concluded that the Tasmanians originated from a southeast Asian 'negrito' race.[27]

Mulvaney's 1961 paper was in large part written to counter Tindale's entire theoretical approach to Aboriginal archaeology. While he commended Tindale for recognising cultural change, he found that his successive phases were dependent upon artefact typology and lacked any real chronology. Mulvaney was calling for a new approach to Australian archaeological practice, one that used professional and precise dating and sequencing methods. If Rocky Cape was central to a century-old debate over Australian Aboriginal origins and antiquity, then someone qualified should excavate it thoroughly.[28]

Rocky Cape

Jones read Mulvaney's 1961 paper on his sea journey to Sydney. By the time he arrived, Rocky Cape had become, he remembers, '*the* urgent project'.[29] While the dates were yet to be confirmed, in 1962 Mulvaney had potentially broken the 'Pleistocene barrier' at Kenniff Cave, North Queensland.[30] At the base of Mulvaney's sequence were stone tools that looked remarkably Tasmanian. 'Everything was pointing again,' Jones remembers, 'to the question of [the] … Tasmanians as the ancestors of the mainland Australians.'[31]

Jones went south in December 1963, taking with him fellow students Ron Wild, Jim Allen and Bob Reece, among others. Contrarily, '[t]he one site' he 'was determined *not* to dig was Rocky Cape.'[32] Local politics meant that the directors from Tasmania's two museums stipulated they supervise any excavation of Rocky Cape. Then there was Jones's own sense of being a 'bit intimidated' by the site's significance. So he chose to first excavate at nearby Sisters Creek.[33]

Jones could see Rocky Cape from the Sisters Creek beach, and was reminded of the urgency of what he was meant to find. He pushed his team hard, digging big holes. Jones wanted his Pleistocene date 'in one go'.[34] Most of the team were men in their early twenties, and members of the Sydney Push: 'We were bearded, we were rough,' Jones remembered, '… and we were drinking very heavily.' Reece and Allen sang AL Lloyd folk songs and espoused Lawson's late-nineteenth century Australian socialism. In hindsight, Jones reflected that this liberalism was also realised in their 'tremendous freedom of enquiry', which was due, in his mind, to the absence of any Aboriginal consent to excavate sites and remove artefacts which would later become requisite for all archaeological research in Tasmania. The only Aboriginal people Jones remembers seeing in Tasmania in 1963 were in Jimmy Sharman's boxing tent in Burnie—punters were invited to 'come and hit a darkie'.[35]

In January 1964 they got news from Canberra that Mulvaney's Kenniff Cave dig had confirmed a date of 14,500 years. This was 'crucial', Jones remembers, 'there were humans in Australia older than … Bass Strait.'[36] Allen remembers, 'That night, as we gazed northwards over Bass Strait, we knew … people had walked, dry-shod, to Tasmania … more than 8,000 years ago.'[37]

Rhys Jones's archaeological team at West Point, north-western Tasmania, late January 1965. From left: Rhys Jones, Harry Lourandos, Annie Bickford, Bill Rodman, Alan Thorne and Dorothy Bingham. [courtesy Betty Meehan]

At the end of this first season Jones decided on a whim to visit
Rocky Cape. The many previous excavations had left it looking like
'the Iraqi frontline after a couple of B52s had been on top of it,'
but Jones scraped the edge of a pit with his trowel and found the
sequencing still had 'integrity'.[38] In the summer of 1964 to 1965,
Jones returned to excavate West Point and the southern caves of
Rocky Cape. He reported his initial findings to the 1965 Australian
Archaeology Conference in Hobart, confirming Mulvaney's assertion that Tindale's 'Kartan' theory was unfounded. A doyen was in
the audience: Tindale 'rose majestically' to pronounce, 'I bow to a
younger generation.'[39]

'Slow strangulation'

Throughout the 1960s, Australia's 'empty' temporal map began, as
Mulvaney had hoped, to be filled, and at an exciting pace. Excavations
across the country began to yield Pleistocene dates of Aboriginal
occupancy of Australia, some even older than that of Kenniff Cave; up
to 25,000 to 30,000 years before present (BP). Jones's north-western
Tasmanian excavations, which continued throughout the 1960s,
though, did not. It wasn't until 1974 that Sandra Bowdler demonstrated
a Pleistocene occupation on Hunter Island in north Tasmania.[40] Jones
admitted to archaeologist Mike Smith in 1991 that he had felt like
he had 'failed', and nearly did not submit his PhD.[41] But his 1971
dissertation, 'Rocky Cape and The Problem of the Tasmanians', made
a significant impact on his field. I remember an Aboriginal person
in Tasmania telling me, in the course of my own PhD research, how
offensive they found the title; how could Jones refer to the Aborigines
as a 'problem'? But the use of that word did not suggest an innate
deficiency. It referred to the older debate over the Tasmanians' origins.
As Jones had 'solved' that problem more by logical deduction than
by chronological sequencing, that was not the real reason his thesis
became renowned. It was due to a new 'problem' that Jones set out to
answer: the effects of isolation on Tasmanian culture.[42]

The Rocky Cape excavations had revealed thousands of fish
bones. At first Jones thought the finds countered the oft-repeated

ethnological observation that the contemporary Tasmanian Aborigines never ate scaled fish. Then he sequenced his findings: after 3500 BP, Jones identified only one fish bone.[43] He concluded that the Tasmanians had, in just a few generations, stopped eating scaled fish.[44] Finding no clear environmental reasons (the fish were still bountiful), and noting that bone awls too had disappeared in the sequence, Jones asked if this was a society 'becoming simplified ... and losing some of its "useful arts"?'[45] While his discipline agreed that Jones had meticulous evidence for the cessation of deposited scaled fish bones in middens, they disagreed profoundly with his reasoning, preferring explanations in the realm of cultural adaptation to regression. It became one of Australian archaeology's longest and most-cited debates.[46] Jared Diamond and Tim Flannery, however, have since suggested an isolation-induced regression in Tasmania. Notably, neither made direct reference to Jones's work, nor have they received the same critical response that he did. This is perhaps because they did not make a figurative connection, as Jones had, between a millennia-long regression and a modern history of colonial devastation.[47]

Jones's perspective was also heavily influenced by his research in mainland Australia. Following excavations in Lake Mungo, Jones accompanied his partner Betty Meehan on fieldwork with the Gidjingarli of Arnhem Land during 1972 and 1973. They learned the Aboriginal language, and formed close and lasting relationships with the community.[48] Going north, Jones told me, changed how he saw Tasmania. He was struck by contrasts. Meehan calculated that over one month scaled fish comprised 62 per cent of the Gidjingarli's meat. In a 1978 paper, Jones quotes Frank Gurrmanamana's response to the idea that the Tasmanians did not eat fish: 'Silly bugger, eh?'[49] As Jones reworked parts of his dissertation for publication, the Tasmanian Aborigines became even simpler: they lost not only bone tools and fishing skills, but even the ability to make fire.[50]

Jones researched the recent past as thoroughly as he examined his excavations. He read Westlake's notebooks when he visited the Pitt Rivers Museum in 1968. This is demonstrated by his attempts to reconstruct Westlake's interview questions in his 1971 PhD thesis:

'Did the Tasmanians know how to make fire, did they have edge ground axes ...'[51] Westlake did not write down his questions, so Jones must have deduced them from the answers given. In those responses Jones would have found evidence to directly challenge his assertions that the Tasmanian Aborigines neither ate scaled fish nor made fire. However, Jones remained confident of his thesis and did not include these contrary sources. This is probably because he did not consider the informants to be reliable witnesses of traditional Tasmanian culture, having been interviewed more than a century after first settlement. It is a significant body of evidence to overlook.

Westlake had read Roth's *The Aborigines of Tasmania* before going to Tasmania and was aware of his conclusion that the Tasmanians never ate scaled fish.[52] But when he posed this idea to several of his interviewees, almost all disagreed. In 1909, Charles Smith of Launceston said it was '*altogether wrong* to say that [they] never eat fish with scales'. The first records that suggested the Aborigines did not eat fish came from the French explorers and from Captain James Cook, who reported how offers of their food were refused on the beaches.[53] But was the reason a fear of explorers, or, at least, of their gifts? Edward Stevens told Westlake that 'the Blacks (as regards refusing to eat fish) refused to eat anything offered them fearing that because a white man killed it there might be danger in eating it.'[54]

Henry Beeton was emphatic: 'I've *seen* them eat fish with scales ... blue head and parrot fish wouldn't eat fish with no scales (except eels).'[55] This was a memory acquired from returning to Country. Philip Thomas explained, too, that, 'as a child', accompanying his mother at Cape Portland, he had seen the fires lit on the sea shores to attract the fish so they could spear them. Thomas's testimony appears to echo what Captain Nicolas Baudin's men reported in 1802: that Aboriginal people were using 'torches' to catch fish on the beach. NJB Plomley, however, suggests that the French saw the Aboriginal people catching stingrays rather than scaled fish.[56]

How then to discount the memories of Thomas and Beeton? When Jones and Plomley were working on Aboriginal Tasmania in the 1960s and 1970s, they echoed the historiographical approach suggested by Walker to Roth in the 1890s: drawing a chronological line across the Tasmanian historical record, with sources dating from after the 1840s, when the Tasmanian Aborigines were living either on the government mission or in the sealing communities in the Bass Strait, deemed unreliable and predominantly excluded. A feature argument is that the culture observed from this time may have been learned by new influences.[57] A comment by Henry Beeton to Westlake seems to underline this possibility, when he said to Westlake that the Aboriginal people, 'caught with the line after [they] got with the white people'.[58] But the reverse is also true: they caught fish by other means before they encountered white culture, with spears and with fire.

In 1939 Cliff Everett told Norman Tindale that he 'knew that white men believed the Tasmanians did not eat fish'; implying that, despite this belief, they in fact did.[59] It is with incredulity that Aboriginal Cape Barren Islander Buck (Brendan) Brown writes in 1999: 'there is actually an archaeological argument that Tasmanian Aboriginal peoples did not eat fish, which is hogwash ... I grew up eating scale-fish as a large part of my diet all my life. There are fish traps throughout Tasmania ... This evidence is ignored by archaeologists.'[60]

Archaeologist Jim Stockton did study the fish traps on Tasmania's northern coast, and historian Ian McFarlane has followed up with further research that points to the traps being Aboriginal made.[61] And how much does it really matter if the Tasmanian Aboriginal people did not eat fish? While in 1978 dropping fish from their diet was a 'grossly maladaptive strategy', in 1995 Jones made a gracious retraction: he had 'missed' important evidence revealed by Bowdler, that crayfish and large abalone had amply replaced scaled fish on the north and west coasts of Tasmania at that time. Indeed, the Tasmanian Aboriginal women's ability to dive for these fish, Jones acknowledged, made 'effective occupation of the west coast possible'.[62]

Perhaps the most provocative aspect of Jones's degeneration thesis was the idea that the Tasmanian Aborigines had lost the ability to make fire. 'Fire was carried ... in smouldering slow burning fire-sticks,' Jones wrote, 'but the Tasmanians did not know how to make it,' and if their sticks went out, they had 'to go to their neighbours for a re-light'.[63] In making this statement, Jones relied on the one entry in Robinson's diary from which such an interpretation could be drawn. It is from 28 December 1831, written as Robinson was making one of his five epic treks across Tasmania with 'his mission' Aborigines:

> As the chief always carries a lighted torch I asked them what they did when their fire went out. They said if their fire went out by reason of rain they [were] compelled to eat the kangaroo raw and to walk about and look for another mob and get fire of them. They must give fire and sometimes they would fight afterwards. MANNALARGENNA said that the two men in the sky first gave the natives fire, that they stood all round. WOORADY said PARPEDER gave fire to the Brune [Bruny] natives.[64]

Almost all the historical sources on fire making, from as early as 1773, support the idea that the Tasmanian Aborigines made fire. The few nineteenth century sources to state that they could not were evidently influenced either by a Tasmanian Aboriginal creation story in which fire is said to come from the sky or by the hardness, and possibly wetness, of Tasmanian timbers.[65] Both of these factors make Robinson's journal entry in late 1831 highly ambiguous. Mannalargenna was possibly unwilling to divulge what may have been a secret ritual related to a mythical story, or was unable to make fire in the rain, or both.

The greatest body of historical evidence for Tasmanian fire making is contained in the Westlake papers. Of the ninety-five people Westlake noted conversations with in Tasmania, twenty-seven recounted methods by which the Aborigines made fire. 'I have seen them making fires by rubbing pieces of wood together,' Philip Thomas said. 'I used to watch them doing it.' Thomas was careful to qualify that his memory came from 'before they were on Flinders'.[66]

Thomas could also explain the process in detail: the stick was held at an angle of about forty-five degrees, and also trimmed to that angle 'so as to fit in the groove'. 'Very fine powder like the ashes from a pipe' is placed into the groove, and 'turn black and catch fire very quickly'.[67] The description echoes closely those given to JB Walker by settlers GH Rayner and Edward Cotton. Reassured by Walker the information could be 'relied on', Roth included the accounts exactly in his second edition.[68] Walker did not know that the settlers' memories tallied with that of the Islanders. Having dismissed Thomas's community as being '<u>not</u> Aborigines' Walker never heard their memories. He paradoxically considered the white settlers to be more authoritative witnesses.[69]

Extinction had been an ingrained scholarly fact for nearly a century when Jones began his research. If Ryan, and others, began to see the inaccuracy of this idea in the mid 1970s, it is valid to ask why Jones did not too. Why, in Ryan's words, he chose not to recognise the Tasmanian community as 'Aboriginal in an anthropological sense'.[70] I too have asked why Jones discounted as unreliable most anthropological sources dating from the mid-nineteenth to late-twentieth centuries, including testimonies by Tasmanian Aborigines that stated they could make fire, and continued to eat scaled fish. The sheer quantity of this disregard is academically problematic, and for Tasmanian Aboriginal people it is simply erroneous. For them there is no absolute disconnect between pre- and post-settlement history; they are the living proof of that continuity.[71]

Tasmania's history was too devastating for Jones to recognise this continuity. 'Instead of distinguishing extermination from extinction,' as Ryan put it, 'Jones compounded it.'[72] But if the Tasmanian Aborigines' extinction was a fact for Jones during the 1970s, it was not one he considered the result of any natural deficiency. Jones took his cues principally from Clive Turnbull's 1948 *Black War*, which in turn was influenced by nineteenth century historian James Bonwick.[73] Both writers concluded unequivocally that the cause of the Tasmanian Aborigines' extinction was the policies and actions of the British administration. Ann Curthoys reasons that Turnbull would probably have used the term genocide had he known of it. *Black War* was published some time after it was written, by which time Raphael Lemkin had coined the term, citing Tasmania as one of the clearest cases of historical genocide.[74] Jones felt, in following Bonwick and Turnbull, he need only summarise that Tasmania's 'sorry tale' was one 'of psychopathic sadism, of punitive man hunts, of sexual mutilation'. To this he added a cautionary note: 'lest we strike too strong a moral pose, Buchewald [sic] and My Lai remind us that things are much the same nowadays.'[75]

Jones's anti-colonialism was inspired by the same politics that stirred his left-leaning, folk-singing cohort, but it was also informed by his Welsh nationalism. Jones's first language was Welsh, and he continued to publish academic papers in Welsh throughout his career.[76] He said to me in a jocular tone that being Welsh made him indigenous. In 1990, Jones 'lodged' a 'land claim' as 'a British Aboriginal' for Stonehenge at the World Archaeology Conference.[77] More seriously, Jones believed that being Welsh gave him a sense of empathy for other colonised peoples. Thus Jones was inspired to counsel his colleagues with an idea radical for its time: 'It is time we tried to look at an Australian landscape through Aboriginal eyes.'[78] His Welshness suggested this was a less daring assumption.

For anthropologist Carmel Schrire, Jones wrote straight from his Welsh heart. He:

> understood what it felt like to look out across a grey sea, whether from Bangor or Burnie, and feel your back pressing against the wall of what you thought was your own land. He had a very good idea what it might mean to feel ringed in by an implacable ocean and colonised by a hostile intelligentsia.[79]

Looking from Burnie, on the north coast of Tasmania, across the Bass Strait reminded Jones of the Tasmanians' cultural paucity, and made it seem perilous and dramatic; the rising seas at the end of the Pleistocene a 'trauma':

> Like a blow above the heart it took a long time to take effect, but slowly but surely there was a simplification ... a squeezing of intellectuality. The world's longest isolation, the world's simplest technology ... Even if Abel Tasman had not sailed the winds of the Roaring Forties in

1642, were they in fact doomed—doomed to a slow strangulation of the mind?[80]

It is beautiful prose. Tasmania is indeed heart-shaped, and to imagine its pulse fading is an effective, if dramatic, idea. Jones intended the chapter, he told me, to read 'like a novel'. But, Schrire admitted, 'the pairing of "intellectuality" and "squeezing" raised a red flag,' and the oft-quoted final sentence gave Jones much grief.[81] Thinking of the enormous controversy his words stirred, Jones said to me, 'I shouldn't have written the bloody thing.'[82]

'On our land'

It is doubtful that the closing words of a chapter in an edited academic book would have been so controversial if they had not resonated in Tom Haydon's 1978 film, *The Last Tasmanian*. Jones starred in the film, as narrator and explorer. He is captured making stone tools, building a bark shelter, and sinking slowly on a bark canoe off Hunter Island to demonstrate its limited efficacy.[1] He speaks of rising seas as a 'catastrophe' that 'sealed' the Tasmanians' 'doom'.[2]

The educative prehistory of the film flows into a dramatic history of colonisation. As the camera sweeps over the beautiful Tasmanian landscape, Leo McKern's masterful narration informs us that it is a land bereft of its original peoples. This is how Jones imagined Tasmania as he looked down from Australia's far north: a *judenrein*—a land of post-Holocaust emptiness. Jones stands in deep valleys and speaks of the wars waged there and describes how the Aborigines were 'suddenly ... wiped out ... a terrible thing'.[3]

The film was part of a broader intellectual attempt to break what WEH Stanner condemned in 1968 as a 'Great Australian Silence' over the nation's history of frontier violence. It was in direct response to Stanner's reproach that Bernard Smith called on Australians in his 1980 Boyer Lecture to heed 'The Spectre of Truganini', whose story 'must stand ... for all those that will never be written.'[4] Smith followed David Boyd's seventeen portraits of Truganini shown at the 1959 Antipodeans Exhibition in Melbourne. Inspired by Turnbull's *Black War*, Boyd thought Truganini offered an 'Australian theme' when Australian art needed to look to its own history—'a story in which we are all involved'—in order to 'make its own way'. Playwright Bill Reed followed more than a decade later, in 1970, with a three-part play, *Truganini*.[5]

Truganini was reified; elevated from local legend—the begging old woman of The Reverend Atkinson's repeated story of a broken promise—to become, as Onsman puts it, an 'icon of new consciousness'.[6] Ryan summarises that 'Trukanini has been the subject of more than fifty poems, a number of novels and plays, several histories and biographies, at least fifty paintings and photographs and nearly fifty scientific articles.'[7] She has appeared on countless posters, on a postage stamp and has several places named after her, including a Melbourne suburb. Midnight Oil's 1993 hit song 'Truganini' questioned the very point of Australia's colonisation. She became, as Bernard Smith first suggested she should, the nation's 'tragic muse'. She is the poster girl of our national story of indigenous dispossession. The woman whose story we recount 'for what it tells us about European ideology and actions,' Reynolds explains, 'rather than for what she believed in and for what she did in life.'[8] As Suvendrini Perera puts it, Truganini has a disturbingly powerful 'foundational authority' in the 'discourses of [Australian] national identity'.[9]

Despite these words of admonition, still we turn to Tasmania to summarise our guilt. JM Coetzee's Elizabeth Costello struggles before a panel of judges to make the statement of belief that will release her from purgatory, and is asked:

'What of the Tasmanians?'
   'I have always found them decent people …' He waves impatiently.
'I mean the old Tasmanians, the ones who were exterminated? …'
   The extermination of a whole people … of the old Tasmanians by her countrymen, her ancestors. Is this, finally, what lies behind this hearing, this trial, the question of historical guilt?[10]

Tasmania's frontier was arguably no more violent, nor disastrous, for Aboriginal people than other Australian frontiers, but the idea of extinction has made it seem so, made it seem a clear case of genocide. In this popular context, and also within the growing area of international genocide studies, there emerged, Curthoys notes, 'some slippage' between the ideas of extinction and genocide: 'everyone "knew" that Tasmania was a clear case of colonial extinction; therefore it seemed to follow that it must be a case of genocide.'[11]

In the context of *The Last Tasmanian*, this slippage was straightforward surrogacy.[12] Its tag line was, 'the story of the swiftest and most destructive genocide on record'.[13] For many Australians it was first time they encountered a history of colonial violence, and their emotional cues were assured by its association with a history they probably knew far better: 'Our own awful holocaust,' declared *The Sun*. 'Sheer bloody murder!' exclaimed the *TV Times*.[14]

Ann Curthoys argues that the Tasmanian Aborigines did not become extinct, but they did suffer genocide. She is joined in this argument by James Boyce, and by Ryan in 2012. This was a marked revision for Ryan, whose earlier history made only a single passing reference to genocide. Henry Reynolds, however, has carefully questioned the broad assumption that genocide occurred in Tasmania.[15] Still, Ryan and Reynolds were targets in the first shots fired in the 'History Wars' in 2000. It was arguably the popular presentations of Tasmania's past that were Keith Windschuttle's true marks; what inspires shame tempts controversy.[16] While conservative voices have found traction, and white Australia has shown impatience with black armband guilt, Tasmania remains the bloodiest chapter in our history. But is it 'our' history, or is it 'their' history: part of what has made Tasmania, in Jim Davidson's words, 'always seem ... "different"'?

Cut off and seemingly distant, mainlanders have long imposed their own myths and converse realities upon their island state. It is not part of the 'sunburnt country'; it is the politicised and historicised wilderness of mountains and mists; a place haunted by a tragic past of brutalised convicts and eradicated Aborigines. A story of extinction allows white Australians to share the old Tasmanians' shame, as

Westlake recorded from the settlers—the memories of a 'land soaked with blood'—with the added convenience of living somewhere else. Truganini can still symbolise the guilt of a nation, but she also belongs to another island, from a place so unlike us it is not really part of us at all. 'Our own little Gothic repository,' as Davidson puts it.[17] An off-shore historical dumping ground. Or in the words of Onsman (paraphrasing Martin Flanagan), 'By accepting that the Tasmanians exterminated "their" Aborigines, the rest of Australia can heap its collective guilt upon the island state, secure in the knowledge that they, at least, weren't as bad as that.'[18]

Tasmania has been useful in shaping a cleaner, whiter Australia. But who has borne the cost of such cleansing? If the film *The Last Tasmanian* was a turning point for the construction of a new national identity, what did it mean to those whom it claimed were no longer there?

Banners pasted over posters of *The Last Tasmanian* proclaimed, 'RACIST!: This film denies Tasmanian Aborigines their LAND RIGHTS'. Protests were staged at cinemas in Hobart, Melbourne and Sydney. 'How can a film be damned as "racist" when its main burden is an indictment of the whites of what they did to the blacks?' asked Tom Haydon.[19] Midnight Oil's songwriters asked a similar question when Tasmanian Aborigines objected to the description of Truganini as 'the last Tasmanian' in their *Earth and Sun and Moon* album sleeve notes.[20] Tasmanian Aboriginal leader Michael Mansell explained, 'Whites today must be shown the irreparable damage that their ancestors did to our heritage.' But *The Last Tasmanian* 'perpetuates past myths … undermines the current struggle of Aboriginal people for recognition of our rights and identity.'[21]

The film did not exclude contemporary Aborigines; it misrepresented them. Since 1973 the Commonwealth government had funded an Aboriginal legal service as part of the Tasmanian Information Centre, which by 1977 was called the Tasmanian Aboriginal Centre (TAC). Haydon knew this, and sought members of TAC, among others, to participate. They are filmed scattering Truganini's ashes in 1976 but their forthright voices are edited out. When they speak it is to deny their Aboriginal identity. Cape Barren Islander Annette Mansell tells the camera while plucking a muttonbird, 'I'm not an Aboriginal. I'm only a descendant of one. Just compare the Aboriginals that were here with the descendants living today—there's a hell of a difference.' The statement might have been edited by Haydon to underpin the idea of extinction, but it also challenges it. It echoes Nancy Mansell's determined words to Westlake on Cape Barren Island in 1908: 'it's no concern of mine what the natives did out here + all her remarks refer to practices of the half casts.'[22] Both women look to the differences between the former traditional people and themselves, but they do so to show their ancestors respect. They define themselves as the inheritors of a lineage. If they speak of difference, they also acknowledge the continuation of tradition: Nancy Mansell speaks of continuing 'practices'; Annette Mansell acts them out as she cleans a muttonbird.

Jones told me that the film's title should have had a question mark, but why should their survival be posed as a question? 'We trusted and we were betrayed,' TAC representative Rosalind Langford despaired; 'we helped portray the story which denied our existence.'[23]

Haydon manipulated the contemporary Aboriginal voices in his film not to absolve white guilt but to shock; a story of survival would have dulled the impact. But in doing so Haydon undermined his project. Here the word 'genocide' could come to mean its opposite: a euphemistic colonial apology. The ire was focused foremost on Jones; he was the film's presenter and the proclaimed expert who spoke of rising seas sealing the Tasmanians' 'doom', a word hauntingly reminiscent of the 'doomed race theories' that had conveniently explained the Aborigines' disappearance not so many decades earlier.[24] Langford told the audience of the 1982 Australian Archaeology conference in Hobart:

> We all know the severing of William Lanne's [sic] skull, and ... the digging up of Truganini ... all done in the name of science. And that is not in the past. It has continued ... I speak of course of Dr Rhys Jones and his association with the film-maker Tom Haydon.[25]

Thus Jones came to represent all that Tasmanian Aboriginal people had suffered, and were still fighting to overcome.

The first time I met Jones was in early 1998 in the Australian National University's beer garden. When he learned I had just begun a PhD in Tasmanian Aboriginal history he told me: 'I am ... hated by [the Tasmanian Aboriginal people] ... Do you know what I was known as? I am the FWC!' Someone at our table tried to unpick the acronym: 'Fucking white ...?' 'Cunt!' Jones chimed in.[26] It was less the expletives that shocked me than it was the extent of discord they revealed between a leading Australian archaeologist and the Aboriginal community whose past he had researched for more than thirty years. If Jones had only excavated and measured the past he would perhaps never have offended so deeply. His abilities to write and perform—even before a camera—and to turn complex and dry ideas into simple and poetic images were expensive traits. So too, conversely, was his sense of historical empathy. Schrire asks, 'Who better to convey the drama [of the Tasmanian story] than this witty, elegant, even elegiac Welshman?'[27] One might mischievously ask, who worse?

Four years later Jones helped to realise the Pleistocene occupation of Tasmania's south-eastern region. The Franklin River was subsequently not dammed, and a formative environmental campaign won.[28] But the 'political context,' Meehan explains, had become 'far too difficult and negative to allow research to be carried out successfully'. Jones was unable to gain the now compulsory Aboriginal permission. He complained to Mike Smith in 1991 that 'not only can you not work in Tasmania without the full permission of the community, you de facto have to have somebody along with you as a commissar.'[29] Only the year before, Jones had stopped working in Tasmania completely, despite having 'a lot of unfinished work there'.[30]

His sense of frustration is still raw when, in 1999, Jones implores me, 'I gave them their history!' His words echo with shocking arrogance. But in the sense of the wider recognition of that history, Jones is right. As Mulvaney puts it, the Tasmanian Aborigines' 'invective was directed against the person who did more than any other non-indigenous person to demonstrate the antiquity, cultural significance and humanity of their ancestors.'[31]

Jones was among the first scholars to read the journals of GA Robinson (something Westlake had wanted to do). This primary source transformed Tasmania's historiographical landscape.[32] Jones mapped this information into language-groups that formed the basis for the 1994 Encyclopaedia of Aboriginal Australia's 'Tasmanian Regions' map, and the basis for the clan organisation in Ryan's 1981 and 1996 editions of The Aboriginal Tasmanians, and in her 2012 history.[33] Jones wrote in 1995 that archaeologists and Tasmanian Aborigines could create a 'synergistic partnership,' but that their 'desire … to control research into and interpretations of their heritage' might instead 'end up fatally constricting the … freedom of inquiry that has allowed such a flowering of knowledge of the past generation.'[34]

Jones's empathetic historical interpretation, which had led him to emphasise extinction before survival, had made him a figurehead in the early Aboriginal fight for recognition. As debates extended to questions of control over heritage sites, Jones remained a representative foe. As the emblematic 'FWC', Jones did not give Tasmanian Aboriginal people a history, he denied them a presence, and a future. As one Elder said to me in 1999, 'No man has damaged our struggle for existence more than Rhys Jones.'[35]

Scientific racism

Some of the fiercest criticism of Jones came from the closest quarters. Annie Bickford, a member of the archaeological team Jones took to northern Tasmania in the summer of 1964–65, wrote that The Last Tasmanian 'reflects 19th century racist ideology'.[36] Sandra Bowdler, one of Jones's doctoral students in the 1970s, stated that the theoretical basis of Jones's Tasmanian prehistory 'derives from nineteenth century social Darwinism'.[37] Ryan, who was inspired by conversations with Jones to take up research of Tasmanian Aboriginal colonial history in the 1960s, said 'scientists have helped to expiate the guilt of dispossession'.[38]

Through the 1970s these scholars worked v
munity and so they witnessed, first-hand, th
Aboriginal people to be recognised as havin
with that community a sense of dismay wl
reiterated the myth of extinction. Ryan joir
a robust public debate with Jones and Haydc
sion forum *Monday Conference*.[39] Bickford made the banners that were
pasted over the posters of the movie because she believed that unless
they were called 'Aborigines' they could not win land rights.[40] There
is a feminist strain to these criticisms, too, as Laurajane Smith and
Hilary du Cros noted that Pleistocene archaeology had been long
dominated by men—the bearded blokes competing for the earliest
date; the 'cowboys'.[41] The idea of Jones as 'social Darwinist' was cast in
the crucible of late 1970s radical race and gender politics.

There were different politics at play when Ryan reiterated her
critique of Jones as advancing 'scientific racism' in her 2012 *Tasmanian
Aborigines*. Ryan makes an accurate assessment when she reflects that
her footnotes were never the real 'tinder' that generated the 'heat' of
the History Wars in 2000. It was that she, like Reynolds, had written
histories 'deeply influenced' by the Tasmanian Aboriginal campaign
for the recognition of their survival. The History Wars were 'a
conservative response' to the end of the myth of extinction, 'to the
overturning of the doctrine of scientific racism'.[42]

Rutledge M Dennis defined 'scientific racism' in 1995 as the
use of science 'as a justification to propose, project, and enact racist
social policies'. This definition is founded in Black North American
history and traces the scientific justifications of slavery to contemporary intelligence tests.[43] Ryan places Jones within a list of scholars
who, since the 1850s, she considers have thus used science to justify
the demise of the Tasmanian Aborigines. Jones's place in this list of
scholars seems accurate only when quoted by Windschuttle who takes
Jones's allegorical 'slow strangulation' of the Tasmanian Aboriginal
cultural 'mind' to argue that their society was not merely technically
but also morally regressed: they bartered the women with sealers for
dogs and flour and thus lost the mothers of future children. They were

'internally dysfunctional', and therefore to blame for the collapse of their 'precarious society' in the face of colonisation.[44] As Ryan points out, it is in Windschuttle that we find the clearest case of fabrication and scientific racism. It is in his writing that we find the colonial apology of which Jones was wrongly accused. In Jones we find comparisons between Tasmanian colonisation, Buchenwald and My Lai. To the idea that his ideas helped expiate colonisation, Jones replied reasonably in 1992, 'I have never said this.'[45]

'Inheritors of a deep real past'

Jones did say, however, that the Tasmanian Aborigines had 'the world's simplest technology'. As archaeologist Tim Murray observes, Jones's idea of the Tasmanians as the 'last refuge' of a culture of 'immense … stability', does have a 'familiar Tylorean ring about it. The feeling that the archaeology of the 1960s had collided with the interpretive framework of the 1860s.'[46] Peter White and James O'Connell describe Jones's regression thesis as being 'at one' with Lubbock and Sollas, while Ian McNiven and Lynette Russell find it bridges the ideas of Lubbock and Tylor.[47] Jones wrote in his dissertation, 'We seem once more to be turning back to the classic problem of the Tasmanians as seen by Tylor.'[48]

If we look more closely at the meeting point between Jones and Tylor, we begin to see it also as the launching point into their differences. Jones saw evidence of slow cultural decline. 'Of degeneration,' Tylor wrote of Tasmania, 'there is at present no evidence.' For Tylor stasis seemed a more likely explanation for the Tasmanians' cultural simplicity.[49] Jones might have agreed, but as Murray puts it, he 'had it both ways': that the Tasmanian Aborigines 'degenerated (because of isolation) and that they were static (because of isolation)'.[50] But when we look at what it was that Jones and Tylor considered was static, we find their fundamental difference. To return to Jones's own comparison: 'We seem once more to be turning back to the classic problem of the Tasmanians as seen by Tylor. Can we now look to the Tasmanians, not so much as the representatives of Palaeolithic man, but of late Pleistocene Australian man?'[51]

Jones was suggesting a shift of continents, and the realisation of Australia's antiquity. He did not continue Tylor's older view of Tasmania, nor the justification of colonisation that such a view has been widely assumed to hold. He undid the paradox that meant the Tasmanians could illuminate Europe's beginnings but have no history of their own. Jones had held a cast of the Taunton Scraper, and reflected how it had turned them into a 'changeless relic'.[52] He had stood at Rocky Cape and looked over Bass Strait, at a history of change that a flooded Pleistocene connection meant. He thus joined an older antipodean view of it, in which Australian archaeologists, since Howitt, had looked down to it as a key to the question of their own country's antiquity. Jones had effectively solved the 'Problem of the Tasmanians'.

Solving that older 'problem', though, 'paled into insignificance,' Murray writes, 'alongside the startling discovery, by Jones and others, of a Pleistocene human occupation in the frozen wastes of southern Tasmania in 1981.'[53] This discovery revealed a very different picture of Tasmanian prehistory than that imagined by Jones ten years earlier. The kutikina excavations, Jones explains, divulged 'a totally different' stone implement industry to that of Rocky Cape. It was part of the unique culture of the 'southernmost humans on Earth', which had changed when warmer temperatures at the end of the Pleistocene brought denser forests and higher seas, enclosing grassy plains and flooding coasts.[54] At the other end of the temporal span was a late Holocene Tasmania that, scholars have agreed, witnessed a cultural renaissance. Aboriginal people began exploring new parts of Tasmania, including off-shore islands, and developing new styles and media in their art.[55] Murray and Christine Williamson explain that the 'complexities of late Holocene variation in Tasmania ... were well understood by Jones,' who argued that after 2500 BP the Aborigines had 'expanded their social and cultural universe'.[56] Jones reported in 1995 that evidence had recently been found that bridged the early Pleistocene and late Holocene with the discovery in Tasmania's mid north of a site with continued habitation from 33,000 BP.[57]

'The Aborigines of Tasmania,' Jones concluded, 'long constructed as an abstract frozen metaphor for Palaeolithic man, are now seen as inheritors of a deep real past.'[58] The shift away from Tylor's metropolitan view—the view that took Westlake to Tasmania—was total, and yet it recalled that older perspective in a new way: Tasmania now had an antiquity equal with that of Palaeolithic Europe. It was now possible to carry out, as Jones put it, 'intercontinental comparisons that relate directly to the questions of global colonization and adaptation by modern people.'[59] This mutual antiquity reignited Jones's sense of a shared indigeneity. When he first entered kutikina cave he was 'strongly reminded of caves of a similar ambience and antiquity … in the … Gower Peninsula' in South Wales. But foremost it reinforced 'the perspective of the Pleistocene archaeologist' that Tasmania's antiquity demonstrates that 'there is a fundamental unity in the history of humankind'.[60]

This was the philosophy instilled in Jones by his Cambridge teacher. Clark taught a concept of history that 'sprang from despair in the depth of the Second World War'. Far from reiterating 'scientific racism', Clark inspired his students to find that 'over-riding sense of human solidarity such as can come only from a consciousness of common origins.'[61] 'It is a philosophy,' Mulvaney writes, 'which regrettably runs counter to much current indigenous belief.'[62] It challenges fundamentally the notion of a singular indigenous claim on Pleistocene prehistory and has ignited disputes over the reburial of repatriated human remains and of control over heritage sites. In 1990 Mulvaney argued that the reburial of skeletal ancestral remains disinterred from Kow Swamp and held in the National Museum of Victoria was not just 'vandalism', but part of a new 'black intellectual totaliatrianism'. The skeletons, dated to be Pleistocene heritage, were too ancient to belong to one community; they were part of a universal heritage.[63]

Mulvaney considers that Jones, 'correctly', remained 'steadfast' to a disciplinary global perspective.[64] Late in his life, remembers Tim Flannery, Jones warned his colleagues that 'if we lose sight of a global view, then we lose the whole point of the game.'[65] Jones was 'not afraid to express opinions which fail the test of political correctness,' reflects Mulvaney. 'Future Australians, indigenous and immigrant, will commend his fortitude.'[66]

Jones's tenacious message has in fact been reiterated by his fiercest critics. In 2009 Bowdler reflected that discovery at kutalayna, (also known as the Jordan River Levee), north-west of Hobart, of a human antiquity dating back around 41,000 BP extended previous understanding of the 'southernmost' Pleistocene humans, and thus 'highlight[s] again the range of environments to which modern humans were able to adapt.' Ryan concludes that 'in global terms the site is significant in adding to our current understandings of human evolution.'[67] When it came to protecting this archaeological discovery, however, 'the best [the Tasmanian State Government] could come up with', writes journalist Andrew Darby, 'was $12 million for a highway bridge over it.'[68] The Brighton Bypass opened in November 2012 to divert traffic away from the Hobart suburbs. It was well into construction by the time the levee's archaeological and cultural value was assessed and realised. Calls to re-route the road failed. So too did the protests that occupied the site for months.[69] When the bulldozers came in, the protesters, including Jim and Aaron Everett, knew it was 'cultural vandalism'.[70] They were captured in social and national media expressing feelings of deep-seated sadness. It was not theirs alone.

Genetic connections

Does the revelation of a 'deep real past' give the Tasmanian Aborigines a history, or does it, in the ambition to find our 'common origins', make them disappear all over again? 'If we go sufficiently far back, everyone's ancestors are shared,' writes Dawkins. What is 'sufficiently'? The question is the point of his book, *The Ancestor's Tale*, and he (with Yan Wong) models an answer with Tasmanian geography. When rising seas at the end of the Pleistocene isolated the Tasmanians they became, Dawkins posits, the first group of humans geographically removed from a previously shared global gene pool. The last Tasmanian generation or, more symbolically, the last Tasmanian 'mother' to bridge the separated populations potentially encompassed the genes of all humanity. She is our 'Mitochondrial Eve'.[71] I wonder: does this make us all Tasmanian Aborigines? Or, by the same reasoning, does it make no one a Tasmanian Aborigine? Or is the question absurd? The concepts of 'Tasmanian' and 'Aborigine', and even the geography that shaped them, did not exist at the end of the last Pleistocene.

The irony is that DNA is used to differentiate indigeneity. In the United States, Kimberly TallBear explains how blood tests are taken to 'measure who is truly Indian' and to 'justify cultural and political authority'.[72] Laboratories advertise the service. The University of Arizona laboratory took some samples from the Tasmanian Aboriginal community in 2002 to determine a genetic ancestral connection. The tests grew out of controversy.

In 1996, the TAC questioned the identity of several elected representatives of the former indigenous government body (ATSIC). A 1998 Federal Court hearing referred the decision back to the community. Justice Merkel found that identity was 'a social, rather than a genetic, construct'.[73] At the next community elections, it was ruled that only those on an electoral roll could vote. The Independent Indigenous Advisory Committee, unheeding Merkel's finding, requested all those on the roll be DNA tested to prove their Aboriginal ancestry. The tests were stopped due to community outrage; it was likened to the colonial-era theft of Aboriginal ancestral remains.[74] But the samples were not stolen as relics of an extinct race. They were sent willingly to prove who was a living Aborigine.

What remained in place was an eligibility test. To identify as an Aborigine and be recognised as eligible for specific programs and services offered by the state government, it was necessary to meet the Commonwealth three-part criteria—self-identification, descent and recognition by community. But what comprised 'community' was confined to recognised Aboriginal groups. This changed from July 2016, when the state government allowed communal recognition to broaden and for self-determination to be more widely accepted.[75] While welcomed by many people who had felt excluded, others felt the change meant their Aboriginal community would be 'swamped with white people'.[76]

'Access to the public purse demands ... proof of blood,' reflected Flanagan.[77] It was blood that once denied Tasmanian Aborigines their existence, so is it enough to determine their identity? Or is it enough to irradiate identity? Like a Pleistocene past, can blood—or more specifically the genetic information it contains—distinguish us, or connect us to the point of making indigeneity dissolve?

Identity must emerge at some point. Jones felt Welsh. His indigeneity gave him empathy—to dare to look 'through Aboriginal eyes'.[78] He can feel connected to kutikina because it reminds him of his home. But his land claim to Stonehenge was made in jest; his sense of indigeneity does not compromise his 'global view'. But still Jones knows what it feels like to be colonised. Is this then the demarcation of what shapes indigeneity: to have known and to have survived the other side of the frontier?

Jim Everett explained to me that in his community survival 'is no longer a useful word'. During the first wave of radical self-determinism it had meaning; now it suggests a kind of coping, a culture defined by struggle, when in reality it is so much richer. 'The politics of survival are not our culture,' Greg Lehman explains, 'they are a measure of the days we live in. Our true culture is where we stand—on our land.'[79]

The sentiment does not answer to the requirements of legal identity, and there lies its strength. It is a vestige of colonisation that forces indigenous communities to link biology to identity for reasons of politics and access to funding resources. Lehman's definition ignores that entire history. It draws a line between community and Country rather than blood and money. But who gets to draw the line? I have asked Lehman this, curious that his definition of culture must by extension of logic require if not a legal definition then at least some call to biological essentialism. He agreed it must, but the problem seemed to trouble me more than him. My concern is akin to me cleaning a muttonbird in my freezing hands—submerged in culture— yet still wanting to reach for my notepad and record the moment and its context and meaning in order to validate it.

Europeans have a long history of defining and studying the Tasmanian Aborigines with a principal reason being to understand their own culture and history. Westlake searched for European antiquity in Tasmania. Jones searched, and found, Aboriginal antiquity, but by drawing connections between the deep past and recent colonial history, he made the search also about exculpating white shame. Even the realisation of Aboriginal deep time became about, and had to be shared with, the coloniser. But Mulvaney's steadfast insistence that we accept archaeology's global perspective is an important challenge for all communities to try to meet. The celebration of deep time in the cause of white national identity is, however, worth questioning.[80]

The search for human antiquity in Tasmania has long been about discovering the European self, looking inwards, or downwards—from Britain, from the mainland of Australia, from somewhere else at least than on the land that Lehman rightfully claims. But by traversing the land, as Westlake did, by digging into it, as Jones did, the enduring Aboriginal lifeworld cannot help but come into view. Westlake looked for stones of a dead people and collected their living Aboriginal voices. Jones looked out over the Bass Strait and remembered that the eyes looking out have long been Aboriginal. And so the search to collect, to possess, at least momentarily, offers up opportunities to see and to understand.

Epilogue: The return

kutalayna, 31 August 2016

Jim untwists the thin piece of wire that holds the gate closed and steps onto the land. He has driven past and stopped once, he tells me, but this is the first time he has walked back on since the day he was arrested.

The grass is thick and green. Our shoes get a bit wet as we walk towards the river. The sun feels wonderful. It has been a long winter. We stop when we reach the remains of the healing ceremony fire. 'I thought the bulldozers would have been all through here,' Jim says. It is a good surprise. The grass has grown between the stones that surround the hearth. Three large green squares of corrugated iron form a triangle around us, the points several paces apart. The archaeological excavations, Jim explains. The metal lids are screwed down onto wooden frames and we cannot see the trenches underneath. I go to take a step, and Jim suddenly calls, 'Look out, Rebe!' A patch of brown fur in the grass is next to my foot. Something dead? A rabbit bolts towards the distant fence line where sheep are grazing. No grass is growing where it was nestled. How long had it been there? 'That's its burrow. They don't dig where the ground is wet,' Jim tells me.

This is a levee. The Jordan River has long risen, and fallen, covering millions of meals, fires, moments and lives.

On the way to kutalayna Jim needed to drop off something to his son Aaron, who now works as an Aboriginal community nurse. We stood on the street as Aaron explained to me that the archaeological dates for kutalayna lay beyond the carbon-dating barrier. They were obtained using Optically Stimulated Luminescence, which reveals the last time sunlight fell on the sand before it was covered again. Each deposit of river mud acted like a seal, encasing stone artefacts and human Aboriginal activity, like a slice of time.

The state government paid for the archaeological digs, but Aaron thought they weren't happy with the extreme depth of antiquity. It made it harder to justify building the bridge. In the end they called the bridge 'conservation'. A joke. They had to change legislation, Aaron explains, in order to construct pylons that close to a waterway.

Jim Everett by the healing fireplace, kutalayna, Rebe Taylor, April 2016

Then they cut through layers of human occupation, destroying an integral part of what Jim calls a 'cultural library'. Aaron hasn't gone back to the site. Jim has gone only once. He and his family will never drive on the bypass.

Jim and I look up at the huge bridge. I notice that the cars and trucks pass infrequently. 'What is the point of it?' I ask. 'It cuts five to ten minutes off the drive from Launceston,' Jim responds. Five to ten minutes saved; 41,000 thousand years of human occupation damaged. The difference in the value and meaning of time is too vast for me to fathom.

Jim steps into the cold fireplace and sits down on a rock. I ask him if the place feels healed. 'It has a quiet energy,' he answers. He picks up a handful of ash. 'The Tent Embassy ashes,' he says, triumph in his voice, 'they are still here.' He stands up to let them fall through his fingers, back into the hearth, back into the land. When he turns his face back towards me I see there are tears in his blue eyes. 'We should return to this place,' he says to me. 'We should *reclaim* it.'

Acknowledgements

For a book that is largely about the search for human antiquity, it seems appropriate that writing the acknowledgments feels a bit like an archaeological dig. I was surprised when the rough outline of a book emerged nearly two years ago, for it has its antecedents in several other guises that span nearly two decades. I first encountered Ernest Westlake as a doctoral student in 1999, and I owe much to those at the Australian National University who guided my first stumbling attempt to tell the story of his journey to Tasmania, foremost my wonderful supervisor, Tom Griffiths, and also the many colleagues and friends who made up our inspiring community: Chris Blackall, Frank Bongiorno, Tim Bonyhady, Gordon Briscoe, Ann Curthoys, John Docker, Bronwen Douglas, Kirsty Douglas, Rani Kerin, Amanda Laugesen, Darrell Lewis, Nicole McLennan, Ann McGrath, Mark McKenna, Howard Morphy, Peter Read, Deborah Rose, Tiffany Shellam, Tim Sherratt, Barry Smith, Tim Rowse, John Thompson and Paul Turnbull. It was a privilege to be among the students taught by Greg Dening and Donna Merwick, and I was very fortunate to be able to listen to Rhys Jones tell his story with boundless passion.

It was early in my research that I had the honour to meet members of the Tasmanian Aboriginal community who became invaluable teachers and good friends. Jim Everett, Patsy Cameron and Greg Lehman welcomed me into their homes and hearts and spent many hours talking to me and reading my work over the years. I acknowledge Jim's invaluable help in writing the Prologue and Epilogue. Buck (Brendan) Brown, Bob Hughes and David Sainty taught me how to clean mutton birds on Cape Barren Island, which gave me an insight into culture I could not find in a book. Other Islanders who helped me understand Westlake's papers include Chris Mansell, Claude Mansell, Hilda Thomas, and Morton and Sue Summers. I have enjoyed wonderful conversations with Tony Brown, Julie Gough, Caroline Spotswood, Maggie Walters and Lyell Wilson. My heartfelt thanks to Clinton Mundy for helping me understand the culture and history of Fanny Smith and her family. Thanks also to Cheryl Mundy for introducing me to Clinton, and for her contribution.

Writing about Westlake would not have been possible without going to England and reading his papers and meeting his family. I appreciate the warm hospitality offered by Jean Westlake and Chris Charman in Hampshire. It was a privilege to research in the Pitt Rivers Museum, where I was given expert and extensive help by Jeremy Coote, Elizabeth Edwards, Philip Grover, Chris Morton, Mike O'Hanlon and Alison Petch, and by the staff at the Balfour Library. I also appreciate the help offered by the staff at the Oxford University Museum of Natural History, especially librarian Stella Brecknell, and at the British Museum and Manchester Museum. My thanks go to Chris Gosden, who supervised me while I studied at Oxford; to Derek Roe, who taught me how to look at eoliths; and to Justin Delair, who was my forerunner.

I began my Australian Research Council postdoctoral Fellowship at the University of Melbourne with the goal to publish Westlake's entire archive digitally. I could not have achieved this without the incredible expertise and creativity of my co-creators of *Stories in Stone*, Gavan McCarthy and Mike Jones. Also critical was the assistance of Ailie Smith, Helen Morgan and all the staff at the eScholarship Research Centre, where I have been welcomed and supported as an Honorary Fellow and friend.

I have benefited from the collegial and interdisciplinary environment of the Australian Centre. Kate Darian-Smith was a great mentor and friend, and Michael Cathcart, Helen MacDonald and Sara Wills were very supportive. I am thankful to Clive Blazey and Tim Herbert, respectively brother and partner of Peter Blazey. As the recipient of the 2015 Peter Blazey Fellowship I was able to write the first draft of this book. The School of Historical and Philosophical Studies assisted with funds to reproduce images in this book and also offered me an Honorary Fellowship.

I owe a debt of gratitude to all the historians and archaeologists whose work has inspired me, many of whom have talked to me and read my work, including Bain Attwood, Annie Bickford, Shayne Breen, James Boyce, Richard Cosgrove, Kate Darian-Smith, Jim Davidson, Billy Griffiths, Tom Griffiths, Katie Holmes, Philip Jones, Betty Meehan, Stuart Macintyre, Peter McPhee, Andrys Onsman, Cassandra Pybus, Henry Reynolds, Lynette Russell, Lyndall Ryan, Mike Smith and Chips Sowerwine. Further thanks to Betty Meehan and Mike Smith for the photographs of Rhys Jones.

Parts of this book have appeared in earlier forms in journals and edited books, and I acknowledge the creative guidance of their editors, in particular Juilee Decker of *Collections*, Helen Gardner and Robert Kenny of the special edition of *Oceania*, Anna Johnston and Mitchell Rolls of the companion essays to *Friendly Mission*, Ingereth Macfarlane of *Aboriginal History*, Zora Sanders of *Meanjin* and Christina Twomey of *Australian Historical Studies*.

It has been a fantastic experience working with Melbourne University Press. I am indebted to CEO Louise Adler for her enthusiasm for my proposal, to executive publisher Sally Heath for her elegant and pitch-perfect editing, to copy editor Joanne Holliman for her indefatigable patience and keen eye, to Louise Stirling for managing the project with aplomb and to Perri Palmieri for publicising the book.

I have spent many hours over the last two years writing alone in my converted garden shed and I owe a great deal to the friends and family who have offered essential companionship when I have emerged, and who have been patient when I haven't. Kathleen Birrell, Susan Brennan,

Michael Golding, Martin Leckey and Peter McPhee have been generous and important friends throughout. My parents, John and Ariette, and my sister, Juliet who live nearby have often helped me so I can write. My brother, Ingmar, and sister-in-law, Louise, have always shown keen interest from Sydney. My children, Hugo and Neve, have been such enthusiastic supporters and so patient when their mum has struggled to balance it all. This book is dedicated to them, and also to my partner, Peter, who deserves the most gratitude and thanks of all. His love and support have been vital and unflagging.

Thank you.

Rebe Taylor
Yarraville, Victoria, December 2016

'To Mum for when you've finished
your book', Neve, aged 5, 2015

Notes

Acronyms

DPE, BM: Department of Prehistory and Europe, British Museum, London.

ML: Mitchell Library, State Library of New South Wales, Sydney.

MM: Manchester Museum, Manchester.

RAI: Royal Anthropological Institute of Great Britain and Ireland, London.

TP/PRM: Tylor Papers, Manuscripts Collections, Pitt Rivers Museum, Oxford.

UTAS: The University of Tasmania, Hobart.

WP/OUMNH: Westlake Papers, Oxford University Museum of Natural History, Oxford.

WP/PRM: Westlake Papers, Manuscripts Collections, Pitt Rivers Museum, Oxford.

WP/SIS: *Stories in Stone: An annotated history and guide to the collections and papers of Ernest Westlake (1855–1922)* at www.westlakehistory.info.

Note: the archival notes in this book usually refer only to the physical version of the Westlake Papers, not WP/SIS (see Westlake Papers in 'Bibliography' for more details).

Prologue: The gift

1   Paton.

The decision

1   British Museum, 1908, p. 76.

2   ibid., pp. 105, 107.

3   ibid., p. 232.

4   This may have been an oil-on-canvas portrait of Woureddy by Benjamin Duterrau, 1834, Tasmania, acquired by the British Museum in 1883. For details, search 'Woureddy' in the Research Collections at www.britishmuseum.org.

5   In 1908 the British Museum had a collection of around 100 stone implements from Tasmania, acquired between 1899–1906. My research in 2008 identified the collectors, their correspondence and their artefacts. Parts of this collection are available online, including the artefacts sent by CG Wilkinson: search 'Wilkinson Tasmania' in the Research Collections at www.britishmuseum.org.

6   WP/PRM, Westlake to children, 22 November 1908, f. 41v.

7   ibid., 14 May 1910, f. 237; 11 November 1908, ff. 37–37v.

8   Plomley's changes included collating interviews held separately with the same individual, reordering notes by placing them under subject headings, correcting grammar and excluding text, all without any indication. Plomley justifies these changes, saying, 'the whole record is almost unreadable in the original and its defects, it is suggested, relate to Westlake's view that there was little worth recording'; Plomley, 1991, p. 7. Neither is entirely true. While the notes are rough and disorderly, Westlake's handwriting is arguably legible, and while he believed much of the information about the Tasmanian Aborigines was irretrievably lost, Westlake was largely pleased by the quality and volume of the information he recorded.

9   ibid., pp. 7–8.

10 ibid., p. 8.

11 Jones, 1977b.

12 Haydon, 1978.

13 Jones, 1971, pp. 36, 39.

14 Cameron, pp. ix, 101–108.

15 Delair, 1981, 1985.

16 Taylor, 2000c.

17 Taylor, 2004.

18 Edgell.

The collector

1   Sackett, p. 1.

2   Griffiths, 1996, pp. 9–10.

3   Grayson; Roe.

4   RAI, 1910; 1912; WP/PRM, Westlake to children, 27 February 1909, f. 69 v.

5   Lanne's cranium was removed and replaced with that of another man laid out in the death house, however, it never surfaced in any collections or records. When Truganini died in 1876, it was decreed that her body be left to rest. The Royal Society of Tasmania later applied to have her remains disinterred in order that they would be 'accessible ... to scientific men for scientific purposes'. For the ninety-eight years her skeleton was in the museum in Hobart, little research was ever carried out on them: MacDonald, pp. 136–82; Petrow, pp. 39–40; Fforde and Hubert.

6   WP/PRM, Westlake to children, 12 December 1908, f. 51; Taylor, 2000a, 2000b; Edgell, pp. 10–11.

7   *The Times*, 29 July 1869, quoted in Lawson, p. 171.

8   MacDonald, p. 10; see also Lawson, p. 162.

9   Gough, p. 45; Lawson, pp. 157, 162. The names of the residents in the photograph of Oyster Cove residents is sourced from Gough, p. 20. Gough provides a more complete list of residents on pp. 34–36.

10 Lubbock, pp. 336–37.

11 Tylor, 1878, p. 195.

12 Darwin, 1871, p. 238; Lawson, p. 162.

13 WP/PRM, Westlake to children, 11 November 1908, ff. 39–39v.

14 ibid., 11 May 1909, ff. 94–94v.

15 Lawson, p. 162.

16 Tylor, 1895, p. 340, quoted in WP/PRM, 'Exercise Book 17' (WP/SIS, Image 4).

17 ibid., 1899, p. viii, quoted by Westlake in 'Exercise Book 17'.

18 Noetling, p. 2, wrote that 'only quite recently' Rutot had written to him explaining the comparative similarity of Tasmanian implements to eoliths found in Belgium. Balfour, 1925, p. 3; Daniel, pp. 230–31; Grayson, pp. 101, 131; Rutot, 1907; 1908.

19 WP/PRM, Westlake to children, 29 May 1910, f. 246.

20 ibid., 6 December 1908, f. 46.

21 ibid., 22 November 1908, f. 42.

22 ibid., 27 February 1909, f. 69v.

23 ibid., 11 November 1908, ff. 37–37v.

24 ibid., 22 November 1908, f. 42v.

25 ibid., 14 February 1909, f. 67v.

26 Griffiths, 1996, pp. 77, 85.

27 WP/PRM, Westlake to children, 22 November 1908, f. 42v; 1 June 1910, f. 248v.

28 Griffiths, 1996, pp. 19–21.

Leaving home

1 WP/PRM, 'Westlake (draft) letter to *SS Afric*, 13 September 1908' in 'Notes regarding French "eoliths" and geology', Folder 1a, Box 3; Westlake to children, 17 October 1908, f. 17.

2 Westlake, 1903.

3 Westlake, 1889, p. 21.

4 Hale, (no page numbers).

5 Westlake, 1903, second and final pages.

6 Delair, 1981, p. 134.

7 Westlake, 1889, pp. 3–4.

8 Delair, 1985, p. 39.

9 Westlake, 1921c, p. 19.

10 Light and Ponting, 1997, p. 41.

11 Hoare, pp. 6–7, 200–201.

12 Richard Westlake, pp. 2–3.

13 ibid.

14 Jean Westlake, 2000, pp. 11–13.

15 ibid.

16 ibid., p. 13.

17   ibid., Jean Westlake, 1982, p. 6; Westlake, 1910, p. 33.

18   Westlake, 1921c, p. 20; Jean Westlake, 2000, p. 13.

19   Westlake, 1921c, pp. 20–22.

20   Jean Westlake, 2000, p. 14; Gil, S, *Stumbling blocks to stepping stones*, 'Quaker Alphabet Blog 2014 – B for A Neave Brayshaw', 24 January 2014, stumbling stepping.blogspot.com.au/2014_01_01_archive.html; *Rowntree Family*.

21   Jean Westlake, 2000, p. 11.

22   Thomas Westlake, 1885.

23   Richard Westlake, p. 6; Brayebrook Observatory, 'History of English silvered-glass reflecting telescopes: The Equatorial Reflecting Telescopes of Browning, Horne & Thornthwaite, Calver & Irving', www.brayebrookobservatory.org/ BrayObsWebSite/HOMEPAGE/HISTORY.html.

24   Richard Westlake, pp. 6–7, 9.

25   Power.

26   Taylor, email from Carol Bowen, Records Assistant, University College London, 8 March 2001, personal collection. Hogg's address is listed in the *Report of the Fourth International Ophthalmological Congress, Held in London, August, 1872*, books.google.com.au/books?id=njIAAAAAQAAJ&pg.

27   *British History Online*, 'No 1 Bedford Square', www.british-history.ac.uk/ survey-london/vol5/pt2/pp152-153.

28   Camden History Society.

29   WP/PRM, Westlake to children, 13 December 1908, f. 51v.

30   Jean Westlake, 2000, p. 14; 'John Tyndall', en.wikipedia.org/wiki/John_Tyndall.

31   Edgell, p. 2, believes these essays are not in Westlake's handwriting, but it is not that different from other examples by Westlake in the same period, such as his geographical notes regarding London clay in which the Ts are crossed with the same long stroke. Edgell dates the essay as 1876 but this could not be substantiated, which may be because the notes were reorganised when transported from the University of Southampton to OUMNH. WP/ OUMNH, 'Geological notes—early material', Folder iv (i) (WP/SIS, Image 2, WEST00365, Series 16).

32   Aubrey Westlake, 1956, p. 4.

33   Delair, 1981, p. 133; Geological Society of London, Ernest Westlake's Application Form to join the society, 10 March 1879; Sollas, 1923.

34   Delair, 1981, pp. 134–35.

35   Aubrey Westlake, 1956, p. 4.

36   Delair, 1985, p. 39. A collection of Westlake's chalk fossils is housed in the Salisbury Museum.

37   Westlake, 1888; Delair, 1981, p. 134; Barrois. It was realised in 1975 that Westlake had discovered a previously unknown fossil sea urchin that was subsequently named after him, *Micraster westlakei*, Stokes, p. 814.

38   Westlake, 1889, p. 26.

39   Richard Westlake, p. 4.

40   Isichei, p. 12; Abbott, et al., p. 156.

41   Isichei, pp. 10, 12–13.

42   Joseph John Gurney, whose writings inspired the Quaker evangelical movement, was influenced and impressed by the wealth and social standing of Anglican evangelicals; Isichei, pp. 4–5, 13.

43   Richard Westlake, pp. 4–5, 8.

44   Thomas Westlake, 1847.

45   Richard Westlake, pp. 4–5.

46   Westlake, 1921c, p. 20.

47   Richard Westlake, pp. 3, 6–7, 9.

48   Westlake, 1889, pp. 10, 6, 12.

49   Richard Westlake, pp. 3, 5.

50   Westlake, 1921c, p. 21.

51   Westlake, 1910, pp. 20, 65; WP/PRM, Westlake to children, 31 May 1909, f. 103.

52   WP/PRM, Westlake to children, 30 October 1908, f. 30.

53   Westlake, 1910, pp. 20, 65.

54   Hoare, pp. 198, 160, 348, 280, 191; 'New Forest Shakers', Wikipedia, en.wikipedia. org/wiki/New_Forest_Shakers.

55   'Auberon Herbert', Wikipedia, en.wikipedia.org/wiki/Auberon_Herbert; Hoare, pp. 188, 201.

56   Hoare, pp. 415–16.

57   WP/OUMNH, 'On the Paranormal—particular cases 1888-94', Box 6 (WP/ SIS, WEST00409, Series 17).

58   ibid., 'Letter to Mrs Harbord from Westlake, 12 June 1888'; Letter to Westlake from Mr Cormick, 25 July 1894'.

59   ibid., Letters to Westlake from William Crookes, 18 May and 28 July 1894; Letter to Westlake from John W Judd, 30 July 1894'; 'Westlake notes on building a "Rheostat"'; see also Oppenheim, pp. 344–48.

60   Taylor, 2000a.

61   Oppenhiem 1985, pp. 3, 319, 339; Westlake, 1910, p. 58.

62   Hoare, p. 201.

63   Hardy, pp. 22, 208–14.

64   ibid., pp. 22–23, 206–208.

65   WP/PRM, Westlake to children, 21 January 1910, f. 199.

66   WP/PRM, Westlake to children, letter started 17 October 1908, f. 19; Edgell p. 6.

67   Westlake, 1910, pp. 98–99.

68   ibid., pp. 37–38.

69   Edgell, p. 6; Jean Westlake, 1982, pp. 5–6; 2000, p. 16.

70   Jean Westlake, 1982, p. 15.

71   Westlake, 1910, pp. 9, 14.

72   ibid., pp. 7–9.

73   WP/PRM, Westlake to children, 4 April 1910, f. 220.

74   Westlake, 1910, pp. 101–102.

75   Jean Westlake, 1982, p. 7.

76   ibid., p. 15; Westlake, 1910, pp. 35–41.

77   Edgell, p. 6; Westlake, 1910, p. 51; Jean Westlake, 1982, p. 15.

78   Delair, 1985, p. 42.

79   Westlake, 1910, p. 58.
80   Westlake, 1921a, Part III, Chapter XVIII, 'The Crossing', no page numbers.
81   Westlake, 'Memoir of Thomas Westlake', pp. 11–12.
82   Westlake, 1921a, Part III, Chapter XVIII, 'The Crossing', no page number.
83   ibid., pp. 79–80.
84   Westlake, 1910, pp. 44–48; Wiltshire and Swindon History Centre, 'Wilton on the Carpet', www.wshc.eu/blog/item/wilton-on-the-carpet.html.
85   Letter from Ernest Westlake to Richard Westlake, 1901, quoted in Jean Westlake, 2000, p. 17.
86   Westlake, 1910, pp. 46, 60–67.
87   Letter from Ernest Westlake to Richard Westlake, 1901, quoted in Jean Westlake, 2000, p. 17.
88   Jean Westlake, 2000, p. 75.
89   Westlake, 1910, pp. 81–83.
90   ibid., pp. 90–91.
91   Letter by Ernest Westlake to Richard Westlake, 1901, quoted in Jean Westlake, 2000, p. 17.
92   Westlake, 1910, pp. 92–93. The sedative effects of morphine can cause respiratory depression if the lungs are compromised by infection and the patient is overweight, Whang, et al.
93   Westlake, 1910, p. 92.
94   Westlake, 1921a, Part III, Chapter XVIII, 'The Crossing', no page numbers.
95   Westlake, 1910, pp. 30, 66.
96   'Letter by Ernest Westlake to Richard Westlake, 1901', quoted in Westlake, 2000, p. 17.
97   Jean Westlake, 1982, p. 20.
98   ibid., p. 16.
99   Delair, 1981, p. 136.
100   ibid; Westlake, 1903, second page.
101   Westlake, 1889, p. 20; Westlake, 1903, second page.

The same science

1   WP/PRM, Westlake to 'Aunt' and children, 24 September 1908; (no day) October 1908, ff. 1, 4, 4v, 12.
2   Westlake to 'Aunt' and children, 24 September 1908, ff. 1v, 4.
3   Westlake to children, no date, October 1908, f. 10v.
4   ibid., letter started 17 October 1908, ff. 20–20v.
5   Jean Westlake, 1982, p. 20.
6   ibid., pp. 20–21.
7   WP/OUMNH, '"The Eoliths from the Upper Miocene deposits of the Cantal, Central France" by J Red Moir' (unpublished manuscript), Folder III (iii) (WP/SIS, Image 4, WEST00364, Series 16).
8   Delair, 1985, p. 41; Edgell, p. 11; Jean Westlake, 2000, pp. 19–20.
9   Jean Westlake, 1982, pp. 20–21.
10   ibid., pp. 28–29; Edgell, pp. 8–9.

11   Grayson, pp. 94–103; Hazzledine Warren, p. 356; De Bont, p. 608.
12   Hazzledine Warren, p. 337.
13   ibid., pp. 352–53, 345, 358, 346.
14   Grayson, pp. 99–101.
15   ibid., pp. 94–103.
16   WP/PRM, Westlake to children, 11 November 1908, f. 36.
17   ibid., f. 38v; Maltezos.
18   WP/PRM, Westlake to children, 4 November 1908, f. 35v.
19   ibid, 11 November 1908, ff. 37–37v.
20   Griffiths, 1996, pp. 68, 72.
21   ibid., pp. 67, 70.
22   WP/PRM, Westlake to children, 11 November 1908, ff. 37–37v.
23   Griffiths, 1996, pp. 68, 72.
24   ibid., p. 78.
25   ibid., pp. 62–63; Howitt.
26   Griffiths, 1996, p. 72.
27   ibid.
28   ibid., p. 68.
29   WP/PRM, Westlake to children, 11 November 1908, f. 39.
30   ibid., f. 39v.
31   McGregor, p. 50; Brantlinger, p. 5.
32   Morphy, pp. 31, 42.
33   Darwin, 1871, p. 238.
34   WP/PRM, Westlake to children, 11 November 1908, f. 39.
35   ibid, f. 39v.

Collecting stones

1   *The Mercury*, 14 November 1908. This newspaper clipping is held in WP/PRM, Box 1, Folder 1b, f. 20.
2   WP/PRM, 'Westlake to Fritz Noetling, 23 November 1908', Box 1, Folder 1b, f. 26v.
3   Jean Westlake, 1982, pp. 17, 28.
4   WP/PRM, Westlake to children, 16 November 1908, f. 40.
5   Tylor, 1900, p. 258, quoted WP/PRM 'Exercise Book 17', WP/SIS, Image 6; Westlake also mentions here Tylor's notes of Moir's findings of special 'gravers'.
6   Westlake to children, 8 May 1910, ff. 234–35.
7   Westlake to children, 22 November 1908, ff. 43, 41v.
8   WP/PRM, Westlake, 'Notebook 1', p. 28.
9   UTAS Correspondence, 'Moir to Walker, 11 January 1898', W9_c4_1(47)(1). Moir explains to Walker that he has written to Johnston and Morton as well. See also Johnston, 1888.
10   WP/PRM, Moir to Tylor, 23 January 1899, Box 2, Folder 2, f. 36–36v.
11   Petch, 2005; Holdsworth.
12   WP/PRM, Moir to Tylor, 21 March 1899, Box 2, Folder 2, f. 45.
13   ibid., 26 November 1900, f. 66v.

14 Tylor, 1890, pp. v–vi.
15 Tylor, 1899, p. ix.
16 ibid., pp. v–vii; Tylor, 1878, p. 195.
17 Tylor, 1890, pp. v–vii.
18 UTAS Correspondence, 'Roth to Walker, 18 October 1891', W9C19_1.
19 In the hope of a more profitable swap, Williamson offered Tylor a skull from the Aboriginal cemetery at Oyster Cove, which Tylor declined—WP/PRM, Correspondence, Williamson to Tylor, 6 August 1893–16 October 1897. Tylor's brother-in-law, the renowned mountaineer Francis Fox Tuckett, visited Williamson in 1895 and described his museum in a letter to Tylor: TP/PRM, 'Correspondence S–Y and Miscellaneous' Tuckett to Tylor, 13 February 1895'. See also Petch, 2005(?).
20 Tylor, 1894; 1895; 1898; 1899; 1900a; 1900b.
21 WP/PRM, Moir to Tylor, 12 May 1905, Box 2, Folder 2, f. 79v.
22 Quoted in Mulvaney, 1990, p. 45.
23 Griffiths, 1996, pp. 25–26.
24 Tylor, 1871, p. 1.
25 Griffiths, 1996, p. 45.
26 Tylor, 1894, p. 148.
27 Stocking quoted by Keen, p. 89.
28 Griffiths, 1996, pp. 10, 45.
29 Darwin, 1871, p. 238.
30 DPE/BM, Wilkinson to Read, 18 April 1901; Read to Wilkinson, 30 May 1901; Outletters 1901.
31 Tylor, 1900a, p. 258.
32 WP/PRM, Moir to Tylor, 14 May 1905; Roth to Tylor, 13 February 1899, both in Box 2, Folder 2, ff. 81v, 41; Roth, 1899, p. 145; MM, Tylor to Roth, 26 February 1899, 27 February 1899, 1 March 1899, all in XVI 'Various MSS'; UTAS, Roth to Walker, 30 May 1899, W9C19_32.
33 Tylor, 1899, p. viii.
34 ibid.; Murray, 1992, p. 735.
35 TP/PRM, Pitt Rivers to Tylor, 7 August 1898.
36 Ibid. Stocking writes that Tylor's last book was based on the Gifford Lectures he presented in 1889 and 1890 and was to be published in 1907; Tylor, 1994, pp. xxiii–xxiv.
37 Stocking refers to printed galleys of some chapters. I have seen only rough drafts in boxes 5 and 10 in TP/PRM. According to a letter to Moir it was to be called *Growth and Spread of Culture*—draft letter by Tylor to Moir, 25 July 1905, WP/PRM, f. 83v.
38 DPE/BM, St George Gray to Read, 29 April 1905.
39 WP/PRM, Moir to Tylor, 12 May 1905, Box 2, Folder 2, f. 80v.
40 Mulvaney, 1990, p. 46.
41 UTAS, 'Quaker Life in Tasmania'.
42 WP/PRM, Westlake to children, 23 December 1908, f. 52.
43 ibid., 4 January 1908, ff. 56, 59.

44   DPE/BM, Wilkinson to Read, 18 April 1901.
45   Griffiths, 1996, pp. 67–73.
46   ibid., pp. 77–78.
47   WP/PRM, Westlake to children, 25 March 1910, f. 52.
48   Lourandos; Bowdler.
49   WP/PRM, Westlake to children, 27 April 1910, f. 232.
50   ibid., 22 April 1910, f. 223v.
51   ibid., 29 May 1910, ff. 245–46.

Collecting memories

1   *The Mercury*, Hobart, 7 December 1908, nla.gov.au/nla.news-article12656953;
    WP/PRM, Westlake to children, 6 December 1908, f. 45v.
2   WP/PRM, Westlake to children, 16 November 1908, f. 40.
3   ibid., 8 June 1910, f. 251v.
4   ibid, 14 and 27 February 1909, ff. 65, 68.
5   WP/PRM, Exercise Book 7, is filled with notes by Joseph Paxton Moir.
6   Rae-Ellis, p. 265, says that Beattie searched for the manuscripts between 1909
    and 1918 but 'failed to locate them'.
7   ML, Westlake to Mitchell Librarian, 11 August 1909, ML 90, 'Inward Letters
    1906–1909'; 28 February 1910, 26 April 1910, ML 91, 'Inward Letters 1910'.
    WP/PRM, Westlake to children, 22 April 1910, f. 226. Westlake also wrote to
    Roth, asking if he would act as valuer, and suggested that they might publish the
    journals together, as well as offering Roth the exclusive rights to do so alone.
    Roth did not seem interested; in a note written next to his copy of Westlake's
    letter in his archive Roth stated, 'I am under the impression that Robinson's
    journal was once offered to Tylor but in such a mysterious way that Tylor
    doubted its authenticity or its completeness. The alleged owner wanted cash
    before delivery, and would not allow it to be seen unless purchased'—MM,
    Letter to Roth from Westlake, 8 March 1910, XVI, 'Various MSS'.
8   Plomley, 1966, p. 3; Johnston and Rolls.
9   ML, Letter to the Mitchell Librarian from Ernest Westlake, 28 February 1910,
    ML 91, Inward Letters 1910.
10 WP/PRM, Westlake to children, 27 February 1909, f. 69v; MM, Letter to Roth
    from Westlake, 8 March 1910, XVI, various MSS.
11 Roth and Walker's extensive correspondence from 1891 to 1899—part of the
    Roth Papers in Manchester Museum—contributed to a much-altered second
    edition of *The Aborigines of Tasmania* including a map of Aboriginal tribal
    boundaries. See also McDougall.
12 Roth, 1899, p. 151. WP/PRM, Westlake, 'Notebook 2', p. 25; WP/PRM lists of
    stone implement collecting sites, Related Documents, 1934.83-86.
13 Roth, 1899, Appendix H, p. 1 xxxix; MM, Walker to Roth, 10 June 1896,
    24 April 1897, 17 October 1897, 1 November 1897, 26 December 1897,
    20 May 1898, XX, 'JBW'.
14 WP/PRM, Westlake to children, 12 December 1908, f. 51.
15 ibid., 6 December 1908 f. 56.

16   MM, Walker to Roth, 24 April 1897, 17 October 1897, 1 November 1897, 26 December 1897, XX, 'JBW'.

17   MM, Walker to Roth, 20 May 1898, 11 June 1898, XX, 'JBW'; UTAS Correspondence, Roth to Walker, 4 August 1898, W9C19_29.

18   MM, Walker to Roth, 30 January 1897, 24 April 1897, 3 October 1897, 20 May 1898, XX, 'JBW'; UTAS Correspondence, Roth to Walker, 15 August 1897, W9C19_18; Harper and Clarke, p. 99.

19   MM, Walker to Roth, 3 October 1897, 20 May 1898, XX, 'JBW'.

20   UTAS, Roth to Walker, 13 April 1898, W9C19_27.

21   MM, Walker to Roth, 3 October 1897, 12 December 1897, XX, 'JBW'; UTAS, Roth to Walker, 23 September 1898, W9C19_31.

22   MM, Walker to Roth, 15 June 1895, XX, 'JBW'; Walker's remarks on Bonwick's *Daily Life of the Tasmanians* are in his 'Notes respecting writers on the Aborigines of Tasmania', XVII, 'Various MSS'.

23   Felton, p. 1; Neil Smith, 'Walker, James Backhouse'.

24   MM, XIII, 'Jas. B. Walker'; UTAS, Roth to Walker, 13 April 1898, W9C19_27; Felton, p. 24; McDougall, p. 51; Griffiths, 1996, pp. 68, 72.

25   MM, Walker to Roth, 14 March 1897, XX, 'JBW'.

26   MM, Walker to Roth, 30 September 1893, XX; Walker to Roth, 24 September 1899, XX, 'JBW'; Tylor to Roth, 14 February 1899, XVI, 'Various MSS'; UTAS, Roth to Walker, 3 August 1895, W9C19_6.

27   MM, Walker to Roth, 14 August 1899, XX, 'JBW'.

28   WP/PRM, SA Hughes to Westlake, 8 December 1908; FB Shandlands to Westlake, 18 November 1908, 'Correspondence 1889–1911', Box 1, Folder 1b, ff. 21–22, 27. Shandlands' name is barely legible in the original and may not be the correct spelling here.

29   Ryan, 2012, pp. 219, 251–56.

30   Westlake, 'Notebook 2', pp. 29, 32.

31   ibid., p. 30. Ryan notes that archaeological research at Oyster Cove shows how the Aboriginal residents 'used bottle glass to make scrapers and collected local stone to make stone artefacts': 2012, p. 259.

32   The translation of the same report in the Tasmanian archives, as noted by Ryan, is different, and perhaps more accurate: '*Parrawa:* "Go away you white buggers"': Ryan, 2012, pp. 106 (n. 1), 370. WP/PRM, Westlake, 'Exercise Book 17', WP/SIS image 14.

33   WP/PRM, Westlake, 'Notebook 2', pp. 38, 40.

34   Gough, pp. 44–45. Westlake took notes from Annie Benbow about the photograph in 'Notebook 2', p. 39.

35   WP/PRM, Westlake, 'Notebook 2', pp. 38, 40.

36   ibid., 'Notebook 6', p. 8.

37   ibid, p. 42.

38   ibid., 'Notebook 4', p. 114.

39   ibid., p. 94.

40   ibid., 'Notebook 5', pp. 48–49, 52.

41   See also Westlake's interviews with Bernard Shaw of Hobart, who told Westlake that 'Natives killed by bushrangers (= escaped convicts) ... take women + that

sort of thing', WP/PRM, 'Notebook 2', p. 9; and Joseph Archer of Launceston, who said, 'no doubt very badly treated especially by whalers who took the ginns', 'Notebook 3', p. 68.

42 Ryan, 2012, pp. 49–51.

43 Bonwick, 1870, p. 35; Turnbull, 1948, p. 34; Elder, 1998, p. 32; Lehman, 1992, p. 45. Lehman tells that 'over a hundred were killed that day', but he subsequently redrafted this publication in the course reading material he wrote for first-year students at the University of Tasmania, in which he estimates about fifty Aborigines were killed. Keith Windschuttle (2002, p. 26) concludes that only three Aborigines were killed, and at least one wounded.

44 Bolger, p. 17.

45 WP/PRM, Westlake, 'Notebook 3', pp. 70, 71.

46 WP/PRM, Westlake to children, 14 March 1909, ff. 64v–65.

47 WP/PRM., Westlake, 'Notebook 3', p. 58.

48 ibid., p. 51.

49 ibid., p. 47.

50 Windschuttle, 2002, p. 26.

51 WP/PRM, 'Notebook 3, p. 70.

52 ibid., p. 58.

53 ibid., 'Notebook 4', pp. 100–101.

54 ibid., p. 4.

55 WP/PRM, Westlake, 'Exercise Book 17', WP/SIS image 12.

56 'Talks with a Naturalist', 1905, published in *Church News*, quoted in WP/PRM, 'Exercise Book 14'.

57 ibid.

58 ibid.

59 WP/PRM, 'Notebook 2', p. 1.

60 ibid.

61 Ryan, 2012, p. 269.

62 Boyce, 2014, p, 109.

63 Ryan, 2012, pp. 269–70.

64 Boyce, 2014, p. 109; McLean, p. 65.

65 Boyce, 2014, p. 109; Condon.

66 Ryan, 2012, pp. 313–14.

67 WP/PRM, Westlake, 'Notebook 2', pp. 2, 5; 'Loose-leaf copy of an Interview with The Reverend Atkinson', 27 November 1908, Box 1, Folder 4a, f. 81a.

Fanny Smith

1 Sections of this chapter (in a different version) have appeared in Taylor, 2016b.

2 While she is widely remembered as 'Fanny Cochrane Smith', she introduced herself as 'Fanny Smith' in the recordings of the songs made in the 1890s, and that is what Westlake and the people he spoke to called her.

3 The benefit concert poster and soap advertisement come from Clinton Mundy who sent them to me in September 2016. They are from Hobart and date from about the 1890s.

4 Barnard, p. 60.

5   McGregor, pp. 51, 53.

6   Barnard Davis; Griffiths, 1996, p. 63; Huxley, p. 18.

7   Roth, 1889, p. 105.

8   Felton, p. 21; McDougall.

9   UTAS, Roth to Walker, 18 October 1891, W9C19_1.

10   Fforde and Hubert, p. 86.

11   MM, Walker to Roth, 20 December 1891, XX, 'JBW'.

12   ibid., 12 March 1893, 30 September 1893.

13   ibid., 23 September 1893.

14   ibid., 12 October 1894.

15   Taylor, 2016a, July 2016.

16   UTAS, Roth to Walker, 3 August 1895, W9/C1/9_14; Roth, 1899, p. 1xxxvi.

17   MM, Beattie to Roth, 2 November 1896, XIX, 'JWB'.

18   MM, Holden to Beattie, 3 January 1897 (mistakenly dated as 1896 by Holden),
     XVI, 'Various MSS', forwarded to Roth, 11 January 1897, XIX, 'JWB'.

19   MM, Geeves to Beattie, 21 October 1896, forwarded to Roth, XIX, 'JWB'.

20   MM, Beattie to Roth, 10 July 1897 (see also 27 February 1897), XIX, 'JWB'.

21   ibid., 4 December 1897.

22   ibid., 27 February 1897; Walker to Roth, 12 December 1897, XX; UTAS, Roth
     to Walker, 14 April(?) 1898, W9C19_25.

23   Roth, 1899, p. ixxxiv.

24   UTAS, Roth to Walker, 14 April(?) 1898, W9C19_25.

25   MM, Walker to Roth, 14 August 1899, XX, 'JBW'.

26   McDougall, pp. 57–58.

27   MM, Walker to Roth, 12 March 1893, 30 September 1893, XX, 'JBW';
     Browne.

28   WP/PRM, Westlake, 'Notebook 6', pp. 54–55.

29   WP/PRM, Westlake to children, 14 May 1910, f. 238.

30   ibid., f. 237.

31   WP/PRM, Westlake to children, 8 June 1910, f. 251v.

32   WP/PRM, Westlake, 'Notebook 6', pp. 54–55, 69, 125.

33   ibid., p. 124. Westlake noted that Joseph Smith called this native potato 'Lerner-
     merners', and Tasman and William Smith referred to them as 'Lúnna-búnnas';
     pp. 69, 54, 61.

34   ibid, pp. 55, 69. For references to 'tooreēla', see pp. 61, 64, 79, 120, 124.

35   ibid., pp. 124, 61, 55, 58.

36   ibid., pp. 63, 68, 72 (from Flora Stanton, Mary Miller and William Smith).

37   ibid., pp. 63, 72, 73.

38   ibid, p. 72.

39   ibid., pp. 66, 67.

40   ibid., p. 54.

41   Colleen Mundy's description of basket making features in a permanent
     exhibition at the Tasmanian Museum and Art Gallery.

42   WP/PRM, Westlake, 'Notebook 6', p. 56. Clinton Mundy requested that his
     Uncle Walter's story about Truganini be included in this chapter. Clinton

has been telling it for many years. He says his Uncle Walter should always be acknowledged as its teller.

43 WP/PRM, 'Notebook 6', p. 79.

44 ibid.

45 ibid., p. 75.

46 ibid., p. 92.

47 Plomley 2008, pp. 399–400, 406, 425, 432, 433, 435, 497, 500, 503, 895, 926; Taylor, 2016a, August 2016; Gantevoort. See also Gantevoort et al.

48 Clinton Mundy read this chapter, and other sections of this book.

49 WP/PRM, Westlake, 'Notebook 6', pp. 66, 67, 72, 77, 78, 83. Westlake's symbols and pronunciation are hard to reproduce in text. He has added 'gn?' under the first 'n' in 'withanunny'. It helps to see his original notes for Tasman's song on p. 83 (WP/SIS, Image 44, WEST00006, series 3).

50 ibid, p. 83.

51 ibid, p. 74.

52 For variations of 'carni', see Plomley, 1976, p. 399, palawa kani is the Tasmanian Aboriginal language program in the Tasmanian Aboriginal Centre: tacinc.com. au/programs/palawa-kani.

53 WP/PRM, Westlake, 'Notebook 6', pp. 62–63.

54 ibid., pp. 56–57.

55 ibid., p. 119.

56 ibid., pp. 74, 80, 58.

57 ibid., pp. 71, 75; WP/PRM, Westlake to children, 22 May 1910, f. 239.

58 WP/PRM, Westlake, 'Notebook 6', pp. 71, 80.

59 WP/PRM, Westlake to children, 14 and 22 May 1910, ff. 237, 239v.

60 ibid., 22 May 1910, f. 240. See also Backhouse.

61 WP/PRM, Westlake, 'Notebook 6', pp. 92–93.

62 MM, Holden to Beattie, 3 January 1897 (mistakenly dated as 1896 by Holden), XVI, 'Various MSS', forwarded to Roth, 11 January 1897, XIX, 'JWB'.

63 'Port Cygnet', *The Mercury*, 4 May 1889, Trove, trove.nla.gov.au/ndp/del/article/9211556.

64 Clark, 'Smith, Fanny Cochrane (1834–1905)'.

65 Taylor, 2016a, August 2016.

66 WP/PRM, Westlake, 'Notebook 6', pp. 94–97.

67 MM, Beattie to Roth, 4 December 1897, XIX, 'JWB'.

68 WP/PRM, Westlake, 'Notebook 6', p. 64.

69 Clinton Mundy prefers to use a capital 'L' for Layrappenthe Country. He also wrote to me that Tanganooturra's names vary. They include Dinudara, Ploorernelle, Tibb, Tarenootairrer, Tingnooterrunne, Jackanoothara, Sarah and more. Her name was recorded as Tanganooturra by her great-granddaughters, Pearl Mundy and Dot Heffernan in 1971. The palawa kani language program of the Tasmanian Aboriginal Centre has reconstructed her name as Tanganutara. Taylor, 2016a, August 2016.

70 WP/PRM, Westlake to children, 8 June 1910, f. 252.

71 WP/PRM, Westlake, 'Notebook 6', p. 82.

72   WP/PRM, Westlake to children, 22 May 1910, f. 240v.
73   Plomley, 1991(?), p. 8.
74   WP/PRM, Westlake, 'Notebook 6', pp. 66, 67, 72, 77, 78, 83.
75   ibid., p. 75.
76   ibid., p. 82, as written down while talking to Frederick Smith. Westlake noted
     this phrase as 'neena toolabri my carni' from Gus Smith, and 'nēēna toonábri my
     cárne' from William Smith, pp. 79, 61.
77   WP/PRM, Westlake to children, 14 May 1910, f. 237.
78   Taylor, 2016a, August 2016.
79   Clinton is quoting family members from the past.
80   Bert Mundy's full name was Bert Herbert Tasman Mundy, named after his
     Uncle Herb Smith and Grandfather Tas Smith.
81   Taylor, 2016a, August and October.
82   Libby Lester, 'Aborigines Find Rallying Point', *Sunday Examiner*, 19 January
     1986.
83   WP/PRM, Westlake to children, 22 May 1910, f. 241.

The Islanders
 1   WP/PRM, Westlake to children, 14 February 1909, ff. 64–64v.
 2   WP/PRM, Westlake, 'Notebook 3', p. 43. In 1898 Cook interviewed Fanny
     Smith in Port Cygnet and the transcript dated June 1898 was copied by
     Westlake from Beattie's papers into 'Exercise Book 4', WP/SIS image 9.
 3   WP/PRM, Stephens to Westlake, 5 February 1909, 'Loose items taken from
     Notebook 6', Folder 4a, f. 81b.
 4   Roth, 1899, pp. 176–77.
 5   MM, Walker to Roth, 3 October 1897, XX, 'JBW'.
 6   Walker thought there were only about three 'native' necklaces left in the colony:
     ibid., 30 January 1897.
 7   UTAS, Roth to Walker, 6 May 1897, W9C19_15.
 8   WP/PRM, Westlake, 'Notebook 3', pp. 63–70.
 9   WP/PRM, Westlake to children, 7 February 1909, f. 61.
10   Cameron, pp. ix, 97, 122, 154.
11   ibid., pp. ix, 101–108.
12   ibid., pp. ix, xii, 130.
13   WP/PRM, Westlake, 'Notebook 3', pp. 73, 76.
14   ibid, pp. 79–80.
15   ibid., 'Notebook 4', p. 21.
16   ibid., 'Notebook 3', pp. 79–80.
17   ibid, pp. 81–84.
18   ibid., pp. 74–75.
19   WP/PRM, Westlake to children, 14 February 1909, ff. 67–67v.
20   Cameron, p. 44.
21   ibid.
22   ibid., pp. 95–96; Ryan 1996, p. 67.
23   Cameron, quoting Ryan (1996, p. 67), p. 96.

24 *Hobart Town Gazette*, 26 August 1826. For a more extensive discussion of this and other related historical sources, see Taylor, 2008c, pp. 44–58.

25 West, p. 274.

26 Clark, p. 187.

27 Blainey, pp. 106–107.

28 Molony, p. 31.

29 Hughes, p. 333.

30 Windschuttle, 2002, pp. 317, 386.

31 Clements, pp. 193–95.

32 ibid., pp. 198–203.

33 Taylor, 2016a, August 2016.

34 Ryan 1996, p. 257.

35 ibid., p. 71.

36 Cameron, p. ix.

37 Boyce, 2008, p. 19.

38 Russell, p. 133.

39 Cameron, p. 120.

40 Cameron, pp. 108, 122.

41 MM, Beattie to Roth, 22 September 1893, XIX, 'JWB'.

42 Tindale, 1953.

43 Tindale 1936–1965, p. 95.

44 By the 1940s Birdsell had abandoned his theories of racial classification because he found them scientifically untenable and because he was horrified by the realisation of these theories in the Holocaust: Anderson, p. 234.

45 Tindale 1936–1965, p. 69. Plomley echoes this sentiment in his introduction to *The Westlake Papers*, writing that the Islanders were a 'community of European Christian peasants, having the strengths and weaknesses of such people', p. 8.

46 Tindale 1936–1965, p. 95.

47 Cameron identifies the Aboriginal name of Cliff Everett's ancestor, p. 136.

48 Tindale 1936–1965, p. 119.

49 ibid., p. 117.

50 AJ Campbell, Dr Charles Ryan and Captain SA White were also part of Mattingley's expedition. Charles Ryan expressed a concern regarding the health of the Islanders, but it seems more likely that Captain White requested the Aboriginal words. White had not only recorded words from other Aborigines in an expedition to Oodnadatta, but he reputably had an authoritarian attitude that may have offended the Islanders; telephone conversations with Libby Robin, 7 March 2004 and 9 December 2004; Robin, pp. 26–28, 366; McCarthy; 'Death of AHE Mattingley', *Wild Life*, November 1950, p. 496.

51 Tindale 1936–1965, field notebooks, p. 121.

52 Taylor, 2003, pp. 45–46.

53 Ryan, 2012, p. 288.

54 ibid., p. 292.

55 Taylor, 2003, pp. 4, 6.

56 WP/PRM, Westlake, 'Notebook 3', p. 88.

57 WP/PRM, Letter to children, (no day) February 1909, f. 66v.
58 ibid., 27 February 1909, ff. 70v-72.
59 WP/PRM, Letter to children, 27 February 1909, f. 70v. This is a paraphrase from Chapter XIII, Book of Isaiah, Old Testament.
60 The name 'Victoria' comes from 'West, Ida'.
61 WP/PRM, Westlake, Tasmanian Notebook 4, p. 20.
62 WP/PRM, Westlake to children, 21 March 1909, ff. 78–78v.
63 ibid., 14 and 21 March 1909, ff. 75 v, 78–78v.
64 ibid., 14 March 1909, f. 76.
65 ibid., 12 July 1909, f. 119.

Photographing stones

1   WP/PRM, Westlake to children, 14 March 1909, f. 77. Westlake photographed 230 artefacts. He noted The Reverend Wilkinson had 'lent' him 255 implements, but this was in order to photograph, not to take to England: 'Notebook 6', p. 8.
2   WP/PRM, Westlake to children, 14 February 1909, f. 65.
3   ibid., 21 November 1909, f. 182.
4   ibid., 21 March 1909, ff. 78v–79; 5 April 1909, f. 82v; 27 April 1909, f. 89.
5   ibid., 5 April 1909, ff. 82–82v.
6   MM, Tylor to Roth, 27 February 1899, XVIII.
7   WP/PRM, Westlake to children, 23 May 1909, f. 100v.
8   ibid., 27 April 1909, f. 89v. Carbon arc light in ibid., 27 April, 21 November 1909, f. 181.
9   ibid., 31 May 1909, f. 102. The cards included the fields for their collection location, the type of rock, colour, the type and angle of fracture and size. There was also a shorthand description, seemingly of Westlake's own devising, in which letters indicated the tool's shape; for example, H = hollow, R–B = round-backed. On the reverse of each card was the traced outline of the stone implement to indicate its actual size. The entire collection of photographs can be viewed at WP/SIS series 8, 9 and 10. Plomley identified fifty of Westlake's photographs as of artefacts in the Wilkinson collection, which had been acquired earlier by the Museum: Plomley, 1991(?), p. 5.
10 WP/PRM, Westlake to children, 5 April 1909, f. 81v.
11 ibid., 24 September 1909, f. 150.
12 ibid., (no day) October 1909, f. 161.
13 ibid., 9 August 1909, f. 133.
14 ibid., 21 November 1909, f. 182v.
15 ibid., f. 181v.
16 ibid., 21 November 1909, f. 183.
17 ibid., 25 July 1909, f. 125.
18 Davis, 1986; WP/PRM, Westlake to children, 9 August 1909, ff. 133–34.
19 WP/PRM Westlake to children, 25 July 1909, f. 126–27.
20 ibid. 28 November 1909, f. 186.
21 ibid., 5 April 1909, f. 82v; 21 November 1909, f. 181v.

Such sweepings

1 WP/PRM, Westlake to children, 8 June 1910, f. 251v.
2 WP/PRM, 'Notebook 6', pp. 130–31; Westlake to children, 8 June 1910, f. 253.
3 Ryan, 2012, p. 112.
4 ibid., pp. 19, 27, 39.
5 ibid., pp. 74–75, 89, 100, 103–104.
6 Reynolds, 2004, p. 53, quoted by Ryan, 2012, p. 112.
7 Ryan, 2012, pp. 180, 243.
8 WP/PRM, Westlake, 'Exercise book 10', WP/SIS image 13.
9 ibid.
10 WP/PRM, Westlake to children, 8 June 1910, f. 251v.
11 ibid., f. 254.
12 Reynolds, 2004, p. 1.
13 ibid.
14 Reynolds, 2011, p. vi.
15 MM, Beattie to Roth, 12 March 1897, XIX, 'JWB'; Walker to Roth, 14 and 27 March 1897, XX. UTAS, Roth to Walker, 6 May 1897, W9C19_15.
16 Roth, 1899, p. 151.
17 WP/PRM, Westlake, 'Notebook 2', p. 25; WP/PRM lists of stone implement collecting sites, Related Documents, 1934.83-86.
18 Roth, 1899, p. 151.
19 WP/PRM, Westlake to children, 8 June 1910, f. 255.
20 ibid., ff. 253–56.
21 ibid., 16 June 1910, f. 261v.
22 ibid., 22 May 1910, f. 245v.
23 ibid., 16 June 1910, f. 257.
24 ibid., ff. 257v–258.
25 RAI, 1910; 1912.
26 WP/PRM, Westlake to children, 8 June 1910, f. 252v.
27 ibid., 16 June 1910, f. 258.
28 ibid, 11 November 1908, ff. 37–37v.
29 WP/PRM, Westlake, 'Notebook 4', p. 120.
30 Taylor, 2000a.
31 Taylor, 2000b; Edgell, 1992, pp. 10–11.

Going home

1 WP/PRM, Westlake to children, 22 April 1910, f. 228.
2 WP/OUMNH, 'Ernest Westlake's notes and correspondence: Woldringham Sanatorium plans, 1913', Folder: II.3 (WP/SIS, image 21, WEST00361, Series 15).
3 Jean Westlake, 1982, pp. 28–29.
4 WP/PRM, Westlake to children, 29 May 1910, ff. 245–46.
5 WP/PRM, Moir to Westlake, Box 3, Folder 1, 21 August 1910, f. 2.
6 ibid, 14 January 1911, f. 14; 2 April 1911, f. 18.
7 ibid., 14 January 1911, ff. 10–14.

8   ibid., 2 April 1911, f. 18; 5 June 1911, f. 22; 7 August 1911, f. 29.
9   Jean Westlake, 1982, p. 29.
10   ibid., pp. 29–31.
11   WP/PRM, Moir to Westlake, 14 January 1912, Box 3, Folder 1, ff. 35–36.
12   ibid., 8 July 1912, f. 55; 5 August 1912, ff. 58–59.
13   WP/OUMNH, 'Ernest Westlake's notes and correspondence: Woldringham Sanatorium plans, 1913', Folder II.3.
14   ibid.
15   ibid.
16   ibid.
17   Jean Westlake, 1982, pp. 38–39.
18   ibid.
19   WP/PRM, Memorandum to Ernest Westlake from Port of London Authority, 4 June 1915, Box 3, Folder 2, f. 44.
20   ibid., FA Bather to Westlake, 17 June 1916, f. 60
21   WP/PRM, Secretary of George Wheatley & Co. to Westlake, 9 June 1915; draft letter to Secretary of George Wheatley & Co. from Westlake, June 1915, both in Box 3, Folder 2, ff. 40–42.
22   Aubrey Westlake, 1956, pp. 4–5.

A new order

1   Aubrey Westlake, 1956, pp. 4–5.
2   Aubrey Westlake, 1956, p. 5.
3   Carpenter, 1891, p. 1; WP/PRM, Westlake to children, no date (early November 1909).
4   Hardy, p. 215.
5   WP/PRM, Westlake to children, 19 September 1909.
6   Aubrey Westlake, 1979, p. 3; Edgell, pp. 21–23.
7   ibid., Westlake, p. 7; Edgell, p. 24.
8   Edgell, pp. 28–30; Evans, pp. 47–48; Hutton, p. 163.
9   Taylor, 2000a.
10   Hutton, p. 166.
11   Order of Woodcraft Chivalry, pp. 58–60.
12   Seton accepted the Grand Master invitation in 1917, but later wrote to Ernest and Aubrey Westlake that he needed to gain confirmation of this role from his Council, Edgell, pp. 35–36.
13   Order of Woodcraft Chivalry, p. 46.
14   ibid., p. 18.
15   Jean Westlake, 1982, p. 24.
16   Evans, p. 50–51; Scott and Bromley, p. 153.
17   Scott and Bromley, p. 153.
18   James, p. 79; Scott and Bromley, p. 153.
19   Aubrey Westlake, 1979, pp. 6–7.
20   Order of Woodcraft Chivalry, pp. 3–4; Aubrey Westlake, 1979, pp. 6–7.
21   Edgell, p. 21; Scott and Bromley, p. 152.

22 Aubrey Westlake, 1933; Scott and Bromley, p. 152; Westlake, c. 1922, p. 12.

23 Edgell, p. 21; Scott and Bromley, p. 152.

24 Aubrey Westlake, 1956, pp. 7–9

25 Richard Westlake, pp. 2–3; Westlake, 1889, pp. 10, 6, 12.

26 Jean Westlake, 1982, p. 41.

27 ibid., pp. 42–43. Rake remained the sole occupant, but for his servants, until his death in 1947. Oaklands was bequeathed to Aubrey, but only for the amount Rake paid for it. Death duties demanded Aubrey pay the difference between his bequest and the property's actual value. Forced to sell, Aubrey undertook some essential renovations, by which time the market had fallen and he sold at a loss. See also Jean Westlake, 2000, p. 10.

28 Jean Westlake, 1989, p. 24; 2000, pp. 21–22.

29 Seton, p. 9.

30 Aubrey Westlake, 1979, p. 9; Westlake, 1927, p. 20.

31 Aubrey Westlake, 1956, pp. 4–5.

32 ibid., p. 6.

33 Order of Woodcraft Chivalry, p. 3; Westlake, c. 1922, p. 10.

34 Seton, p. 8.

35 WP/PRM, Letter to Aubrey Westlake from Donald Baden-Powell, 14 January 1963 (copy in WP/OUMNH), f. 11; WP/PRM, 'Biographical Notes on Ernest Westlake', 13 August 1976, both kept in Box 1, Folder 2b.

36 Aubrey Westlake, 1956, p. 5.

37 Order of Woodcraft Chivalry, pp. 58–60.

38 WP/PRM, Westlake, 'Notebook 2', p. 49; 'Notebook 5', pp. 53–54.

39 ibid., 'Notebook 1', pp. 1–2; 'Notebook 2', p. 42; 'Notebook 3', p. 74. There are other references to this: Thomas Dunabin thought the Aborigines 'could see remarkably well—could track an animal where white man couldn't see any sign', 'Notebook 4', p. 110; Eliza Brownlow thought the Aborigines had 'very keen hearing', 'Notebook 6', p. 100; Thomas Riley said they had 'very sharp eyesight and hearing (the tame blacks)', 'Notebook 4', p. 108; George Davis thought the Aborigines were 'very quick in the hearing and sight', 'Notebook 6', p. 29; Mrs Elmer also thought the Aborigines had better sight than whites, which explained why they were employed as whalers; 'Notebook 6', p. 46.

40 WP/PRM, Letter to children, 22 August 1909, f. 135v.

41 Margaret Westlake, p. 17.

42 PW/PRM, Letters to children, 30 October 1908, f. 31v; 13 March 1910, ff. 211–211v.

43 Westlake, 1921b, p. 25.

44 Westlake, 'The Forest School', p. 10; Jean Westlake, 2000, p. 21.

45 Westlake, 1927, p. 17.

46 Quoted in Hutton, p. 166.

47 Harrison, 1908, pp. 444–45.

48 ibid.

49 Westlake, 1927, pp. 9, 17.

50 WP/PRM, Letter to children, 22 May 1910, f. 240v.

51   ibid., 14 and 22 May 1910, ff. 237, 240–240v.
52   Carpentier, p. 55.
53   WP/PRM, Letter to children, no date (c. early November 1909) f. 174.
54   Aubrey Westlake, 1956, p. 5.
55   ibid., p. 5; Westlake, 1910; Taylor, 2000b, p. 66.
56   Westlake, 1910, p. 5.
57   WP/PRM, Letter to children, no date (c. November 1909), f. 174.
58   WP/PRM, Letter to children, 13 March 1910, f. 212 v: 'I wish my study hadn't taken me so far away—I must get through with it, and take to something such as the ghostly world which is nearer to hand, or can at any rate be best done in Europe.'
59   Aubrey Westlake, 1979, p. 4.
60   Evans, p. 48.
61   Aubrey Westlake, 1979, p. 7; Hardy, pp. 218, 221; Scott and Bromley, p. 153.
62   Hardy, p. 220.
63   Fowler, p. 20; Jeffries, p. 53.
64   Hardy, pp. 223–24.
65   Hutton, p. 163; Hardy, p. 225.
66   Hutton, p. 163.
67   Aubrey Westlake, 1956, p. 9.
68   WP/OUMNH, Letter to Aubrey Westlake from Ernest Westlake, 11 November 1920, Box 1, Folder 1.4.
69   Westlake, 1921a, parts 1–4, c. 1912.
70   Letter to Aubrey Westlake from Henry Savage, no date, Jean Westlake's papers.
71   Letter to Ernest Westlake from George Allen, 9 May 1913, found between the pages of 'About Snakes', Jean Westlake's papers.
72   Edgell, p. 168.
73   Margaret Westlake, 1918.
74   Taylor, 2000a.
75   Westlake, 1910, p. 35.
76   Taylor, 2000b.
77   Jean Westlake, 1982, p. 43.
78   Taylor, 2000a.
79   ibid.
80   Jean Westlake, 2000, p. 22; Order of Woodcraft Chivalry, 1923b.
81   Jean Westlake, 2000, p. 11; Order of Woodcraft Chivalry, 1923a.

In his wake

1   Aubrey transferred ownership of Godshill to Margaret: Jean Westlake, 2000, p. 22.
2   ibid; Aubrey Westlake, 1979, pp. 10–11.
3   Hutton, pp. 166–67; see also Aubrey Westlake, 1979, p. 11.
4   Jeffries, pp. 53–54.
5   Scott and Bromley, p. 156; Jean Westlake, 2000, pp. 28–32.
6   De Abaitua, pp. 174–75.
7   Hutton, pp. 168–69; Scott and Bromley, pp. 156–57; Aubrey Westlake, 1979, p. 20.

8   Hardy, p. 224; Scott and Bromley, pp. 154–57, 203; Aubrey Westlake, 1979, pp. 54–56; MacMurray et al.

9   Scott and Bromley, pp. 157, 204–206.

10 Hardy, pp. 223–24.

11 ibid., pp. 165–67.

12 Jean Westlake, 1979, pp. 114–15, 136.

13 Hutton, pp. 169–70.

14 Jean Westlake, 1979, pp. 190–93.

15 WP/OUMNH, WJ Sollas to Aubrey Westlake, 11 September 1923; Aubrey Westlake to WJ Sollas, 10 September 1923. Sollas had successfully outbid another contestant, Mr Crawley of Kent, who wrote to Aubrey barely a month after Westlake's death requesting to buy at least part of Westlake's French collection. Despite writing twice more, and being supported by at least one letter from HP Blackmore, an 'old friend' of Westlake's, as he described himself, Crawley never got any of the French eoliths: Mr Crawley to Aubrey Westlake, 6 December 1923; 19 November 1922; 12 April 1923; HP Blackmore to Sidney Rake, 2 April 1923; HP Blackmore to Aubrey Westlake, 16 April 1923.

16 WP/PRM, Aubrey Westlake to Henry Balfour, 3 September 1923, Box 1, Folder 2b, f. 1.

17 WP/OUMNH, Westlake to Aubrey Westlake, 11 November 1920.

18 WP/OUMNH, Sollas to Westlake, 18 March 1922.

19 WP/OUMNH, Sollas to 'Mrs Charman' (Margaret Westlake), 28 August 1923; 31 August 1923. Either Sollas assumed Margaret's name was Mrs Charman or Margaret took the name out of conventionality, but she did not formally marry Tom Charman.

20 Sollas, 1924, p. 98.

21 WP/OUMNH, Sollas to Aubrey Westlake, 12 December 1926.

22 WP/OUMNH, JA Douglas to Aubrey Westlake, 1 November 1936.

23 WP/OUMNH, J Reid Moir to Aubrey Westlake, 27 January 1937.

24 Reid Moir argued in 1911 that stone tools from the Crag deposit at Suffolk were pre-Palaeolithic, a claim supported by eminent evolutionary biologist Sir E Ray Lankester; Grayson, pp. 106–107; Daniel, p. 231; Baden-Powell, p. 219.

25 WP/OUMNH, Reid Moir to Aubrey Westlake, 27 January 1937; 23 January 1937.

26 ibid., 3 February, 12 February, 20 April, 11 May, 17 June, 20 June 1937; Donald Baden-Powell to Aubrey Westlake, 14 September 1937.

27 ibid., 8 August, 16 August 1937, 10 February, 15 February, 10 November, 18 November 1938.

28 ibid., 23 March, 23 May 1939.

29 ibid., 8 November 1939.

30 WP/PRM, Aubrey Westlake to Derek Roe, 5 January 1977, Related Documents, 1934.83–86.

31 WP/PRM, Westlake, Letters to children, (no day) October 1908, ff. 6, 10v; 17 October 1908, f. 20-20v.

32 WP/OUMNH, G Maynard to Aubrey Westlake, 21 January, 29 January, 4 September, 8 December 1947, 14 December 1948, 25 January 1949, 9 May 1950; Baden-Powell to Aubrey Westlake, 14 January 1963, copy in WP/PRM; P Burkitt to Aubrey Westlake, 12 May 1950.

33 WP/OUMNH, Maynard to Aubrey Westlake, 14 June 1950.

34 WP/OUMNH, Baden-Powell to Aubrey Westlake, 15 November 1952.

35 ibid., 24 May 1953, 10 January 1955.

36 ibid., 10 June 1955.

37 WP/OUMNH, Baden-Powell to Aubrey Westlake, 10 June 1959, copy in WP/ PRM.

38 WP/OUMNH, Aubrey Westlake to Baden-Powell, 17 June, 30 December 1959; 6 February, 23 February 1961; 17 December 1962; 6 February 1963; Baden-Powell to Aubrey Westlake, 13 January 1960, 20 February 1961, 14 January 1963, copies in WP/PRM.

39 WP/OUMNH, Baden-Powell to Aubrey Westlake, 28 June 1963.

40 ibid., 30 November 1967, copy in WP/PRM, Related Documents, 1934.83–86.

41 ibid., Derek Roe to Aubrey Westlake, 19 January 1977.

42 ibid., Ray Inskeep to Aubrey Westlake, 22 January 1977.

43 ibid., Aubrey Westlake to Roe, 21 September 1977.

44 ibid., Roe note to Inskeep, (no day) September 1977.

45 ibid., Inskeep to Curator, OUMNH, 18 October 1977.

46 ibid., David Vincent to Inskeep, 26 October 1977.

47 ibid., Aubrey Westlake to Bryan Cranstone, 4 December 1979; Cranstone to Aubrey Westlake, 26 November, 10 December 1979.

48 ibid., Aubrey Westlake to Cranstone, 3 January 1980.

49 ibid., Roe to Aubrey Westlake, 14 February 1980; Roe, pp. 214–20.

50 Justin Delair to Rebe Taylor, 28 August 2000, personal collection.

51 WP/OUMNH, F Hodson to Aubrey Westlake, 21 February, 24 February, 8 March 1961. The collection was kept in the Oxford University Museum's Newnham Church store in 2000.

52 WP/OUMNH, Delair to Aubrey Westlake, 21 January, 17 May 1981, 27 January 1982.

53 ibid., 28 March 1984.

54 Jean Westlake, 2000, p. 194.

55 Delair to Taylor, 28 August 2000, personal collection.

56 ibid., 15 October 2001.

57 Larson.

58 WP/OUMNH, Henry Balfour to Aubrey Westlake, 4 September, 7 October 1923.

59 ibid., 22 May, 22 July 1924.

60 Balfour, 1925, p. 2.

61 ibid., pp. 3–14. The Mousterian flint industry, discovered in Le Moustier in the Dordogne in 1909, was a Middle Palaeolithic Neanderthal technique. The Aurignacian flint industry, named after a cave site discovered in Aurignac in 1860, was Upper Palaeolithic. It was the work of Cro Magnon, the first modern humans of Europe dating back 25,000 to 35,000 years.

62 See 'Collecting stones' chapter; Mulvaney, 1990, p. 46.
63 Balfour, 1929, p. 315.
64 WP/PRM, Aubrey Westlake Letter to Balfour, 17 August 1926, Box 1, Folder 2b, f. 4.
65 WP/OUMNH, Balfour to Aubrey Westlake, 30 November 1924.
66 WP/PRM, Aubrey Westlake to Balfour, 11 December 1926, Box 1, Folder 2b.
67 WP/OUMNH, Balfour to Aubrey Westlake, 8 August 1926.
68 ibid., 14 December 1926.
69 ibid., 18 October 1931.
70 ibid., 7 January 1934.
71 Balfour Papers/PRM, Henry Balfour, 'Stone Implements of the Natives of Tasmania', 1939, Box 6; TK Penniman and B Blackwood, 'Editorial Note', to Balfour 1939, kept with the manuscript, p. 3 (WP/SIS, WEST00334, Series 14).
72 WP/PRM, TK Penniman to Aubrey Westlake, 14 October 1939, Box 1, Folder 2b.
73 WP/PRM, Westlake to children, 4 January 1909, f. 59.

Below the surface

1   WP/PRM, Rhys Jones to Derek Roe, 3 May 1966, Related Documents, 1934.83-86.
2   ibid.
3   Jones, 1971, p. 39.
4   ibid., pp. 31–32.
5   ibid. Jones is quoting from Tylor, 1899, p. ix.
6   Mulvaney, 1990; Mulvaney and Kamminga, p. 15. Part of this chapter has appeared in Taylor, 2014.
7   Murray, 1998, p. 1.
8   Jones, 1999, pp. 41, 48–49.
9   Douglas, p. 153; Tuniz, et al., pp. 41–44.
10 Jones and Megaw, p. 21; Jones, 1995, pp. 432–33.
11 Roberts, et al.; Jones, 1999, pp. 37–65, 48–49; Roberts, 2001.
12 Roberts, 2001, pp. 91–92.
13 Jones, 1969; Mulvaney, 2001, p. 20; Flannery, 2001; Gammage, pp. 3, 11.
14 Jose, p. 354; Douglas, p. 158.
15 Griffiths, 2000.
16 Jones, 1999, p. 40.
17 Jones and Megaw, p. 15.
18 Griffiths, 1996, p. 92; Griffiths and Bonyhady, p. 6; Mulvaney and Kamminga, p. 15; Jones, 1999, p. 41.
19 Meehan, pp. 8–9.
20 Mulvaney, 2001, p. 19.
21 Jones, 1971, pp. 62–63; Howitt; Griffiths, 1996, p. 72.
22 Griffiths, 1996, p. 72.
23 Wood Jones, p. 11.
24 Jones, 1971, pp. 36–43.
25 WP/PRM, 'Notebook 3', p. 49.

26   Noetling had told Westlake the caves were 'practically untouched', but warned
      only a 'wealthy' man could dig them as one would need a labourer and to pay for
      his keep: WP/PRM, Westlake to children, 7 February 1909; see also 10 February
      1909, 6 April, 22 April 1910, f. 222v. Rocky Cape is listed among the sites from
      which Westlake's stone artefacts were collected: WP/PRM, Related Documents,
      1934.83–86.
27   Jones, 1971, pp. 48–52; Tindale, 1937–41.
28   Mulvaney, 1990, p. 48.
29   Jones and Smith: 1: 2/5 - RJ: 1: 2/7.
30   Jones, 1999, p. 41.
31   Jones and Smith, RJ: 1: 2/5.
32   Jones, 1971, p. 58.
33   Jones and Smith, RJ: 1: 1/2.
34   ibid.; Jones and Megaw, p. 15.
35   Jones and Smith, RJ: 3: 1/5 - RJ: 3: 1/7.
36   ibid, RJ: 2: 1/1.
37   Jones and Meehan, p. 40.
38   Jones and Smith, RJ: 2: 1/3.
39   Jones and Megaw, p. 8; Jones and Meehan, pp. 44, 51.
40   Jones, 1995, pp. 426, 428.
41   Jones and Smith, RJ: 2: 2/5.
42   Jones, 1971, pp. v, 627–28.
43   Jones, 1978, pp. 26–27. For a more detailed discussion on the question of scaled
      fishing in Tasmania, see Taylor, 2007, McFarlane and Johnson and McFarlane.
44   ibid., 44–46; Jones, 1987, p. 38; 1977b, p. 196; 1977a, p. 343.
45   Jones, 1971, pp. 603, 620.
46   Horton; White with O'Connell, p. 170.
47   Diamond; Flannery, 1994, pp. 264–70.
48   Jones and Megaw, p. 24.
49   Jones, 1978, p. 41.
50   Jones, 1977b, p. 197.
51   Jones, 1971, p. 36.
52   Edgell states that Westlake had read the 1890 edition of Roth's *The Aborigines of
      Tasmania* 'even before touching foot on Tasmanian soil', p. 10. Westlake's notes,
      most likely made before he left Tasmania in 1908, include the full reference
      for the second edition (1899) of Roth's book with the note, 'This work is most
      important': WP/PRM, 'Exercise Book 17', WP/SIS, image 4.
53   Jones, 1978, pp. 16–18; Roth, 1899, p. 88.
54   WP/PRM, 'Notebook 3', pp. 63–65.
55   ibid., p. 86.
56   McFarlane, p. 13; Johnson and McFarlane, p. 46; Plomley, 1983, p. 206.
57   Jones, 1974, pp. 319–21; Plomley, 1966, p. 35; Hiatt, p. 101.
58   WP/PRM, 'Notebook 3', p. 86. Fanny Smith's children and acquaintances told
      Westlake how she caught freshwater trout by 'tickling' the fish, although they
      suggested this method was learned from her husband who was from Kent,

England, where the practice was used. See WP/PRM, 'Notebook 6', pp. 31, 56, 122–23.

59   Tindale, Field notebooks, p. 119.
60   Brown, 2003.
61   Johnson and McFarlane, pp. 48–49.
62   Jones, 1978, p. 46; Jones, 1995, p. 428; Dunnett.
63   Jones, 1977b, p. 196. For a more detailed discussion of fire making, see Taylor 2008b.
64   Plomley, 2008, p. 599.
65   Milligan, p. 274; Dove, p. 250; Backhouse, p. 99; Fenton, p. 94; Calder, quoted by Roth, 1899, p. 83.
66   WP/PRM, 'Notebook 3', pp. 87–88.
67   Westlake sketched the stick and groove in his notebook: ibid., p. 87.
68   Roth, 1899, pp. lxxxxviii, 83–84; Taylor, 2008b, pp. 7–9; Walker, 1900, p. 5; MM, Walker to Roth, 10 June 1896, 20 May 1898 and 16 May 1899, XX, 'JBW'; Rayner to Walker (copied by Walker for Roth), 20 April 1898, XXVV.
69   WP/PRM, 'Notebook 3', p. 87.
70   Ryan, 1985, p. 51.
71   Taylor, 2007; Taylor, 2008b.
72   Ryan, 1985, p. 51.
73   Turnbull; Bonwick.
74   Curthoys, pp. 235, 239–40. For a more detailed discussion of the idea of genocide and extinction in Tasmanian history, see Taylor, 2013.
75   Jones, 1971, pp. 2, 8–9.
76   Meehan, pp. 3, 13.
77   Jones, 1990b.
78   Jones, 1985, p. 185.
79   Schrire, 2001, p. 30.
80   Jones, 1977b, pp. 202–203.
81   Schrire, 2001, p. 28.
82   Taylor, interviews with Rhys Jones, Australian National University, 1998–2000.

'On our land'
1   Allen, p. 46.
2   Haydon, 1978. Sections of this chapter (with alterations) appeared in Taylor, 2012.
3   Schrire, 2001, p. 27.
4   Smith, Bernard, p. 10.
5   Ryan, 1997, pp. 161–65.
6   Onsman, p. 45.
7   Ryan, 1997, p. 153.
8   Reynolds, 2004, pp. 203–204.
9   Perera, p. 407.
10   Coetzee, pp. 202–203.
11   Curthoys, pp. 240–41.

12   Taylor, 2013, p. 410.
13   Ronin Films.
14   Tippet, Gary, 1978, 'Our Own Awful Holocaust', *The Sun*, 3 October; *Workers News*, 1978, 'Genocide: How Capitalism Annihilated the Entire Race of the Tasmanian Aborigines', 6 July; *TV Times*, 1978, 'Sheer Bloody Murder!', 30 September.
15   Curthoys, pp. 242–47; Boyce, 2008, pp. 295–96, Ryan, 2012, pp. 144–45; Ryan, 1996, p. 255; Reynolds, 2001, pp. 29–85.
16   Windschuttle, 2000 and 2002.
17   Davidson, p. 310.
18   Onsman, p. 40, paraphrasing Flanagan, 2002.
19   Haydon, 1979, p. 12.
20   Perera, pp. 397–98.
21   Mansell, p. 2.
22   WP/PRM, 'Notebook 3', p. 88.
23   Langford, p. 5.
24   McGregor, pp. 50–51.
25   Langford, p. 5.
26   Taylor, 1998.
27   Schrire, 2001, p. 28.
28   Jones and Megaw, p. 21; Jones, 1995, pp. 430–33.
29   Jones and Smith, RJ: 3: 1/7.
30   Jones, '1995, p. 441; Meehan, p. 12.
31   Mulvaney, 2001, p. 21.
32   Johnston and Rolls; Plomley, 1996 and 2008.
33   Taylor, 2008a, p. 112; Ryan, 2012, pp. 13–14.
34   Jones, 1995, pp. 441–42.
35   Taylor, conversations with Tasmanian Aboriginal Elders and academics, Launceston and Hobart, author notebooks, 1999–2000.
36   Bickford, p. 14.
37   Bowdler, 'Fish and Culture', p. 335.
38   Meehan, p. 13; email to Rebe Taylor from Lyndall Ryan, 21 June 2006, personal collection, Ryan, 1996, p. 254; Jones, 1971, p. 14; Ryan, 1981, p. 2. Ryan 1985 expands this argument.
39   ABC Television, *Monday Conference*, 4 September 1979; O'Regan.
40   Taylor, telephone conversation with Annie Bickford, 31 October 2012.
41   Tuniz, et al., p. 19.
42   Ryan, 2012, pp. xxii–xxiv.
43   Dennis, p. 243.
44   Windschuttle, 2002, pp. 317, 386.
45   Jones, 1992, pp. 59–60.
46   Jones, 1977b, p. 196; Murray, 1992, p. 738.
47   McNiven and Russell, pp. 64–66; White and O'Connell, p. 158.
48   Jones, 1971, p. 630.
49   Tylor, 1894, p. 148.

50   Murray, 1992, p. 738.
51   Jones, 1971, p. 630.
52   Jones, 1995, p. 441.
53   Murray, 1992, p. 739.
54   Jones, 1995, pp. 438–39.
55   Brown, 1991; Bowdler, 1980, p. 339; Clark, 1987.
56   Murray and Williamson, p. 319.
57   Jones, 1995, p. 440.
58   ibid., p. 423.
59   ibid., pp. 441, 423; see also Jones, 1990a, p. 290.
60   Mulvaney, 2001, p. 21.
61   Jones, 1999, p. 57.
62   Mulvaney, 2001, p. 21.
63   Griffiths and Bonyhady, p. 16; see also Griffiths, 1996, pp. 94–100.
64   Mulvaney, 2001, p. 21.
65   Flannery, 2001, p. 39.
66   Mulvaney, 2001, p. 21.
67   Ryan, 2012, p. 360.
68   Andrew Darby, 2009, 'Bridge too far in a fight for cultural heritage', *Sydney Morning Herald*, 27 December 2009, www.smh.com.au/federal-politics/political-opinion/bridge-too-far-in-a-fight-for-cultural-heritage-20101226-1985c.html.
69   Wikipedia, 'The Brighton Bypass', en.wikipedia.org/wiki/Brighton_Bypass.
70   Michael Mansell, quoted on the ABC News, 2009. Michael Mansell, 1978, 'The Last Tasmanian', *Racism in Tasmania*, pamphlet, National Union of Students, Glebe, New South Wales, (also published as: Michael Mansell, 'Black Tasmanians Now', *Arena*, vol. 51, 1978, pp. 5–8).
71   Dawkins, pp. 39–43.
72   TallBear, p. 82.
73   *Shaw v Wolf*.
74   Sanders.
75   Department of Premier and Cabinet, Tasmanian Government, 'Aboriginal Eligibility Policy and Processes: a new approach for determining eligibility from 1 July 2016', www.dpac.tas.gov.au/divisions/csr/oaa/eligibility_policy; ABC News, 'Tasmanian Government relaxes criteria for proving Aboriginality', a report by Felicity Ogilvie for *PM*, 22 January 2016, www.abc.net.au/pm/content/2015/s4393122.htm.
76   ABC News, 'Aboriginality test changes will "swamp the community with white people", Tasmanian Aboriginal Centre fears', 22 January 2016, www.abc.net.au/news/2016-01-22/concerns-for-tasmanian-aboriginality-test-changes/7106664.
77   Flanagan, 2002, p. 15.
78   Jones, 1985, p. 185.
79   Lehman, 1994; see also Everett.
80   Griffiths, 2000.

Bibliography

Ernest Westlake Papers and publications

WP/PRM—Westlake Papers, Manuscripts Collection, Pitt Rivers Museum, Oxford

WP/OUMNH, Westlake Papers, Oxford University Museum of Natural History

WP/SIS—Stories in Stone: An annotated history and guide to the collections and papers of Ernest Westlake (1855–1922) (SIS), www.westlakehistory.info, contains the entire Westlake Papers held in the Pitt Rivers Museum (PRM) and Oxford University Museum of Natural History (OUMNH) as an online web resource, and it also includes papers and records created by other researchers and by the institutions relating to the study, accession and storage of Westlake's Tasmanian and French papers and stone collections. WP/SIS contains 17 series:

Introductory Series

Series 1 Records generated from researching and cataloguing Ernest Westlake's papers in the Pitt Rivers Museum and the Oxford University Museum of Natural History.

Pitt Rivers Museum, The University of Oxford

Series 2 Correspondence: Tasmanian Collection 1893–1916 and French Collection 1923–1976

This series includes Westlake's letters to his children, Aubrey and Margaret Westlake (noted in this book as 'Westlake to children, 10 January 1909, f. 60', as an example). They are stored in Box 2 by date range:

- 24 September to 6 December 1908, Folder 1a, folios 1–47
- 12 December 1908 to 27 April 1909, Folder 2a, folios 48–90
- 2 May 1909 to 19 September 1909, Folder 3a, folios 91–146
- 24 September 1909 to 20 February 1910, Folder 4a, folios 147–203
- 28 February 1910 to 9 October 1910, Folder 5a, folios 204–71

Series 3 Notebooks: Tasmania 1908–1910

This series includes Westlake's interview notes with Aboriginal and settler Tasmanians. Noted as 'Westlake, Notebook 6, p. 65', as an example, they are stored in Box 1 and each was numbered 1 to 6 by Westlake, who also numbered each page.

Series 4 Exercise Books: Tasmania 1909 – 1910

This series includes Westlake's archival research notes made in England and Tasmania. Noted as 'Westlake, Exercise Book 10, WP/SIS image 13', as an example, they are stored in Box 5 and numbered 1 to 20. The pages of the notebooks are not numbered, hence a reference to an image number in WP/SIS.

Series 5 Publications: Tasmanian Stone Implements and Aborigines

Series 6 Publications: Tasmanian Travel and Tourism

Series 7 Photographs: Tasmanian Aboriginal People and Collecting Sites

Series 8 Photographs: Classified Tasmanian Stone Implements (mounted)

Series 9 Photographs: Classified Tasmanian Stone Implements (unmounted)

Series 10 Photographs: Unclassified Tasmanian Stone Implements (unmounted)

Series 11 Maps: Tasmanian

Series 12 Notes and Notebooks: French Collection

Series 13 Westlake Tasmanian Aboriginal Stone Implement Collection Accession Documentation

Series 14 'Stone Implements of the Natives of Tasmania'; unpublished manuscript and plates by Henry Balfour.

Oxford University Museum of Natural History

Series 15 Correspondence and Biographical Papers: English and French Collections 1879–1993

This series includes correspondence concerning Westlake's French eolith collection, mostly with Aubrey Westlake, dating from 1923–1993, stored in Box 1, Folders I.6(i)–I.6(iii).

Series 16 Notes and Notebooks: English and French Collections

Series 17 Notes and Correspondence: Paranormal and Psychical Research 1881–1894

Westlake, Ernest, 1888, *Tubular Index to the Upper Cretaceous Fossils of England and Ireland*, T. Mitchell, Fordingbridge.

——1889, 'Outlines of the Geology of Fordingbridge and Neighbourhood', *Mitchell's Fordingbridge Almanack and Directory*, printed by Titus Mitchell, pp. 1–28.

——1903, 'The Antiquity of Man in Hampshire: Notes on Recent Discoveries in the Valley of the Avon', *Kings Fordingbridge Alamanac*, no page numbers.

——1910, 'About Snakes', Jean Westlake's papers.

——1921a(?), 'Bacchic Eros', Jean Westlake's papers.

——1921b, 'Camping as a Prime Element in Education (a paper read at the Simple Life Exhibition, 1921)', *The Woodcraft Way Series*, vol. 7, pp. 24–28.

——1921c, 'Recollections of Recapitulation (A Paper Read at the January Folkmoot, 1921)', *The Woodcraft Way Series*, vol. 7, pp. 19–24.

——c. 1922, 'The Forest School and other Papers', *The Woodcraft Way Series*, no. 7, published posthumously.

——1927, 'The Place of Dionysos', *The Woodcraft Way Series*, no. 9.

Other resources

Abbott, Margery Post, Mary Ellen Chijioke, Pink Dandelion and John William Oliver Jr, 2003, *Historical Dictionary of The Friends (Quakers): Historical Dictionaries of Religions, Philosophies, and Movements, No. 44*, The Scarecrow Press, Inc., Lanham, Maryland and Oxford.

ABC News, 2009, 'Aborigines label bypass work "cultural vandalism"', 17 September, www.abc.net.au/news/2009-09-17/aborigines-label-bypass-work-cultural-vandalism/1431982.

Allen, Jim, 2001, '"The Last Tasmanian"—A Personal View' in Atholl Anderson, Ian Lilley and Sue O'Connor (eds), *Histories of Old Ages: Essays in Honour of Rhys Jones*, Pandanus Books, Canberra, pp. 45–47.

Anderson, Warwick, 2002, *The Cultivation of Whiteness*, Melbourne University Press, Melbourne.

Backhouse, James, 1843, *A Narrative of a Visit to the Australian Colonies*, Hamilton Adams, London.

Baden-Powell, Donald, 1955, 'The Suffolk Crag', *Transactions of the Suffolk Naturalists' Society*, vol. 9, no. 3, pp. 215–22.

Balfour, Henry, 1925, 'The Status of the Tasmanians Among the Stone-Age Peoples' in *Proceedings of the Prehistoric Society of East Anglia*, vol. 5, no. 1, pp. 1–15.

———1929, 'Stone Implements of the Tasmanians and the Culture-Status Which They Suggest', Hobart, Australasian Association for the Advancement of Science, 1929, pp. 314–22.

Barnard, James, 1889, 'Notes on the last living Aboriginal of Tasmania', *Papers & Proceedings of the Royal Society of Tasmania*, pp. 60–64.

Barnard Davis, J, 1874, *On the Ostelogy and Peculiarities of the Tasmanians*, Haarlem, De Erven Loosjes.

Barrois, Charles, 1876, *Recherches sur le terrain crétacé supérieur de l'Angleterre et de l'Irlande*, Impr. et librairie Six-Horemans, Lille.

Belloc, Hilaire, 1912, *The Servile State*, ESP Haynes, London and Edinburgh.

Bickford, Anne, 1979, 'Superb Documentary or Racist Fantasy?', *Film News*, January, pp. 12–14.

Birdsell, Jospeh B, 1939, 'Harvard–Adelaide Expedition, Tasmanian Journal', held in the South Australian Museum.

Blainey, Geoffrey, 1966, *The Tyranny of Distance: How Distance Shaped Australia's History*, Sun Books, Melbourne.

Bolger, Peter, 1976, 'Reibey, Thomas (1821–1912)' in NB Nairn, Geoffrey Serle, Russell A Ward (eds), *Australian Dictionary of Biography: Volume 6 (1851–1890)*, University of Melbourne Press, Melbourne, p. 17.

Bonwick, James, 1870, *The Last of the Tasmanians or the Black War of Van Diemen's Land*, Sampson Low, Son & Marston, London.

Bowdler, Sandra, 1980, 'Fish and Culture: a Tasmanian Polemic', *Mankind*, vol. 12, no. 4, pp. 334–340.

———1984, *Hunter Hill, Hunter Island*, Terra Australis 8, Canberra, Australian National University.

Boyce, James, 2008, *Van Diemens Land*, Black Inc., Melbourne.

——2014, *God's own country?: The Anglican Church and Tasmanian Aborigines* (2nd edn), Anglicare Tasmania, Tasmania, stors.tas.gov.au/1263690.

Brantlinger, Patrick, 2005, *Dark Vanishings: Discourse on the Extinction of Primitive Races, 1800–1930*, Cornell University Press, Ithaca.

British History Online, 'Parishes: Fordingbridge', www.british-history.ac.uk/vch/hants/vol4/pp567-577.

British Museum, 1892, *A Guide to the Exhibition Galleries of the British Museum* (Bloomsbury), 1892, p. 232, archive.org/stream/aguidetoexhibit07musegoog#page/n4/mode/.

——1908, *A Guide to the Galleries of the British Museum* (Bloomsbury), 8th edition, <archive.org/stream/aguidetoexhibit01musegoog#page/n6/mode/2up.

Brown, Brendan, 2003, 'Some old people taught me' in K Wells (ed.), *Crossing the Strait: Tasmania to the South Coast*, catalogue from exhibition held at the Wollongong City Gallery in February 1999, Continental Shift Association Inc. and Identity and Research Group, University of Wollongong, Orford, Tasmania and Wollongong, New South Wales, p. 31.

Brown, Steve, 1991, 'Art and Tasmanian Prehistory: Evidence for changing cultural traditions in a changing environment' in P Bahn and A Rosenfeld (eds), *Rock Art and Prehistory: Papers Presented to Symposium G, the AURA Congress, Darwin, 1988*, Oxbow, Oxford, pp. 96–108.

Browne, Jackie, 1999, *Tasmanian Place Names and Changes* (updated by Mike Hurburgh and Robert Tanner, October 2002, and by Robert Tanner, August 2003), www.hobart.tasfhs.org/TasNames.html.

Camden History Society, 1997, *Streets of Bloomsbury and Fitzrovia*, www.ucl.ac.uk/bloomsbury-project/streets/bedford_square.htm.

Cameron, Patsy, 2011, *Grease and Ochre: The Blending of Two Cultures at the Colonial Sea Frontier*, Fullers Bookshop, Hobart.

Carpenter, Edward, 1889, *Civilisation: Its Cause and Cure*, Swan Sonnenschein & Co., London.

——1891, *Civilisation: Its Cause and Cure (2nd edn)*, Swan Sonnenschein & Co., London.

Carpentier, Martha C, 2013, *Ritual, Myth and the Modernist Text: The influence of Jane Ellen Harrison and the on Joyce, Eliot and Woolf*, Routledge, London and New York.

Clark, J, 1988, 'Smith, Fanny Cochrane (1834–1905)', *Australian Dictionary of Biography*, National Centre of Biography, Australian National University, adb.anu.edu.au/biography/smith-fanny-cochrane-8466/text14887.

Clark, Julia, 1987, 'Devils and Horses: Religious and Creative Life in Tasmanian Aboriginal Society' in Michael Roe (ed.), *The Flow of Culture: Tasmanian Studies*, Australia Academy of the Humanities, Canberra, pp. 50–72.

Clark, Manning, 1997, *Manning Clark's History of Australia* (abridged by Michael Cathcart), Melbourne University Press, Carlton, Victoria.

Clements, Nicholas, 2014, *The Black War: Fear, Sex and Resistance in Tasmania*, University of Queensland Press, Brisbane.

Coetzee, JM, 2004, *Elizabeth Costello*, Vintage, Sydney.

Condon, Herbert H, 1979, 'Atkinson, Henry Brune', in Bede Nairn and Geoffrey Serle (eds), *Australian Dictionary of Biography: Volume 7 (1981–1929)*, Melbourne University Press, Melbourne, pp. 120–21.

Curthoys, Ann, 2008, 'Genocide in Tasmania: The History of an Idea' in A Dirk Moses (ed.), *Empire, Colony, Genocide: Conquest, Occupation and Subaltern Resistance in World History*, Berghahn Books, New York and Oxford, pp. 229–52.

Daniel, Glyn E, 1952, *A Hundred Years of Archaeology* (2nd edn), Gerald Duckworth, London.

Darwin, Charles, 1859, *On the Origin of Species By Means of Natural Selection*, John Murray, London.

——1871, *The Descent of Man: Selection And Selection in Relation to Sex*, Murray, London.

Davidson, Jim, 1989, 'Tasmanian Gothic', *Meanjin*, vol. 48. no. 2, pp. 307–24.

Davis, RP, 1986, 'Mercer, John Edward (1857–1922)', Australian Dictionary of Biography, National Centre of Biography, Australian National University, http:// adb.anu.edu.au/biography/mercer-john-edward-7558/text 13189.

Dawkins, Richard, with Yan Wong, 2004, *The Ancestor's Tale*, Weidenfeld and Nicolson, London.

De Abaitua, Matthew, 2011, *The Art of Camping: The History and Practice of Sleeping under the Stars*, Hamish Hamilton, London.

De Bont, Raf, 1900–1920, 'The Creation of Prehistoric Man: Aimé Rutot and the Eolith Controversy', *Isis*, vol. 94, no. 4, December 2003, The University of Chicago Press on behalf of The History of Science Society, pp. 604–30.

Delair, Justin B, 1981, 'Ernest Westlake (1855–1922) Geologist and Prehistorian with a Synopsis of the Contexts of his Field Notebooks', *The Geological Curator*, vol. 3, nos 1 & 2, pp. 133–52.

——1985, 'Ernest Westlake (1855–1922): Founder Member of the Hampshire Field Club', *Hampshire Field Club Archaeological Society*, vol. 41, pp. 37–44.

Dennis, Rutledge M, 1995, 'Social Darwinism, Scientific Racism, and the Metaphysics of Race', *The Journal of Negro Education*, vol. 64, no. 3, pp. 243–52.

Diamond, Jared, 'Ten Thousand Years of Solitude', *Discover*, vol. 14, no. 3, 1993, pp. 48–57.

Douglas, Kirsty, 2010, *Pictures of Time Beneath: Science, Heritage and the Uses of the Deep Past*, CSIRO Publishing, Melbourne.

Dove, Rev. T, 'Moral and social characteristics of Aborigines of Tasmanian as gathered from intercourse with the surviving remnants of them now located on Flinders Island', *The Tasmanian Journal of Natural Science*, vol. 1, 1842, pp. 247–55.

Dunnett, Gary, 1993, 'Diving for Dinner: Some Implications from Holocene Middens for the Role of Coasts in the Late Pleistocene of Tasmania' in Mike A Smith, M Spriggs and B Frankhauser (eds), *Sahul in Review: Pleistocene Archaeology in Australia, New Guinea and Island Melanesia, Occasional Papers in Prehistory*, 24, Australian National University, Canberra, pp. 247–57.

Edgell, Derek, 1992, *The Order of Woodcraft Chivalry, 1916–1949, as a New Age Alternative to the Boy Scouts*, The Edwin Mellen Press, New York.

Edgeworth David, TW, 1923, 'Geological Evidence of the Antiquity of Man in the Commonwealth, With Special Reference to the Tasmanian Aborigines', *Papers and Proceedings of the Royal Society of Tasmania*, pp. 109–50.

Elder, Bruce, 1998, *Blood on the Wattle; Massacres and Maltreatment of Aboriginal Australians since 1788*, New Holland Publishers, Sydney.

Evans, IO, 1930, *Woodcraft and World Service: Studies in Unorthodox Education, An Account of the Evolution of the Woodcraft Movements*, Noel Douglas, London.

Everett, Jim, 2000, 'Aboriginality in Tasmania', *Siglo*, vol. 12, pp. 2–6.

Felton, Heather, 2012, 'Writing Tasmanian History: The Case of James Backhouse Walker', *Tasmanian Historical Studies*, vol. 17, pp. 1–44.

Fenton, James, 1884, *A history of Tasmania*, Macmillan, Birchall, Roberston & Co, Sydney, Melbourne, Adelaide, Launceston, London.

Fforde, Cressida, and Jane Hubert, 2006, 'Indigenous Human Remains and Changing Museum Ideology' in Robert Layton, Stephen Shennan and Peter Stone (eds), *A Future of Archaeology*, UCL Press, pp. 83–96.

Flanagan, Martin, *In Sunshine or in Shadow*, Picador Pan Macmillan, Sydney, 2002.

Flannery, Tim, 1994, *The Future Eaters*, Reed New Holland, Sydney.

——2001, 'Brief life of clarity and compassion: Rhys Maengwn Jones', *Australian Archaeology*, vol. 53, pp. 39–40.

——2002, 'The Lost Tribes', *Sydney Morning Herald*, 17 October, p. 15.

Fowler, David, 2011, 'Rolf Gardiner: Pioneer of British Youth Culture, 1920–1939' in Matthew Jeffries and Mike Tyldesley (eds), *Rolf Gardiner: Folk Nature and Culture in Interwar Britain*, Ashgate eBook, Ashgate Publishing Group, pp. 17–46.

Gammage, Bill, 2011, *The Biggest Estate on Earth: How Aborigines Made Australia*, Allen and Unwin, Sydney.

Gantevoort, Michelle, 2015, Stingray in the Sky: Astronomy in Tasmanian Aboriginal Culture and Heritage, Honours Thesis, Nura Gili Indigenous Programs Unit, University of New South Wales.

Gantevoort, Michelle, Duane Hamacher and Savannah Lischick, 2016, 'Reconstructing the Star Knowledge of Aboriginal Tasmanians', *Journal of Astronomical History and Heritage*, vol. 19, no. 3.

Gough, Julie, 2014, 'Forgotten Lives: The First Photographs of Tasmanian Aboriginal People' in Jane Lydon (ed.), *Calling the Shots: Aboriginal Photographies*, Aboriginal Studies Press, Canberra, pp. 20–54.

Grayson, Donald K, 1986, 'Eoliths, Archaeological Ambiguity, and the Generation of "Middle-Range" Research' in David J Meltzer, Don D Fowler and Jeremy A Sabloff (eds), *American Archaeology Past and Future*, published for the Society of American Archaeology by the Smithsonian Institution Press, Washington, pp. 77–133.

Griffiths, Tom, 1996, *Hunters and Collectors: The Antiquarian Imagination in Australia*, Cambridge University Press, Cambridge (England) and New York.

——2000, 'Travelling in Deep Time: *La Longue Durée* in Australian History', *Australian Humanities Review*, June 2000, www.australianhumanitiesreview.org/archive/Issue-June-2000/griffiths4.html.

Griffiths, Tom and Tim Bonyhady (eds), 1997, *Prehistory to Politics: John Mulvaney, The Humanities and the Public Intellectual*, Melbourne University Press, Melbourne.

Hale, Tim, 2011, 'The Salisbury and the Dorset Railway', www.southernrailway westofyeovil.blogspot.com.au.

Harper, Walter R, and Arthur H Clarke, 1897, Notes on the measurements of the Tasmanian crania in the Tasmanian Museum, Hobart, *Papers & Proceedings of the Royal Society of Tasmania*, pp. 97–107.

Hardy, Dennis, 2000, *Utopian England Community Experiments 1900–1945*, E & FN Spon, London.

Harrison, Jane Ellen, 1908, *Prolegomena to the Study of Greek Religion* (2nd edn), Cambridge University Press, Cambridge.

——1913, *Themis: A Study of the Social Origins of Greek Religion*, Cambridge University Press, Cambridge.

Haydon, Tom (director), 1978, *The Last Tasmanian*, Artis Film Productions, Sydney.

——1979, 'A Witness to History', *Film News*, April 1979, pp. 12–14.

Hazzledine, Warren, S, 1905, 'On the Origin of "Eolithic" Flints by Natural Causes, Especially by the Foundering of Drifts', *The Journal of the Anthropological Institute*, vol. 35, pp. 337–64.

Hiatt, Betty, 1968, 'Food Quest and Economy of the Tasmanian Aborigines', *Oceania*, vol. 38, no.1, pp. 99–133.

Hoare, Philip, 2005, *England's Lost Eden: Adventures in a Victorian Utopia*, Fourth Estate, London and New York.

Holdsworth, Chris, 2004, 'Tylor, Sir Edward Burnett (1832–1917)', *Oxford Dictionary of National Biography*, www.oxforddnb.com/view/article/36602.

Horton, David, 1979, 'Tasmanian Adaptation', *Mankind*, vol. 12, no. 1, pp. 28–34.

Howitt, Alfred, 1898, 'On the Origin of the Aborigines of Tasmania and Australia', *Australasian Association for the Advancement of Science*, vol. 7, pp. 723–58.

Hughes, Robert, 1987, *The Fatal Shore: A History of Transportation of Convicts to Australia, 1787–1868*, Collins Harvill, London.

Hutton, Ronald, 1999, *The Triumph of the Moon: A History of Modern Pagan Witchcraft*, Oxford University Press, Oxford, New York.

Huxley, TH, 1870, 'On the Geographical Distribution of the Chief Modifications of Mankind', *The Journal of the Ethnographical Society of London*, vol. 2, no. 4, pp. 404–12.

Isichei, Elizabeth, 1970, *Victorian Quakers*, Oxford University Press.

James, Winston, 2003, 'A Race Outcast from an Outcast Class: Claude McKay's Experience and Analysis of Britain' in Schwarz, Bill (ed.), *West Indian Intellectuals in Britain*, Manchester University Press, Manchester, pp. 71–92.

Jeffries, Matthew, 2011, 'Rolf Gardiner and German Naturism' in Matthew Jeffries and Mike Tyldesley (eds), *Rolf Gardiner: Folk Nature and Culture in Interwar Britain*, Ashgate eBook, Ashgate Publishing Group, 2011, pp. 47–64.

Johnson, Murray and Ian McFarlane, 2015, *Van Diemen's Land: An Aboriginal History*, University of New South Wales Press, Sydney.

Johnston, Anna and Mitchell Rolls (eds), 2008, *Reading Robinson: Companion Essays to Friendly Mission*, Quintus, Hobart.

Johnston, Robert MacKenzie, 1888, *Systematic Account of the Geology of Tasmania*, W.T. Strutt Government Printer, Hobart.

Jones, Rhys, 1969, 'Fire-stick Farming', *Australian Natural History*, vol. 16, no. 7, pp. 224–28.

——1971, Rocky Cape and the Problem of the Tasmanian Aborigines, PhD, University of Sydney.

——1974, 'Appendix: Tasmanian Tribes' in Tindale, Norman, *Aboriginal Tribes of Australia*, Berkeley, Los Angeles, London, University of California Press, vol. 1, pp. 319–54.

——1977a, 'Man as an Element of a Continental Fauna: The Case of the Sundering of the Bassian Bridge' in J Allen, J Golson and R Jones (eds), *Sunda and Sahul: Preshistoric Studies in Southeast Asia, Melanesia and Australia*, Academic Press, London, New York, San Francisco, pp. 317–86.

——1977b, 'The Tasmanian Paradox' in RVS Wright (ed.), *Stone Tools as Cultural Markers*, Australian Institute of Aboriginal Studies, Canberra, pp. 189–204.

——1978, 'Why Did the Tasmanians Stop Eating Fish?' in RA Gould (ed.), *Explorations in Ethnoarchaeology*, University of New Mexico Press, Albuquerque, 1978, pp. 11–47.

——1985, 'Ordering the Landscape' in I Donaldson and T Donaldson (eds), *Seeing the First Australians*, Allen and Unwin, Sydney, pp. 181–209.

——1987, 'Hunting Forebears' in M Roe (ed.), *The Flow of Culture:Tasmanian Studies*, Australian Academy of the Humanities, Canberra, pp. 12–49.

——1990a, 'From Kakadu to Kutikina: The Southern Continent at 18,000 Years Ago' in Clive Gamble and Olga Soffer (eds), *The World at 18,000 BP, Volume Two, Low Latitudes*, Unwin Hyman, London, pp. 264–95.

——1990b, '*Sylwadau cynfrodor ar Gôr y Cewri*: Or a British Aboriginal's land claim for Stonehenge' in C Chippendale, P Devereux, P Fowler, Rhys Jones and T Sebastian (eds), *Who Owns Stonehenge?*, BT Batsford Ltd, London, pp. 62–87.

——1992, 'Tom Haydon 1938-1991: Film Interpreter of Australian Archaeology', *Australian Archaeology*, vol. 35, pp. 51–64.

——1995, 'Tasmanian Archaeology: Establishing the Sequences', *Annual Review of Anthropology*, vol. 24, pp. 423–46.

——1999, 'Dating the human colonization of Australia: Radiocarbon and Luminescence Revolutions', *Proceedings of the British Academy*, vol. 99, pp. 37–65.

Jones, Rhys, and Betty Meehan, 2000, 'A Crucible of Australian Prehistory: The 1965 ANZAAS Conference' in Atholl Anderson and Tim Murray (eds), *Australian Archaeologist: Collected Papers in Honour of Jim Allen*, Coombs Academic Publishing, Canberra, pp. 40–61.

Jones, Rhys and Mike Smith, 1991, Rhys Jones interviewed by Mike Smith, sound recording, and transcript, ORAL TRC 2677 (transcript), National Library of Australia, Bib ID: 628228, TRC 2677.

Jones, Rhys, and Vincent Megaw, 2000, 'Confessions of a Wild Colonial Boy', *Australian Archaeology*, vol. 50, pp. 12–26.

Jose, Nicholas, 1997, *The Custodians*, Macmillan, Sydney.

Keen, Ian, 2000, 'The Anthropologist as Geologist: Howitt in Colonial Gippsland', *The Australian Journal of Anthropology*, vol. 11, no. 1, pp. 78–97.

Langford, Rosalind F, 1983, 'Our Heritage—Your Playground', *Australian Archaeology*, vol. 16, pp. 1-6.

Lawson, Tom, 2014, *The Last Man: A British Genocide in Tasmania*, IB Taurus, London.

Larson, Frances, 2005, 'Henry Balfour' (updated by Alison Petch, August 2011), www.prm.ox.ac.uk/h_balfour.html.

Lehman, Greg, 1992. 'Our Story of Risdon Cove', *Pugganna News*, vol. 34.

——1994, 'Being Black' in G Burenhult (ed.), *Traditional Peoples Today*, St Lucia, University of Queensland Press, p. 89.

——2016, Regarding the Savages: The Visual Representation of Tasmanian Aborigines in 19th Century Art, PhD Thesis, University of Tasmania.

Light, Tony and Gerald Ponting, 1997, *Victorian Journal: Fordingbridge 1837–1901*, Charlewood Press, Fordingbridge.

Lourandos, Harry, 1968, 'Dispersal of activities—The East Tasmanian Aboriginal Sites, *Papers and Proceedings of the Royal Society of Tasmania*, vol. 102, pp. 41–46.

Lubbock, John, 1865, *Pre-historic Times, As Illustrated by Ancient Remains, and the Manners and Customs of Modern Savages*, Williams and Norgate, London.

MM (Manchester Museum), Roth Papers—Roth organised this into sections and assigned Roman numerals; for example, 'XX' includes letters from James Backhouse Walker (JBW).

MacDonald, Helen, 2005, *Human Remains: Episodes in Human Dissection*, Melbourne University Press, Melbourne.

MacMurray, John, Guy W Keeling, Arthur Cobb, Aubrey Westlake and Norman Glaister, 1933, 'The Grith Fyrd Idea', *The Woodcraft Way Series*, no. 19.

McDougall, Russell, 2007, 'Henry Ling Roth in Tasmania', in Peter Hulme and Russell McDougall (eds), *Writing, Travel and Empire: In the Margins of Anthropology*, IB Taurus, London and New York, pp. 42–68.

McCarthy, GJ, 1993, 'Mattingley, Arthur Herbert Evelyn (1870–1950)', *Encyclopedia of Australian Science*, www.eoas.info/biogs/P001279b.htm.

McFarlane, Ian, 2002, Aboriginal Society in North West Tasmania: Dispossession and Genocide, PhD Thesis, University of Tasmania.

McGregor, Russell, 1997, *Imagined Destinies: Aboriginal Australians and the Doomed Race Theory, 1880–1939*, Melbourne University Press, Melbourne.

McLean, John, n.d., *Bruny Island and Adventure Bay: Bruny Aborigines and the Story of Truganini*, Telegraph Printery, Hobart(?).

McNiven, Ian and Lynette Russell, 2005, *Appropriated Pasts: Indigenous Peoples and the Colonial Culture of Archaeology*, AltaMira, Oxford.

Maltezos, Peter, 2014, 'The Victoria Hotel (former Victoria Coffee Palace)' Forum, urban.melbourne.

Meehan, Betty, 2001, 'The Early Life of a New Chum' in Atholl Anderson, Ian Lilley and Sue O'Connor (eds), *Histories of Old Ages: Essays in Honour of Rhys Jones*, Pandanus Books, Canberra, pp. 1–15.

Milligan, Joseph, 1859, 'Vocabulary of dialects of Aboriginal tribes of Tasmania', *Papers and Proceedings of the Royal Society of Tasmania*, vol. 3, pp. 239–74.

Molony, John, 1988, *The Penguin History of Australia* (2nd edn), Penguin, Ringwood, Victoria.

Morphy, Howard, 1997, 'Gillen—Man of Science' in John Mulvaney, Howard Morphy and Alison Petch (eds), *'My dear Spencer': The Letters of FJ Gillen to Baldwin Spencer*, Hyland House, South Melbourne.

Mulvaney, John, 1990, 'The Stone Age of Australia' in Janine Mummery (ed.), *Prehistory and Heritage: The Writings of John Mulvaney*, Australian National University, Canberra, pp. 16–54; first published in *The Prehistoric Society*, vol. 4, 1961, pp. 56–107.

——2001, 'Peopled Landscapes: From Prehistoric Tasmania to Contemporary Arnhem Land' in Atholl Anderson, Ian Lilley and Sue O'Connor (eds), *Histories of Old Ages: Essays in Honour of Rhys Jones*, Pandanus Books, Canberra, pp. 19–22.

Mulvaney, John, and Johan Kamminga, 1999, *Prehistory of Australia*, Allen and Unwin, Sydney, 1999.

Murray, Tim, 1992, 'Tasmania and the Constitution of "the dawn of humanity"', *Antiquity*, vol. 66, no. 252, September 1992, pp. 730–43.

——1998, *Archaeology of Aboriginal Australia: A Reader*, Allen and Unwin, Sydney.

Murray, Tim, and Christine Williamson, 2003, 'Archaeology and History' in Robert Manne (ed.), *Whitewash: On Keith Windschuttle's Fabrication of Aboriginal History*, Black Inc. Melbourne, pp. 311–33.

Noetling, Fritz, 1907, 'Notes on the Tasmanian Amorpholithes', *Papers and Proceedings of the Royal Society of Tasmania*, pp. 1–37.

Onsman, Andrys, 2004, 'Truganini's Funeral', *Island*, no. 96, Autumn, pp. 39–52.

O'Regan, Tom, 1984, *Culture & Communication Reading Room*, 'Documentary in Controversy: The Last Tasmanian', Murdoch University, wwwmcc.murdoch. edu.au/ReadingRoom/film/Tasmanian.html.

Oppenheim, Janet, 1985, *The Other World: Spiritualism and Psychical Research in England, 1850–1914*, Cambridge University Press, Cambridge, New York.

Order of Woodcraft Chivalry, The, 1919, *The Adventurer's Handbook: Being the Manual of The Order of Woodcraft Chivalry*, The Woodcraft Way Series, The Swarthmore Press, London.

——1923a, 'The Passing of the British Chieftain', *Pine Cone*, vol. 1, no. 1, pp. 12–14.

——1923b, 'The Recorder's Annual Report', *Pine Cone*, vol. 1, no. 2, pp. 28–29.

——1924, 'The Dawn Dance of Spring', *Pine Cone*, vol. 1, no. 4.

Paton, Robert, 2010, Draft: Final Archaeology Report on the Text Excavations of the Jordan River Levee Site Southern Tasmania, August, Robert Paton Archaeologial Studies Pty Ltd, Sandy Bay, Tasmania.

Perera, Suvendrini, 1996, 'Claiming Truganini: Australian National Narratives in the Year of the Indigenous Peoples', *Cultural Studies*, vol. 10, no. 3, pp. 393–412.

Petch, Alison, 2005, 'Edward Burnett Tylor: From the Armchair to the Totem Pole', www.prm.ox.ac.uk/e_tylor.html.

——2005(?), *England: The Other Within*, 'Tylor and Technology', web.prm.ox.ac.uk/england/englishness-Tylor-and-technology.html.

Petrow, Stephen, 1997, 'The Last Man: The Mutilation of William Lanne in 1869 and its Aftermath' in *Australian Cultural History*, vol. 16, pp. 18–44.

Plomley, NJB, 1976, *A Word-list of the Tasmanian Aboriginal Languages*, published with the Government of Tasmania, Hobart.

——1983, The Baudin Expedition and the Tasmanian Aborigines 1802, Blubber Head Press, Hobart.

——1991(?), *The Westlake Papers: Records of Interviews in Tasmania, 1908–1910*, Occasional Paper No. 4, Queen Victoria Museum & Art Gallery, Launceston.

——1966, *Friendly Mission, The Tasmanian Journals and Papers of George Augustus Robinson, 1829–1832*, Tasmanian Historical Research Association, Hobart.

——2008, *Friendly Mission, The Tasmanian Journals and Papers of George Augustus Robinson, 1829–1832* (2nd edn), Queen Victoria Museum and Art Gallery and Quintus Publishing, Hobart and Launceston.

Power, D'Arcy, 1901, 'Hogg, Jabez (DNB01)', *Dictionary of National Biography*, en.wikisource.org/wiki/Hogg,_Jabez_%28DNB01%29.

Pulleine, Robert, 1928, 'The Tasmanians and Their Stone-Culture', *Australasian Association for the Advancement of Science*, vol. 19, pp. 294–314.

Rae-Ellis, 1996, Vivienne, *Black Robinson: Protector of Aborigines*, Melbourne University Press, Melbourne.

RAI, 1910, Ernest Westlake's Application to the Royal Anthropological Institute of Great Britain and Ireland (RAI).

——1912, Minutes of the Royal Anthropological Institute of Great Britain and Ireland, 12 April.

Reid Moir, J, 1911, 'The Flint Implements of Sub-Crag Man', *Proceedings of the Prehistorical Society of East Anglia*, vol. 1, no. 1, pp. 17–43.

Reynolds, Henry, 2001, *An Indelible Stain?: The Question of Genocide in Australia's History*, Penguin, Melbourne.

——2004, *Fate of a Free People* (2nd edn), Penguin, Melbourne.

——2011, 'Preface' in Patsy Cameron, *Grease and Ochre*, pp. vi–vii.

Roberts, Richard G, 2001, 'The Celtic Chronologist: Rhys Jones and the Dating of the Human Colonisation of Australia' in Atholl Anderson, Ian Lilley and Sue O'Connor (eds), *Histories of Old Ages: Essays in Honour of Rhys Jones*, Pandanus Books, Canberra, pp. 89–94.

Roberts, Richard G, Rhys Jones and Michael A Smith, 1990, 'Stratigraphy and statistics at Malakunanja II: reply to Hiscock, Peter: How old are the artefacts in Malakunanja II?', *Archaeology in Oceania 25*, no. 3, pp. 125–29.

Robin, Libby, 2011, *The Flight of the Emu: A Hundred Years of Ornithology*, University of Melbourne Press, Melbourne.

Roe, Derek, 1981, 'Amateurs and Archaeologists: Some Early Contributions to British Palaeolithic Studies' in John D Evans, Barry Cunliffe and Conlin Renfrew (eds), *Antiquity and Man: Essays in Honour of Glyn Daniel*, Thames & Hudson, London, pp. 214–20.

Ronin Films, 'The Last Tasmanian Study Guide', www.roninfilms.com.au/get/
    files/987.pdf.
Roth, Henry Ling, 1889, 'A Surviving Tasmanian Aborigine' in *Nature*, vol. 41, no. 5,
    December.
——1890, *The Aborigines of Tasmania*, Kegan Paul, Trench, Trüber & Co, London.
——1899, *The Aborigines of Tasmania* (2nd edn), F. King & Sons, Halifax, England.
Rowntree Family, 'The Reminiscences of George Rowntree 1855–1940 written
    during the winter of 1935–36, Chapter IV, Schooldays, www.guise.me.uk/
    rowntree/george/reminiscences/chapter04.htm.
Russell, Lynette, 2015, *Roving Mariners: Australian Aboriginal Whalers and Sealers in the
    Southern Oceans, 1790–1870*, in SUNY series, *Tribal Worlds: Critical Studies in
    American Indian Nation Building*, Ithaca, State University of New York Press, New
    York, via ProQuest ebrary, 22 November 2015.
Rutot, Aimé, 1907, '*Un Grave Probleme Une industrie humaine detant de l'epoque oligocene
    compariaison des outlis avec des Tasmaniens actuels*' in *Extrait du Bulletin de la Societe
    Belge de Geologie de Paleontogie et D'hydrologie (Bruxelles)*, vol. xxi, pp. 3–46.
——1908, '*La Fin de la Question des Eolithes*' in *Bulletin de la Societe Belge de
    Geolohydrologie (Proces-Verbaux)*, vol. 21, pp. 104–109.
Ryan, Lyndall, 1981, *The Aboriginal Tasmanians*, University of Queensland Press,
    St. Lucia, Queensland.
——1985, 'Extinction Theorists and Tasmanian Aborigines: Apologists for an
    Extermination Policy' in C Schrire and R Gordon (eds.), *The Future of Former
    Foragers in Australia and Southern Africa*, Cultural Survival 18, Cambridge, pp. 47–54.
——1996, *The Aboriginal Tasmanians* (2nd edn), Allen & Unwin, Sydney.
——1997, 'The Struggle for Trukanini 1830–1997', Peter Eldershaw Memorial
    Lecture, *Tasmanian Historical Research Association Papers and Proceedings*, vol. 44,
    no. 3, pp. 153–73.
——2012, *Tasmanian Aborigines: A History Since 1803*, Allen and Unwin, Sydney.
Sackett, J, 2014, 'Boucher de Perthes and the Discovery of Human Antiquity' in
    Bulletin of the History of Archaeology, vol. 24, no. 2, pp. 1–11, at dx.doi.org/10.5334/
    bha.242.
Sanders, Will, 2003, 'The Tasmanian Electoral Roll Trial in the 2002 ATSIC
    Elections', Discussion Paper No.245, Centre for Aboriginal Economic Policy
    Research Australian National University, Canberra.
Schrire, Carmel, 2001, 'Betrayal as a Universal Element in the Sundering of Bass
    Strait' in Atholl Anderson, Ian Lilley and Sue O'Connor (eds), *Histories of Old
    Ages: Essays in Honour of Rhys Jones*, Pandanus Books, Canberra, 2001, pp. 25–34.
Scott, John, and Ray Bromley, 2013, *Envisioning Sociology: Victor Branford, Patrick
    Geddes, and the Quest for Social Reconstruction*, State University of New York Press,
    Albany.
Seton, Ernest Thompson, 1927, 'Woodcraft', *The Woodcraft Way Series*, vol. 1.
Shaw v Wolf, 1998, 163 Australian Law Reports, 205: 211–12.
Smith, Bernard, 1980, *The Spectre of Truganini*, Boyer Lectures, Australian Broadcasting
    Commission, Sydney.

Smith, Neil, 1976, 'Walker, James Backhouse (1841–1899)', *Australian Dictionary of Biography*, National Centre of Biography, Australian National University, adb.anu.edu.au/biography/walker-james-backhouse-4786/text7969.

Sollas, WJ, 1923, 'Obituary for Ernest Westlake', *Quarterly Journal of the Geological Society*, vol. 79, p. 1xii.

——1924, *Ancient Hunters and their Modern Representatives* (3rd edn), Macmillan & Co., London.

Stanner, WEH, 1968, *After the Dreaming: Black and White Australians—An Anthropologists' View*, The 1968 Boyer Lectures, Australian Broadcasting Commission, Sydney.

Stokes, Robert B, 1977, 'The Echinoids *Micraster* and *Epiaster* from the Turonian and Senonian of England', *Palaeontology*, vol. 20, part 4, pp. 805–21.

TallBear, Kimberly, 2003, 'DNA, Blood, and Racializing the Tribe', *Wicazo Sa Review*, vol. 18, no. 1, pp. 81–107, muse.jhu.edu/article/42997, made available by the University of Hawaii, Manoa, copyright of the Association of American Indian Research, www2.hawaii.edu/~rrath/hist460/DNA_Blood_and_Racializing_the_Tribe.html.

Taylor Rebe, 1998, Transcript of conversation with Rhys Jones and others, 13 March, personal collection.

——2000a, Interview with Chris Charman, Godshill, Fordingbridge, Hampshire, 10 July, personal collection.

——2000b, Interview with Jean Westlake, Sandy Balls, Hampshire, 10 July, personal collection.

——2000c, Interview with Justin Delair, Oxford, 20 March, personal collection.

——2003, 'Notebooks, Tasmania', personal collection.

——2004, Island Echoes: Two Tasmanian Aboriginal Histories, PhD, The Australian National University.

——2007, 'The Polemics of Eating Fish in Tasmania: The historical evidence revisited', *Aboriginal History*, vol. 31, pp. 1–26.

——2008a, 'Reliable Mr Robinson and the Controversial Dr Jones' in Anna Johnston and Mitchell Rolls (eds), *Reading Robinson: Companion Essays to Friendly Mission*, Quintus, Hobart, pp. 111–28.

——2008b, 'The Polemics of Making Fire in Tasmania: The historical evidence revisited', *Aboriginal History*, vol. 32, pp. 1–26.

——2008c, *Unearthed: The Aboriginal Tasmanians of Kangaroo Island*, Wakefield Press, Adelaide, 2nd edition.

——2012, 'The National Confessional', *Meanjin Quarterly*, vol. 2, pp. 22–36.

——2013, 'Genocide, Extinction and Aboriginal Self-determination in Tasmanian Historiography', *History Compass*, vol. 11, no. 6, pp. 405–418.

——2014, 'Archaeology and Aboriginal Protest: The Influence of Rhys Jones's Tasmanian Work on Australian Historiography', *Australian Historical Studies*, vol. 45, no. 3, September, pp. 331–349.

——2016a, Conversations and correspondence with Clinton Mundy, May–November.

——2016b, 'The First Stone and the Last Tasmanian: The Colonial Correspondence of Edward Burnett Taylor and Henry Ling Roth', *Oceania*, Special Edition: *Before the Field: Colonial Anthropology Reappraised*, Helen Gardner and Robert Kenny (eds), vol. 86, issue 3, DOI: 10.1002/ocea.5145.

Tindale, Norman, 1936–1965, 'Tasmania and the Part Aborigines of the Bass Strait and Kangaroo Island'. Tindale Collection, South Australian Museum, Adelaide.

——1937–41, 'Relationship of the Extinct Kangaroo Island Culture with Cultures of Australia Tasmania and Malaya', *Records of the South Australian Museum*, vol. VI, pp. 39–59.

——1953, *Growth of a People: Formation and Development of a Hybrid Aboriginal and White Stock on the Islands of Bass Strait Tasmania 1815—1949*, Records of the Queen Victoria Museum, Launceston.

Tuniz, Claudio, Richard Gillespie and Cheryl Jones, 2009, *The Bone Readers: Atoms, Genes and the Politics of Australia's Deep Past*, Allen and Unwin, Sydney.

Turnbull, Clive, 1948, *Black War: The Extermination of the Tasmanian Aborigines*, FW Chesire, Melbourne, 1948 (2nd ed., Lansdowne Press, Melbourne, 1965).

Tylor, EB, 1871, *Primitive Culture*, John Murray, London.

——1878, *Researches into the Early History of Mankind* (abridged version of 3rd edn., published 1964), Paul Bohannan (ed.), University of Chicago Press, Chicago and London.

——1890, 'Preface' in Henry Ling Roth, *The Aborigines of Tasmania*, pp. v–ix.

——1894, 'On the Tasmanians as Representatives of Palaeolithic Man', *Journal of the Royal Anthropological Institute of Britain and Ireland* vol. 23, 1894, pp. 141–52.

——1895, 'On the Occurrence of Ground Stone Implements of Australian Type in Tasmania', *Journal of the Royal Anthropological Institute of Britain and Ireland*, vol. 24, pp. 335–40.

——1898, 'On the Survival of Palaeolithic Conditions in Tasmania and Australia', *Journal of the Royal Anthropological Institute of Britain and Ireland*, vol. 23, 1898, pp. 141–52.

——1899, 'Preface' in Henry Ling Roth, *The Aborigines of Tasmania (2nd edn)*, pp. vii–ix.

——1900a, 'On Stone Implements from Tasmania: Extracts from a Letter by J Paxton Moir', *The Journal of the Royal Anthropological Institute of Great Britain and Ireland*, vol. 31, pp. 257–59.

——1900b, 'On the Stone Age in Tasmania, as Related to the History of Civilisation', *Journal of the Royal Anthropological Institute*, vol. 30, 1900, pp. 33–34.

——1994, *The Collected Works of Edward Burnett Tylor with a New Introduction by George Stocking*, Routledge & Thoemmes, London.

UCL, 'Bloomsbury Project', www.ucl.ac.uk/bloomsbury-project/streets/bedford_square.htm.

UTAS 'Quaker Life in Tasmania', 'Francis Cotton', University of Tasmania, www.utas.edu.au/library/exhibitions/quaker/quaker_biographies/quaker_biog_f_cotton.html.

UTAS Correspondence, from Joseph Paxton Moir, James Backhouse Walker and Henry Ling Roth, dating from the 1890s, University of Tasmania archives, accessed via eprints.utas.edu.au.

Walker, Backhouse, J, 1900, *The Tasmanian Aborigines*, John Vail Government Printer, Hobart.

'West, Ida (1919–?)', *Indigenous Australia*, National Centre of Biography, Australian National University, ia.anu.edu.au/biography/west-ida-17832/text29418.

Westlake, Aubrey, 1933, 'Heart, Hand, and Head: A National Educational Program', *The Woodcraft Way Series*, no. 18.

——1956, 'A Centenary Tribute to Ernest Westlake: An Educational Pioneer', *The Woodcraft Way Series*, vol. 24, pp. 3–15.

——1979, 'An Outline History of the Order of Woodcraft Chivalry 1916–1976', *The Woodcraft Way Series*, London, vol. 25.

Westlake, Jean, 1982, *Gipsy Caravan: A 100-years' Story*, Sandy Balls Press, Godshill, Fordingbridge, Hampshire.

——1988, *A Handbook for Sandy Balls* (2nd edn), Sandy Balls Press, Hampshire.

——2000, *70 Years A-Growing*, Hawthorn Press, Stroud, Gloucestershire.

Westlake, Margaret, 1918, 'The Theory of Woodcraft Chivalry', *The Woodcraft Way Series*, vol. 2, pp. 11–27.

Westlake, Richard, 1892, 'Memoir of Thomas Westlake', reprinted from *The Friends Quarterly Review*, April, West, Newman and Co., London.

Westlake, Thomas, 1885, 'Observatory', *English Mechanic and World of Science*, no. 1041, 6 March, p. 10.

——1847, 'Discussions at Lecture Hall', 11 May, Jean Westlake papers.

Whang, Bo Young, Seong Whan Jeong, Jeong Gill Leem and Young Ki Kim, 'Aspiration Pneumonitis Caused by Delayed Respiratory Depression Following Intrathecal Morphine Administration', *Korean Journal of Pain*, vol. 25, no. 2, 2012, pp. 126–129, published online, 10.3344/kjp.2012.25.2.126.

White, J Peter, with James F O'Connell, 1982, *A Prehistory of Australia, New Guinea and Sahul*, Academic Press, Sydney.

Windschuttle, Keith, 2000, 'The Myths of Frontier Massacres in Australian History', *Quadrant*, 3 parts—October 2000, pp. 8–21; November 2000, pp. 17–25; December 2000, pp. 6–20.

——2002, *The Fabrication of Aboriginal History: Volume One, Van Dieman's Land 1803–1847*, Macleay Press, Sydney.

Wood Jones, Frederic, 1935 *Tasmania's Vanished Race*, The Australian Broadcasting Commission.

Index